Informing a Nation

Informing a Nation

The Newspaper Presidency of Thomas Jefferson

MEL LARACEY

University of Michigan Press
Ann Arbor

For questions or permissions, please contact um.press.perms@umich.edu

Published in the United States of America by the
University of Michigan Press
Manufactured in the United States of America
Printed on acid-free paper
First published March 2021

A CIP catalog record for this book is available from the British Library.

Library of Congress Cataloging-in-Publication data has been applied for.

ISBN 978-0-472-13234-8 (hardcover : alk. paper)
ISBN 978-0-472-12855-6 (e-book)

Library of Congress Control Number: 2020951856

Cover illustration: Copy of lithograph "Politics in an Oyster House" by
Richard Caton Woodville. Courtesy of Indianapolis Museum of Art.

Acknowledgments

Support for this project came through a research f
National Endowment for the Humanities and via r
leaves from the University of Texas at San Antonio
support is gratefully acknowledged. I thank everyou
to this endeavor. I am especially grateful to Fred
Medhurst, Sidney Milkis, Julia Azari, Meena Bose, R
Benson, Gretchen Rose, Jill Butler Wilson, Elizabe
Executive Committee and staff of the University of

Some of the material in this book originally app
Rhetoric and Public Affairs, Presidential Studies Quarte
Supreme Court History.

Contents

Digital materials related to this title can be found on the Fulcrum platform
via the following citable URL: https://doi.org/10.3998/mpub.11533401

CHAPTER 1

Introduction

I am persuaded myself that the good sense of the people will always be found to be the best army. They may be led astray for a moment, but will soon correct themselves. The people are the only censors of their governors: and even their errors will tend to keep these to the true principles of their institution. . . . The way to prevent these irregular interpositions of the people is to give them full information of their affairs thro' the channel of the public papers, and to contrive that those papers should penetrate the whole mass of the people. The basis of our governments being the opinion of the people, the very first object should be to keep that right; and were it left to me to decide whether we should have a government without newspapers or newspapers without a government, I should not hesitate a moment to prefer the latter. But I should mean that every man should receive those papers and be capable of reading them.
  —Thomas Jefferson to Edward Carrington, January 16, 1787[1]

[W]herever the people are well informed, they can be trusted with their government.
  —Thomas Jefferson to Richard Price, January 8, 1789[2]

Although the will of the majority is in all cases to prevail, that will to be rightful must be reasonable.
  —Thomas Jefferson, First Inaugural Address, March 4, 1801[3]

These words from Thomas Jefferson are well known. Less known is that during his presidency Jefferson sponsored a newspaper in Washington, DC, that was widely understood to be speaking on his behalf. The newspaper, called the *National Intelligencer and Washington Advertiser*, was published three days a week for all eight years of his presidency and circulated throughout the country. Thus, Jefferson and his allies actually had a way to carry out their vision for American democracy: they could use the *Intelligencer* to provide Americans with the "full information of their affairs" necessary to ensure that popular, majoritarian control of the government would be "reasonable" (at least from a Republican perspective). The *Intelligencer* was essentially the state-controlled media of its time.

Yet while some scholars have referenced items in Jefferson's presidential newspaper on particular points, there has never been a comprehensive examination of the contents of the paper.[4] This book aims to fill that gap. As will be seen, Jefferson's newspaper was full of material that ranged over a number of topics, including raw campaigning and electioneering (especially during the electoral crisis of 1800); defenses of Jefferson and his administration's policies; and articulations of proper "Republican" (as the party Jefferson and James Madison led was originally called[5]) behavior, philosophy, and constitutional interpretation.

This research provides new insights into the thinking and strategies of Jefferson and his Republican allies during his presidency. As the first comprehensive case study of the contents of a "presidential newspaper," it also shows how extensively such a newspaper, heading up a chain of Republican newspapers that circulated throughout the country, could be used as a mass communication tool. It reveals the details of the virtual political community that Jefferson and his allies were working to establish nationally, using newspapers to construct partisan identity in much the same way Benedict Anderson showed they have been used in constructing national identity.[6] Furthermore, the study provides examples of a real-world, limited version of the "sphere of public policy discourse" envisioned by Jürgen Habermas as essential to a properly functioning democracy.[7]

This book grows out of work by others and myself in the field of presidential communication. The field was jump-started in 1987 with the publication of *The Rhetorical Presidency* by Jeffrey K. Tulis.[8] In his study, Tulis asserted that there was a fundamental difference, based on constitutionally grounded norms, between the communication practices of almost all early presidents (up to Woodrow Wilson) and later ones. The vast majority of pre-twentieth-century presidents, Tulis argued, had understood that their constitutional role was to avoid mass public appeals on policy issues, and to instead direct their ideas to Congress in written messages. Presidential communications behavior then changed when Wilson articulated a new understanding of the president's place in the constitutional order that virtually mandated routine direct presidential appeals to the public on policy matters.

Tulis's work prompted a flurry of scholarly research on whether there really had been such an "original" constitutional understanding and whether "premodern" presidents had in fact avoided speaking publicly on policy matters. While the debate on the first question may never end, much research on the second has shown that many early presidents were, either directly or indirectly, making their policy preferences known publicly. Regarding the direct way, several scholars found that early presidents made many more policy-oriented speeches or other communications than Tulis had considered. In my previous research, I focused on a different, indirect means by which many early presidents, even when they did not make speeches or issue public pronouncements, were still able to present their views publicly in an indirect way. As I showed in my first book, *Presidents and the People: The Partisan Story of Going Public,* they did this through the publication of anonymous or pseudonymous commentaries in presidentially sponsored newspapers that were widely understood to be speaking on behalf of a president's administration.[9]

Thus, many early presidents were able to engage in a form of mass political communication. Although by modern standards this would not seem possible, America by the beginning of the nineteenth century had a robust form of national political communication carried out by party-sponsored newspapers. Found in virtually every town, and available via postage-free circulation to other newspaper editors, these newspapers were stridently partisan, promoting party positions and commenting on national affairs from a particular political viewpoint.

These newspapers were not "newspapers" as we commonly understand them today. Rather than trying to provide their readers with a wide, fairly objective range of information about current events, these papers had a very different mission: to advocate on behalf of a particular party or political figure. That is what their sponsors (the political parties and their leaders) wanted them to do. In performing these functions, newspapers became essentially the political lifeblood of the early American Republic. They were the "political system's central institution," as Jeffrey Pasley has described them. The papers and their editors "were purposeful actors in the political process, linking parties, voters, and the government together, and pursuing specific political goals."[10] They were, in Joanne Freeman's assessment, "the key centralizing link in early efforts to build a national party organization," and powerful political agents that could "shape public opinion on a massive scale."[11] They provided adherents with a common strategy and set of principles and policies to follow and advocate. As Philip Converse famously put it in a different context, these newspapers told partisans "what goes with what."[12]

The most prominent and effective partisan newspapers were subsidized through the award of contracts to publish, "By Authority," the government's new laws, decrees, and notices.[13] Political messages in the newspapers circulated quickly throughout the country by being loosely paraphrased, excerpted, or even reprinted in full in other friendly party papers, whose editors received all newspapers postage free under federal law.[14] In 1800, a Federalist newspaper editor wrote scathingly of how, "with much punctuality and rapidity, *the same opinion* has been circulated" throughout the country via the Republicans' newspapers, so that a "perfect union of opinion was established."[15]

At the presidential level, using a newspaper as a thinly veiled means of trying to influence public opinion was also a clever way around the problem created by the Founders when they invented the office of the president but failed to anticipate how it might be impacted by the rise of political parties. From the very beginning of the American Republic, there was a commonly held view—rooted in the original conception of the president as a sort of "Patriot King," a leader "above parties"— that presidents ought to avoid obvious involvement in partisan politics. On the other hand, also beginning with Washington himself (mostly via Alexander Hamilton's establishment of a pro-administration newspaper during Washington's first term), presidents saw the need to try to influence public opinion on policy matters).[16] This need became a virtual imperative with the development of political parties in the 1790s, because suddenly the president was also very much "in the party," as the head of a nationally organized alliance that could only attain power by influencing voters' opinions. As Jefferson said a year after the end of his presidency,

> In a government like ours, it is the duty of the Chief Magistrate, in order to enable himself to do all the good which his station requires, to endeavor, by all honorable means, to unite in himself the confidence of the whole people. This alone, in any case where the energy of the nation is required, can produce a union of the powers of the whole, and point them in a single direction, as if all constituted but one body & one mind.[17]

Hence the use of presidential newspapers. Through them, presidents could get their positions and rationales presented to the public in a format that was known to be coming from the president himself, or with the president's tacit approval, but that also did not manifest this reality too obviously. In this way, a politically active president like Jefferson could fulfill both conceptions of the presidency. Any politically knowledgeable person would have known that the real truth lay behind the flimsiest of disguises. Nevertheless, the accommodation worked for more than sixty years—the lifetime of the presidential newspaper in American politics.

The value that Jefferson saw in such a newspaper is demonstrated by his boldness in getting one established in the nation's new capital. Before he even knew if he had won the presidential election of 1800, Jefferson convinced Samuel Harrison Smith to move with his new wife Margaret to Washington to establish the *National Intelligencer*.[18] When the *Intelligencer* was established, it would have been the only Republican newspaper in Washington.[19] Smith began publishing the newspaper in late October 1800, just in time for it to serve unexpectedly as the Republicans' public relations outlet during the political crisis that ensued when Jefferson and his running mate, Aaron Burr, tied in the Electoral College vote.

Jefferson's encouragement to Smith was part of the effort of the Republicans to establish and nurture a supportive chain of newspapers across the country to promote their principles and candidates.[20] As Jefferson put it in a letter to James Madison on February 5, 1799, the press was to be the "engine" in their effort to free America from the grip of Federalism.[21] Jefferson's Attorney General Levi Lincoln of Massachusetts echoed that assessment of the power of political newspapers in a July 28, 1801, letter to Jefferson. Just a few months into Jefferson's new administration, Lincoln said he saw signs everywhere that political divisions had "meliorated," and that "the ruffled surfaces, of political circles, are tranquillized." All that was needed, he said, was continued firm adherence to "those great republican principles," coupled with "seasonable explanations and statements, to exhibit Government to the view of the people, on the real principles, on which it is administered." Massachusetts was ready to become Republican, and the rest of New England would follow, he said: "A few more republican newspapers, and the thing is accomplished."[22]

On a sheer political level, then, Jefferson would have wanted a newspaper like the *Intelligencer* to carry out the straightforward functions of defending and promoting himself and his administration. As will be seen, the newspaper performed those functions energetically. On controversies including the presidential electoral deadlock of 1800, Jefferson's appointments and removals policies, the Louisiana Purchase, and the impeachment of Supreme Court Justice Samuel Chase, the *Intelligencer* printed dozens of explanations and defenses of the actions. Whenever Jefferson came under attack from Federalists, the newspaper was always ready with spirited responses.

On a deeper level, a newspaper like the *Intelligencer* was essentially the only feasible solution to a difficulty in Jefferson's democratic theory. A core tenet was that he "regarded large numbers of people—all the citizens—as the 'rulers' in the body politic."[23] But a corollary to that theory was, as Jefferson said in his first inaugural address, "Although the will of the majority is in all cases to prevail, that will to be rightful must be reasonable." After all, as Benjamin Barber observed, "without education, democracy may mean little more than the tyranny of opinion over wisdom."[24]

Jefferson, Madison, and others recognized that having an "informed citizenry" was crucial to making representative democracy work, because control of the government ultimately rested with "the people."[25] Therefore, to avoid potential disaster, it was obvious that "the people" would need to be educated in two ways. They would have to be provided with the "principles of their political creed," as Jefferson put it in a letter to Joseph Priestley in 1802 regarding the importance of a written constitution.[26] They would also, as he wrote in his letter to Edward Carrington quoted at the beginning of this book, have to be given "full information" about the actions of their government. Only in this way could popular control of the government make sense.[27]

How, though, was this to be accomplished? While scholars have focused extensively on Jefferson's plans for educating the citizenry, those plans were never realized; in 1800, the nation's educational system was a patchwork affair at best.[28] Moreover, even well-educated citizens would need the right information, properly explained and contextualized, to do their job as "censors" of the government. These obvious realities have led some scholars, most notably Jean M. Yarbrough, to critique Jefferson's concept of statesmanship.

> Jefferson seems to underestimate the moral duty of statesmen not simply to inform but also to educate the people about their rights and responsibilities as citizens.
>
> . . . Jefferson seems to rely far too much on the spontaneous reso-

lution of these questions by a moral sense brought to full flowering under republican institutions, an agrarian economy, and universal education. Yet preserving our rights requires more than a reliance on the innate decency of the American people and their vigilant, but (for Jefferson) benign, spirit; it requires statesmen who will instruct citizens in the true meaning and ground of their rights. The statesman is not simply the people's advocate; he is, more important, their educator. For it is only when citizens understand these principles correctly, and especially in all their limitations, that republican self-government is truly possible.[29]

Yarbrough was of course correct that responsible democratic self-governance requires an educated and informed citizenry. Jefferson (and Madison, as will be discussed later) was saying the same thing more than two hundred years ago. As Jefferson put it in 1788 in the quotation at the beginning of this book, "The basis of our governments being the opinion of the people, the very first object should be to keep that right."[30] Like many other scholars, however, Yarbrough did not consider the solution to this problem that Jefferson himself identified in the same quotation: newspapers that would "penetrate the whole mass of the people" and "give them the full information of their affairs."[31] This is how the opinions of the people would be kept "right," making democratic popular rule safe for America.

As Colleen Sheehan has shown, James Madison detailed this very solution a few years later, in a series of essays published in 1793–94 in the *National Gazette*, the newspaper that he and Jefferson had established in Philadelphia to counter the pro-Federalist newspaper established there by Alexander Hamilton.[32] In those essays, Madison addressed the problem of how to make popular control of government "safe." If, as Republican theory held, governments should be subject to the "will of the people," what could be done to guard against that popular "will" being decided wrongly?

The solution, Madison asserted, was to make the development of public opinion subject to the "reason of society." In what Sheehan calls an "original, momentous insight," Madison said this could be accomplished via a "new conception of the politics of communication."[33] Madison "envisioned newspapers serving as vehicles for circulating the ideas of the literati to the people of the extensive American republic, resulting in the refinement and enlargement of the public views and the emergence of an enlightened public opinion." In this way, the "ideas of the educated and patriotic members of society" could be conveyed to the "people at large." Those "literati," then, would be acting as "civic educators in Madison's republic." They would, in his words, be the "cultivators of the human mind—the manufacturers of useful knowledge—the agents of the commerce of ideas—the censors of public manners—the teachers of the arts of life and the means of happiness."[34]

To do such massive shaping of public opinion in an organized, consistent fashion, there obviously would have to be a central approved information source and a way to communicate it nationally. This is where the aptly named *National Intelligencer* would have come into play. Material generated by Jefferson, Madison, and their Republican allies could be placed in the newspaper. Then copies of the paper would be sent, postage free, to other Republican newspapers across the country. Editors of those other newspapers, confident that what was printed in the *Intelligencer* was the approved Republican position, could then follow the political cues from the newspaper in their own commentaries or simply reprint excerpts from the *Intelligencer*. Thus, Republican principles, positions, and information could be spread across the country, newspaper by newspaper, just as envisioned. The result during Jefferson's presidency was, as described by Robert Johnstone, a practically "optimum use" of a national newspaper network to "mobilize partisan loyalties" by transmitting Republican values, political intelligence, and symbolic representations to "millions of Americans."[35]

So Jefferson's statement about the fundamental role of newspapers in the American system of government was not, as it has been commonly interpreted, just a philosophical paean to the value of a free press. It actually expressed his and Madison's dream of using newspapers to educate and inform the nation politically—in Jefferson's succinct formulation, conveying to the "whole mass of the people" the "full information" that would keep their opinions "right."[36]

That was precisely the role claimed for the *Intelligencer* in Samuel H. Smith's introductory note to readers in the first issue, published on October 31, 1800: "The design of the National Intelligencer is to *diffuse* correct information through the whole extent of the union." The *Intelligencer*, Smith said, would only publish "unperverted facts, and correct political ideas." In effect, Smith was the precursor to the modern presidential press secretary. Instead of having to appear before potentially hostile media reporters and deal with their questions, though, Smith had the easier task of just publishing material that supported his presidential sponsor and then, when necessary, written responses to whatever criticisms were levied against Jefferson or his policies. That most of the material Smith would print was written by others made his job even easier.

As will be shown, Jefferson and his allies devoted much attention to the *Intelligencer*. They ghostwrote many commentaries that were published in the paper, and the paper was commonly understood to be reflecting the views of Jefferson and the Republican Party. Thus, it seems clear that the *Intelligencer* was the cornerstone of the Jeffersonian Republican effort to guide public opinion nationally.[37] A study of the contents of the newspaper therefore offers a unique, contemporaneous guide to the thinking and strategies of Jefferson and his allies and to the core principles of democratic and constitutional theory they were trying to promote in the early American Republic. Since the newspaper was the public face of Jeffersonianism, it could not have veered far from the preferences of its sponsor. It therefore arguably represents a sort of distillation, for public consumption, of what was regarded by Jefferson and his allies as most important to be communicated to the American people to keep their opinions "right."

In this regard, consider how Jefferson and Madison envisioned another form of public education, in the university setting. In their discussions of hiring a professor of government and law, they agreed that care needed to be taken to only appoint someone who had acceptable political (i.e., Republican) views. As Adrienne Koch put it, they were "unwilling to allow the entry of political doctrines contradictory to the cherished freedoms of democratic society and Republican ideology."[38] As Jean Yarbrough has observed, Jefferson evidently believed "that what is useful to the republican cause and what is true are largely the same."[39] If Jefferson only wanted good Republican principles taught in college, then surely he must have thought the same about how the rest of America should be educated and informed through his presidential newspaper.

From a simple pragmatic perspective, Republican leaders needed a means for countrywide promotion of the official, standardized version of Jeffersonian Republicanism. Massachusetts Republican Barnabas Bidwell made that need clear in a letter to Vice President Aaron Burr in July 1801.

> An opposition, not yet very much systematized, is intended against the present administration. Every popular prejudice will be seized and wielded with as much effect as possible. I trust the measures of administration will bear a strict examination; but people at large have not the means of examining. They must judge from impressions,

communicated thro News-papers principally. The true explanations
of controverted measures should be communicated and circulate.
They should be uniform in all parts of the United States. I mean
essentially so. For this purpose there ought to be one authentic paper,
from which the Republican editors can take their Texts, on which
they and their correspondents may comment, with all their variety of
amplifications. It is not to be expected that they will otherwise act in
any good degree of concert, in explaining, defending and enforcing,
to the people, the views and measures of government, so as to counteract false impressions on the public mind.[40]

Bidwell followed up his suggestion with a related question: Could the
National Intelligencer be "relied on" as the kind of politically "authentic
newspaper" he had in mind? Burr assured him it could: "The Washington paper edited by Smith has the countenance and support of administration. His explanations of the Measures of Government and of the
Motives which produce them are, I believe, the result of information and
advice from high Authority."[41]

The research presented in this book proceeds from Burr's simple
point that what was being published in the *Intelligencer* reflected "information and advice from high Authority." Viewed in this way, a systematic
examination of what was printed in the newspaper is bound to reveal
more information about the views and strategies of Jefferson and his
Republican allies once they achieved political power in the election of
1800. As the following description of the book's chapters shows, the
research produced significant material that provides valuable contextual
background and some entirely new information on Jefferson, his presidency, and Jeffersonian Republicanism.

Chapter 2 describes a series of the *Intelligencer's* overlooked commentaries that vividly express Madison's theory of the role of informed public
opinion in republican self-government. Although the commentaries are
anonymous, they are so similar to the essays examined by Sheehan that
it seems Madison himself could well have authored them. Of significance
to scholars of presidential communication, the chapter also shows that
Jefferson was publicly linked with and held responsible for the contents
of the *Intelligencer.* That linkage undermines the central thesis of Tulis's
The Rhetorical Presidency, as Tulis himself has acknowledged would be the
case. Finally, the chapter identifies an 1804 article in the *Intelligencer*
in which Samuel Smith recounts a meeting in which Jefferson showed
him his original draft of the Declaration of Independence to prove he

had been its author. Although Jefferson's authorship has been debated almost from 1776 and been the subject of much research, scholars have apparently not previously noted this particular account.

Chapter 3, which focuses on how the 1800 electoral deadlock was portrayed in the *National Intelligencer*, identifies the public Republican response to the Federalist newspaper commentary that advocated making John Marshall the new president and that Bruce Ackerman speculates, in his book *The Failure of the Founding Fathers*, was authored by Marshall himself. The chapter also examines how Federalists were responding, through their capital newspaper the *Washington Federalist*, to the aggressive Republican rhetoric regarding the electoral crisis. It demonstrates that, contrary to the previous assertions of some historians, Federalists clearly understood that Republicans were threatening violence and revolution if the crisis was not resolved—and that Federalists were responding in kind. The chapter also shows just how vividly Republicans were promoting the "plebiscitary" concept of the presidency, less than twenty years after the Founders at the Constitutional Convention had explicitly rejected that concept.[42]

Chapter 4 discusses the remarkably detailed guidance the *Intelligencer* provided its readers on proper Republican behavior—for both citizens and presidents. That guidance reflects Jefferson's moral theory of self-discipline in society. It also seems to be a clear reflection, previously unnoted, of Madison's plan to "anchor public opinion in the morals and manners of Republicanism," as identified by Sheehan and discussed in chapter 2.[43] Similarly, the guidance obviously reflects elements of civic virtue and republican statesmanship that nevertheless were not mentioned in Yarbrough's book *American Virtues: Thomas Jefferson on the Character of a Free People*.[44] The research presented in chapter 4 also reveals the newspaper's previously undiscovered explanation of why Jefferson delivered his first Annual Message to Congress in writing rather than as a speech as his predecessors had done. That explanation further undermines the reinterpretation of Jefferson's action that was a centerpiece of Tulis's *The Rhetorical Presidency*.

Chapter 5 examines how the *Intelligencer* defended Jefferson's actions in removing and appointing federal officers. Federalists' complaints that Jefferson was not acting in a politically impartial manner are well known. The chapter shows how Republicans publicly embraced the "unitary theory of the presidency," with the *Intelligencer* arguing that Jefferson had absolute control over important executive branch decisions such as whether to initiate or terminate federal criminal prosecutions. The com-

mentaries in the *Intelligencer* even grounded this assertion on the plebiscitary claim that Jefferson as the newly elected president embodied the
new national will and was entitled—indeed obligated—to appoint other
executive branch officials (i.e., Republicans) who could be counted on
to act in accordance with that change in public opinion. Chapter 5 also
shows that Federalists rejected the idea, complaining that it violated constitutional and rule-of-law principles if applied to federal law enforcement actions.

Chapter 6 examines how the idea of judicial review was presented
in the *Intelligencer*. The analysis reveals a surprisingly mixed approach.
The newspaper carried strident commentaries against the idea, but also
printed commentaries that invoked favorable judicial actions and decisions as conclusive evidence of the constitutionality of some Republican
actions.

Chapter 7 focuses on the impeachment of Supreme Court Justice
Samuel Chase as it was "reported" in the *Intelligencer*. The case study
reveals that rather than remaining publicly silent before his Senate trial
(as scholars such as Richard E. Ellis asserted), Chase published a scathing attack on Jefferson in the *Intelligencer* and other newspapers around
the country. Never since has there been such a public, personalized conflict between a Supreme Court Justice and a president. The newspaper's
issue-by-issue, months-long coverage of the proceedings against Chase,
almost always from a pro-impeachment stance, implicitly demonstrated
to the public the Jefferson administration's attitude regarding Chase's
removal. The use of the newspaper for this kind of messaging further
undermines Tulis's claim about the supposed constitutional significance
of differences in the "forms" or "modes of rhetoric" employed histori-
cally by presidents in their public communications. Put simply, all readers of the *Intelligencer* were assured of the Jeffersonian Republican position on Chase's fitness for office, without Jefferson ever uttering a word
about it publicly.

Chapter 8, on the Louisiana Purchase, finds that while Jefferson
remained publicly silent about the possible use of military force to resolve
the dispute over the closing of the port of New Orleans to American
commerce, the *Intelligencer* was printing reports of Jefferson's determination to use force if necessary. Those reports would have served several
purposes. In addition to reassuring anxious Americans and undercut-
ting Federalists' criticisms of Jefferson's timidity, the reports supplied
ambassadors with material to send promptly to European capitals as indi-
cators of Jefferson's true intentions.

Chapter 9, on the campaign to reelect Jefferson in 1804, shows how nationalized and nasty elections had become by then—matching up well with those seen more than two hundred years later. On the other hand, it reveals a very different kind of election campaign, in which the "campaigning" was done not by Jefferson but by anonymous and pseudonymous commentaries published on his behalf in the newspaper. It also discusses a novel effort by Republicans to show how Jefferson had always behaved constitutionally as president.

Beginning on October 31, 1800, the *Intelligencer* was published three times per week, with an occasional special issue, for a total of about 1,300 issues. The present study keeps its analysis to a manageable length, while still conveying the depth of what the newspaper was saying on Jefferson's behalf, by focusing on the contents of the newspaper during Jefferson's first term in office. That term was full of dramatic episodes and endeavors that largely comprise the story of Jefferson's presidency. Most of those are examined in this book.[45] Some topics, though, are not addressed because they were hardly mentioned in the *Intelligencer*. Most notable among those topics are slavery and Jefferson's relationship with Sally Hemings.

Almost every issue of the *Intelligencer* contained advertisements of slaves for sale or rewards for runaway slaves and notices that captured runaway slaves were being held in jail and would be sold if not promptly reclaimed by their owners. But substantive discussion of slavery was rare in the paper, and only once was there a commentary on the subject from the paper itself. On December 19, 1800, the paper reprinted antislavery excerpts from Jefferson's *Notes on Virginia*. In August of 1801, two issues of the paper published antislavery excerpts from Rousseau's *Social Compact*, and two other issues included the opening and closing reports of the national convention of the Society for the Abolition of Slavery.[46] When the *Intelligencer* printed the official US Census results on September 16, 1801, an accompanying commentary marveled at the nation's rapid growth and observed that the population proportion of slaves and "blacks, whether slaves or free," was decreasing "with a rapidity that promises the happiest effects." The paper would make little mention of the topic for the rest of Jefferson's first term. In the fall of 1803, it republished a report on Louisiana (from the *Philadelphia Aurora*) including an antislavery argument, and in the spring of 1804, it carried accounts of the debate in Congress over a proposed federal tax on the importation of slaves.[47]

How the *Intelligencer* handled the topic of slavery mirrors Jefferson's well-known aversion to any public discussion of it. Peter Onuf attributes Jefferson's reticence to the president's conviction that nothing could be done until public opinion had "been more fully enlightened." Jefferson, Onuf writes, believed that "this enlightenment could not be forced or coerced, but must instead spring from below. . . . To dictate to the people, even for the most enlightened and progressive purposes, was to violate the most fundamental principle of republican self-government."[48] The central theme of this book, however, is that the *Intelligencer* was part of Jefferson's effort to provide good Republicans (or any other interested Americans) all the information and guidance they needed to carry out their central role in directing the actions of the national government. The minimal discussion of slavery in the newspaper leads, therefore, to a less noble conclusion: that, for whatever reason, Jefferson was simply not interested in trying to influence public opinion on the issue.[49]

The *Intelligencer* made no attempt to refute the claim about Sally Hemings that James Callender published in his newspaper, the Richmond *Recorder*, on September 1, 1802, alleging that Jefferson had fathered children with her, or other claims Callender later made about Jefferson's personal life.[50] Instead, twice in the *Intelligencer* (on September 29, 1802, and May 2, 1804), Samuel H. Smith broadly condemned the claims (without mentioning any specifics) as being beneath the dignity of any response. On October 27, 1802, Smith also published another newspaper's commentary praising Jefferson's character and attacking Callender's. That was all the newspaper ever said on the matter, ironically confirming Callender's sneering prediction when he had published the charges that "censor Smith" would be "Mute! Mute! Mute! Yes very mute!"[51]

Few subjects in Jefferson's second term are as compelling as those in his first, at least in terms of their coverage in the *Intelligencer*. The Lewis and Clark expedition, which returned in 1806, was barely mentioned in the newspaper until their return and, even then, only in a few issues that mostly reported on the celebrations accompanying their arrival in the capital. Otherwise, Jefferson's second term is distinguished largely by his ultimately unsuccessful efforts to get Aaron Burr convicted for treason and by the president's attempts to enforce his unpopular trade embargo against France and England. Both those topics were addressed extensively in the *Intelligencer*, in predictably supportive fashion. As Jefferson's second term waned, so did the newspaper's energy. In his last two years as president, far fewer commentaries and essays about politics appeared in the paper. Filling its pages instead were dry reports of congressional proceedings and information on foreign affairs gleaned from European newspapers.

Much recent scholarship in the field of presidential studies focuses on presidents as the agents of fundamental change in the American system. The presidency, itself essentially an "invented" office, exerts a powerful influence, capable of fundamental "reconstructions" of the political and constitutional orders.[52] It is, in Stephen Skowronek's vivid metaphor, a "giant battering ram" that, history shows, periodically transforms American politics and its constitutional order.[53]

As scholars such as Skowronek, Ackerman, and Keith Whittington attest, Jefferson's presidency was the classic example of a transformative one.[54] Yet to call it that invites an obvious question: Exactly how did Jefferson manage to make his presidency such a defining moment in American political development? After all, his substantive public communication output during his presidency was meager: he made just two official speeches (at his first and second inaugurations) and issued eight written annual messages to Congress. Those speeches and messages, coupled with a few dozen official proclamations and some published letters, constitute the sum of his public communications. Yet by the end of his presidency, Republicans and Republicanism had swept through most of the country. How could the Republican message have spread so thoroughly and effectively? As this book shows, the answer must lie largely with the important public communication tool Jefferson had at his disposal, his presidential newspaper.

The *National Intelligencer* was obviously the only way that a uniform message could be spread across the country. Its contents therefore had to be acceptable to Jefferson and his allies as somehow furthering their cause. The paper's editor could not have been a "free agent," with the liberty to publish whatever he liked. Rather, he had to have been constrained to only publish material that his sponsor, Jefferson (and his allies), would have liked or wanted published. As Smith's wife put it vividly at the beginning of Jefferson's presidency, the couple's whole "condition in life" depended on Jefferson's political success (see chapter 2).

Imagine if Jefferson had kept a running weekly account of how he and his allies were planning to deal publicly with issues and challenges during his first term in office. That account does not exist, but tracks and traces of it do, in his presidential newspaper. Studying the contents of the newspaper can provide insights into what those plans and priorities must have been.

This book has two goals. The first is simply to provide interested readers an overview of what was being said in the *National Intelligencer*. Very often, of course, how something is said is as important as what is said. Therefore, to best convey a sense of what the messaging in the paper was like, there are many quotations from the articles (with, unless otherwise noted, original spellings, punctuation, and emphases).

The second goal is to analyze how the treatment of various topics in the *Intelligencer* can expand scholarly understanding of the strategies and goals of Jefferson and his allies as they confronted those issues. In all of these cases, as will be seen, how the newspaper addressed these topics adds to our understanding of what Jefferson and his fellow Republicans must have been thinking, and what they thought was important to promote publicly.

CHAPTER 2

Newspapers, Thomas Jefferson, and the *National Intelligencer*

Only a newspaper can put the same thought at the same time before a thousand readers. A newspaper is an adviser that need not be sought out, but comes of its own accord and talks to you briefly every day about the commonweal, without distracting you from your private affairs.

—Alexis de Tocqueville, *Democracy in America*[1]

But who is to give an explanation to the public? Not yourself certainly. The chief magistrate cannot enter the Arena of the newspapers. At least the occasion should be of a much higher order. I imagine there is some pen at Washington competent to it. Perhaps the best form would be that of some one personating the friend of Erving, some one apparently from the North. Nothing labored is requisite. A short & simple statement of the case, will, I am sure, satisfy the public.

—Thomas Jefferson to James Madison, July 3, 1811[2]

Without modern survey research data, it is of course difficult to accurately gauge the impact of newspapers on public opinion during Jefferson's presidency. Moreover, political newspapers were just one tool being used by political leaders to solicit popular support at the turn of the nineteenth century. According to Noble E. Cunningham Jr., Republicans "exploited every available agency of mass communication: official papers such as petitions against governmental measures, public circular letters from congressmen to their constituents, newspapers, pamphlets, handbills, private letters which circulated among leading figures, and personal contacts and word-of-mouth communications."[3]

Nevertheless, judging from the great efforts expended by political leaders to establish newspapers in areas where they wished to improve their party's fortunes, newspapers were considered central to the effort to influence public opinion. Republican leader Elbridge Gerry, writing from the Federalist state of Massachusetts in May 1801, counseled Jefferson, "The multiplying republican presses, is a measure of the utmost importance: I hope it will be attended to in the N England states."[4] As noted in chapter 1, Levi Lincoln, another experienced Massachusetts Republican, agreed, saying that with a "few more republican newspapers" the region could be turned Republican. Jefferson's postmaster general, Gideon Granger, echoed this sentiment in 1802, after traveling "the back road" from Washington to Philadelphia. On the trip of about 190 miles, he saw only one Republican newspaper. This, he wrote Jefferson, "was not altogether pleasing to one who believes that public opinion will in a great measure be governed by that Vehicle of Intelligence."[5]

Federalists in Massachusetts understood the power of the press as well. One of their leaders, Fisher Ames, observed in 1801 that "the majority of citizens form their ideas of men and measures almost solely from the light that reaches them through the magic-lantern of the press." He recommended, "As the newspapers greatly influence public opinion, and that controls everything else, it is not only important but absolutely essential, that these should be used with more effect than ever."[6] As Joyce Appleby and other scholars have noted, these uniform assessments of the power of the press in 1800 reflect that the political climate was changing in a fundamental way in America.

> The Federalists maintained that after voting, citizens should let their elected officials govern, while the Jeffersonians articulated a political philosophy that took popular sovereignty literally, insisting on the people's right to engage in vigorous politicking. Gathering in taverns and coffeehouses, America's new citizens avidly read the papers and, armed with a little information, threw themselves into intense debates about public policy.[7]

In 1795, around 150 newspapers were being published in the United States. Federalists had a major newspaper advantage. Three-fourths of the newspapers were either Federalist supporters of the administration or nonpolitical; there were only 18 or so Republican newspapers, mostly concentrated in large cities.[8] Just five years later, Republicans had essentially achieved newspaper parity with Federalists. In 1800, there were 85 Republican-oriented newspapers out of a total newspaper population of about 260; by the time Thomas Jefferson took office in early 1801, "the Republican cause had a dedicated promoter of its views in every major city and in most of the principal smaller towns of every state."[9]

In his study of the development of the US postal system and the crucial role it played in mass political communication in the nineteenth century, Richard R. John estimated that about 1.9 million newspapers circulated through the postal system in 1800. That number is impressive, considering that the population of the country then was about 5.3 million.[10] Those political newspapers also had a readership that went far beyond the relatively few Americans who subscribed to them. As John found,

> Once newspapers arrived at the post office, they were regarded, by what seems to have been almost universal convention, as less the private property of the subscriber than a kind of public resource to be made available to anyone who wished to catch up on the latest news. "There is scarcely a village or country post office in the United States, particularly if it be kept in a tavern or store," declared one contemporary in 1822, "in which the newspapers are not as free to all comers, as to the persons to whom they rightfully belong."[11]

It seems likely, then, that such a prominent newspaper as the *Intelligencer* could have been found in just about every post office in the country, perhaps even left there intentionally by clever subscribers for others to read for themselves or even aloud to others.

Such sharing would have magnified the influence of newspapers far beyond only the elites who subscribed to them. Word of mouth and personal letters would have spread the information even farther. Thus, by 1800, American politicians, partisans, and newspaper publishers had created effective chains of mass political communication that reached most of the country. The networks continued to expand, as the newspapers became indispensable tools of political persuasion and organization for the early Federalist and Republican parties.[12]

Even before running for president in 1800, Jefferson knew well the value of the partisan newspapers of his era. In 1790, when he returned to the United States from France, he was appalled by the "monarchical sentiments" he encountered everywhere. He attributed this phenomenon to the influence of a newspaper, the *Gazette of the United States*, which Alexander Hamilton had established in the nation's capital to promote the Federalists' agenda during Washington's presidency. Working with James Madison and others, Jefferson quickly established the *National Gazette* to lead the Republican counteroffensive.[13]

For two years, the two party gazettes fought a war of words over the policies and principles that ought to be followed by the new national government. Jefferson used the language of battle, begging Madison to engage Hamilton: "For God's sake, my dear Sir, take up your pen, select the most striking heresies and cut him to pieces in face of the public." Madison did just that in the famous Pacificus-Helvidius newspaper debates of 1793–94. (Jefferson may well have written for the *National Gazette* as well. Hamilton implied it in his counterattacks in the *Gazette of the United States*, prompting Philip Freneau, the editor of the *National Gazette*, to publicly deny Jefferson's involvement.)[14] In his diary later, Jefferson recorded with satisfaction that the *National Gazette*, his first effort at establishing a political newspaper, had "saved our Constitution which was fast galloping into monarchy!"[15] Toward the end of their lives, in 1823, Jefferson reiterated to Madison the value of a partisan system of mass political communication. The Republicans' newspaper network, he wrote, had had an "unquestionable effect" in the "revolution produced on the public mind" that vanquished Federalism.[16]

The *National Intelligencer* was at the apex of that network during Jefferson's presidency. Heading up a Republican "confederation of newspapers," it effectively became the "national newspaper"—in Jeffrey Pasley's term—that Jefferson had long envisioned.[17] Samuel Harrison Smith was Jefferson's logical choice to be the paper's editor and publisher. Smith had published a newspaper in Philadelphia. In 1798, when Jefferson was president of the American Philosophical Society, Smith had won an award from the society for his essay on the ideal "republican system of education."[18] His plan called for the "universal diffusion of knowledge" to produce an "enlightened" citizenry. By "calling into active operation the mental resources of a nation," he maintained, citizens would be "too well informed to be misled, too virtuous to be corrupted."[19] According to Smith's wife, Margaret Bayard Smith, the award led to a warm friendship between Jefferson and Smith.[20]

Jefferson must have been confident that the genteel, classically educated Smith,[21] with a socially connected wife, would be a much more reliable and controllable mouthpiece for elite Republicans than William Duane, the fiery editor of the *Philadelphia Aurora*, which had previously been the flagship publication for the Republican movement. While Duane had been a highly effective Republican propagandist, he had by 1800 antagonized many top Republicans, by often condemning or contradicting their actions and "reserving the right to refuse or alter all anonymous submissions" for his paper.[22] As Duane himself put it, "My independence is my pride."[23] Federalists, of course, thoroughly detested Duane and even prosecuted him under the Sedition Act.[24]

Given Jefferson's vision of a nationally circulated newspaper that would reflect what he and other elite Republicans wanted the country to hear while not unnecessarily antagonizing Federalists, having Duane as its editor would not fit the bill. The twenty-eight-year-old Smith would.[25] Smith's newspaper in Philadelphia, the *Universal Gazette*, had on balance supported the Republican Party, but its "partisan expressions were couched in moderate and inoffensive language."[26] Smith wrote few editorials himself, instead publishing "the usual letters bearing classical signatures from unidentified contributors."[27]

This combination would have been just what Jefferson wanted. As Pasley puts it, the "pliable, genteel" Smith "proved an utterly reliable mouthpiece. Refusing to seek any political role or glory for himself, he allowed administration members to insert articles at will and set the *Intelligencer*'s political line."[28] The nature of the *Intelligencer* was obvious; one competitor derisively described the paper as "Mr. Silky Milky Smith's National Smoothing Plane."[29]

In contrast, as Jefferson reflected in a letter to Madison in 1803 when Duane was badgering them for information to use in his newspaper, Duane's "precipitancy" made him "improper to be considered as speaking the sense of the government."[30] That role, Madison and Jefferson agreed, could only be served by one newspaper, the *National Intelligencer*. As Madison had said in his letter to Jefferson a few days earlier, it would be "improper to make more than one paper the vehicle of informal or formal communications from the government."[31]

This means, of course, that the *Intelligencer* was in fact reflecting the political aims and positions of Jefferson and his allies rather than merely the views of Smith.[32] William Ames, who wrote the history of the *National Intelligencer*, confirms this point via a rather brutal assessment of Smith's intellect and character. According to Ames, Smith had a "general lack of imagination" and no ability for "original political thinking" and therefore had little to do with the paper's political commentaries.

If he had ideas of his own, he submerged them in his complete support of Jefferson. . . . Smith's deficiency of creative power, his blind subservience to a cause, and his mild manner and moderation produced a paper [that] . . . caused many people to regard the *Intelligencer* as merely a mouthpiece for the president and his party and void of any real character contributed by its editor.[33]

Joseph Gales, Smith's onetime business partner and successor, described Smith's pliability just as bluntly, saying, according to Ames, "Smith was so bound to follow the directions of others that he would march directly into a brick wall if ordered to do so by a superior."[34]

The format of the *National Intelligencer* was typical for newspapers of the time. It was four pages, printed on extremely tough and durable paper (volumes of the original issues can still be found in some libraries). Each page, about one-third larger in dimensions than modern newspapers, was filled with four or five columns of dense, small print (in six- or seven-point font). The last page of the paper carried only commercial advertisements and legal notices (including many advertising rewards for runaway slaves and slaves for sale). Some advertisements and notices could be found on the other three pages of the paper as well. Usually, another page or so was devoted to verbatim reports of debates and votes in Congress, as well as publications of new federal laws and official documents such as presidential proclamations, treaties, and reports from government offices. Frequently, the paper carried reprints of reports on affairs abroad from European papers. About two pages were then filled with mostly domestic political material, which commonly included accounts of congressional debates, official government notices, regular anonymous or pseudonymous political commentaries, reprints of commentaries from other Republican newspapers, and the texts of official addresses and messages that had been delivered by governors and legislators in states controlled by Republicans.

After Jefferson had become president, he and James Madison, his secretary of state, even set up a sort of officially sanctioned connection between the *Intelligencer* and a group of friendly Republican newspapers across the country. They did this through a law (ironically passed by Federalists in 1799) that provided for new laws enacted by Congress to be published in one to three newspapers in every state. Madison named the *Intelligencer* the official publisher in the capital of the new laws. He then designated only Republican newspapers to be the paid publishers of the laws in the states and instructed them to take their texts of the laws from those published in the *Intelligencer*. He ultimately selected thirty-five newspapers across the country for this role.[35] Naturally, in addition to consulting the *Intelligencer* for their official texts, the editors of all those newspapers were also receiving the paper's centralized political messages from the Jefferson administration.

The links between Jefferson and the *National Intelligencer* were strong. Jefferson was in close professional contact with Smith. In a letter to her sister in early March 1801, Margaret Bayard Smith reported that her husband had "seen Mr. Jefferson, at least once a week this whole winter."[36] Jefferson also had extensive social contact with the Smiths, who were frequent guests at the White House, attending many of the dinners that Jefferson hosted there[37] and visiting him at Monticello.[38] In turn, the Smiths kept their "cellar and larder well stocked . . . and many political leaders, including the President, frequented the Smith soirees."[39] Their home was a "social center in the new capital."[40] In the words of one biographer, the Smiths seem to have been the original power couple in Washington society. Their home was "the rendezvous of statesmen, authors, musicians, politicians, and editors." Margaret was described as a "charming hostess, happy in married life, capable, intelligent, vivacious, energetic, and positive."[41]

As noted previously, the president's Republican allies in Congress helped Samuel Smith get lucrative government printing contracts that ensured the financial survival of the *Intelligencer*.[42] This of course made the Smiths' economic welfare totally dependent on Jefferson's political success and goodwill, since Jefferson's support could have been withdrawn at any time. Margaret Bayard Smith acknowledged that reality in a letter to her sister in February 1801, after the House of Representatives had named Jefferson president. The news was a great relief, she said, because, through her husband, her "destiny" had been linked to Jefferson's political success. Her "condition in life, my union with the man I loved," she wrote, had depended on Jefferson's "success in the pending presidential election, or rather the success of the democratic party, (their interests were identical)."[43]

The special character of the *Intelligencer* was demonstrated on the first day of Jefferson's presidency. Although Jefferson had delivered his inaugural address in a barely audible voice, the text of the address was readily available in the capital that day—and soon throughout the country. Smith had printed the speech in a special edition of the *Intelligencer*, using the advance copy he had received from Jefferson.[44] In the next issue, on March 6, Smith crowed, "So great was the demand for this address and so considerable the number of citizens surrounding the office in expectation of its appearing that the Press could scarcely keep pace with it. Already thousands have read it."

The close relationship between Jefferson and Smith was displayed in the paper again in 1804, when Jefferson used Smith to respond to the claim of a prominent Federalist newspaper editor, William Coleman, that Jefferson was not really the author of the Declaration of Independence. To rebut the charge, Jefferson summoned Smith and showed him his copy of the original draft.[45] In the July 23, 1804, *Intelligencer*, Smith published the "result of the examination we then made." Based on his viewing of the "original draft, presented to Congress," he assured his readers, it was plainly evident that the document was almost totally the work of Jefferson. Smith said he "found it to be in the hand writing of Mr. Jefferson," with no more than eight or ten alterations by Benjamin Franklin and John Adams. The alterations, he asserted, "did not materially vary the original composition, and, "in every instance, they soften the spirit of the first draft."[46] Readers of the newspaper surely would have been impressed that of all the people to whom Jefferson could have shown his historic draft, the president had chosen Smith.

Smith's account represents an explicit, highly publicized assertion by Jefferson that he was the author of this iconic document. That public claim of paternity by Jefferson appears to have escaped scholarly note. The most recent work on the subject, Robert M. S. McDonald's 2016 *Confounding Father: Thomas Jefferson's Image in His Own Time*, asserts, for example, that although Jefferson famously chose to include the claim in his epitaph, he was "never so crass," while alive, to have publicly claimed authorship of the Declaration.[47] Moreover, it appears Jefferson's claim was quite misleading. As Pauline Maier found, Adams and Franklin indeed made only a handful of minor changes to the original "rough draft" that Jefferson submitted to the committee. However, as she also found, both men had apparently made a number of other, earlier suggestions that Jefferson incorporated into his draft. Those suggestions would not have been evident, because the draft Jefferson submitted to the committee—and showed to Smith—was entirely in his handwriting.[48]

The modus operandi of the *Intelligencer*, like all the other political newspapers of the time, was to publish notes and commentaries that were anonymous, signed with pseudonyms, or portrayed as editorial commentary by Smith himself. While some of this material could have been written by Smith, it is likely (especially if the previously cited assessments of Smith's talents—or lack thereof—are accepted) that most of it was authored by high-level Republicans in Jefferson's administration, including Jefferson himself. According to Jeffrey Pasley, Attorney General Lincoln and Postmaster General Granger were two of the most frequent contributors to the paper.[49] Treasury Secretary Albert Gallatin was involved too; Dumas Malone found an entire commentary by Gallatin published in the *Intelligencer* on October 20, 1802.[50] As suggested previously, it also seems highly likely that James Madison, as secretary of state, would have done much writing for the paper. He is known to have authored a series of commentaries in the paper during Jefferson's second term, on the administration's trade policy, and as will be discussed later in this chapter, several of the commentaries in the paper on the role of public opinion in government echo Madison's writings from the 1790s in the Republican-sponsored *National Gazette*.[51]

Another candidate is Samuel Smith's wife, Margaret Bayard Smith. The letters she wrote to family and friends during Jefferson's presidency describe vividly the social and political scene in the capital and are cited often by historians. The editor's preface to the letters describes her as a prolific writer whose works were often published anonymously or under pseudonyms, and observes intriguingly that, in 1835, she published an anonymous letter in the *Intelligencer* and "probably contributed to this paper on other occasions which cannot be identified."[52] One can easily imagine her having been extensively involved in the editorial operations of the *Intelligencer*.[53]

One example of Levi Lincoln's involvement is found in a letter of July 11, 1801, in which Jefferson asked Lincoln to put together a comprehensive explanation, to be published in the newspapers, of repairs to a French ship, the *Berceau*, done earlier that year. The repairs had been made in haste, without congressional authorization, as part of a settlement with France of the hostilities each country had committed during their "quasi war" from 1798 to 1800. Astonishingly, the work had actually involved the total reconstruction of the ship, because it had been dismantled and sold in January 1801 before being hastily repurchased and reoutfitted for return to France. The whole affair had naturally become fodder for attacks in Federalist newspapers (to which Jefferson referred in his letter to Lincoln, who was in Massachusetts, as "your tory-papers"). An explanation was needed, Jefferson said, to "set the minds of the candid part of the public to rights."[54]

The example Malone found of Gallatin writing for the *Intelligencer* is particularly interesting, because it clearly illustrates how the process worked and Smith's limited role in it. When a Federalist newspaper questioned the legality of the refund of the fine that had been levied on James Callender for his sedition conviction, Gallatin wrote a response for publication and forwarded it to Jefferson for his comments, explaining that his "idea was that Smith should obey the request of 'a plain citizen'" to publish the commentary. Gallatin asked Jefferson to consider "whether it wants any additions, corrections, or curtailing?—I mean as to facts & arguments, not as to style—this Smith must modify."[55]

Although Jefferson was accomplished at concealing many things, there is still much evidence of his direct involvement with the *Intelligencer*. The editors of Jefferson's presidential papers found a note entirely in Jefferson's handwriting, initialed as received by Smith, that was the text for a long, legalistic footnote to Jefferson's first annual message to Congress to be published in the *Intelligencer* on December 9, 1801. Jefferson even provided Smith with a phony line introducing the note, having him say, "The Editor is not very certain to what this refers: but conjectures it is principally to the countervailing act passed by the British parliament in 1797. . . ." Smith published the note verbatim.[56] Similarly, on May 21, 1803, Jefferson sent Smith an analysis the president had written of recent elections in Connecticut, with the notation "Would it not be worth presenting to the public . . . this concise view?" Two days later, Smith published the analysis, virtually verbatim, under the heading "Plain view of the politics of CONNECTICUT."[57]

Another time, in 1804, Federalist editor William Coleman accused Jefferson of having authored and signed a conciliatory, obsequious message from the Continental Congress to the king of England in 1775. Coleman published this charge in the *New York Evening Post*, then the Federalists' flagship newspaper, to detract from Jefferson's growing fame as the author of the Declaration of Independence. Coleman's attack was snide.

> Those who affect to feel such an enthusiastic admiration for every paragraph, sentence, line and comma, in the Declaration of Independence, and who lose no opportunity to extol the prodigious talents and courage of the Immortal Jefferson, as being the penman, are invited to peruse the following extract from an address to the "King of Great Britain," drawn up by that same Immortal Jefferson, only ten months before he, with that singular consistency, which has always happily characterized him and his writings, drew up the Declaration of Independence.

Enraged, Jefferson wrote to Smith on July 19, 1804, asking, "Is it worthwhile to contradict the barefaced falsehood of Coleman in the second page fifth column of the enclosed paper[?]" Jefferson then provided the rebuttal himself: "It is false that I ever <u>drew</u> such a paper as is there ascribed to me. It is false that I ever <u>signed</u> such a paper drawn by another."[58] Smith noted his receipt of the letter the same day, and four days later published in the *Intelligencer* Coleman's charges with the following statement:

> It is on the authority of a friend of Mr. Jefferson, who has long enjoyed his confidence, & acted with him in many of the important scenes of the revolution, that we are enabled to declare,
> *That it is false that Mr. Jefferson ever DREW such a paper as is there ascribed to him.*
> *And that it is likewise false that he ever SIGNED such a paper drawn by another.*

After reading Coleman's actual charges in the *Intelligencer* on July 23, Jefferson wrote Smith another letter, on July 31, that elaborated on and modified his defense of his actions, to respond more precisely to the charges.[59] Smith promptly published the new defense, again as an editor's comment, on August 10.

Scholars have found significant evidence that, in one way or another, Jefferson routinely planted information and commentary in the *National Intelligencer*. Ames, who has written the authoritative history of the newspaper, observed, "As Jefferson admitted, contact between him and Smith was frequent and undoubtedly much information was given to the *Intelligencer* through conversation. Existing records also indicate that Jefferson used the *Intelligencer* not only to give the official point of view on issues but also to place before the newspaper's readers points of view he thought were important to be considered."[60] An example of this technique is found in a note from Jefferson to Smith dated October 23, 1802. Apparently enclosing another document, Jefferson wrote, "The enclosed paper seems intended for the legislative as well as Executive eye; but certainly not to be laid before the former in a regular way. The only irregular one would be in the newspapers. But this must depend on its merit and your opinion of it."[61] Another scholar, Frederick B. Marbut, reported finding several *National Intelligencer* articles with language "practically identical" to the language of letters Jefferson had sent to Smith.[62]

Certainly, Jefferson knew the routine in which high-level political actors wrote commentaries that were masked as coming from another source. In one example just discussed, Smith portrayed Jefferson's defense of himself against Federalist attacks in 1804 as coming not from Jefferson, who had written the defense, but from a "friend of Mr. Jefferson" who had "long enjoyed his confidence and acted with him in many of the important scenes of the revolution." On another occasion during his presidency, Jefferson organized, with Madison and Henry Dearborn, a newspaper response to some hostile commentaries that John Randolph had written under the pen name "Decius." Jefferson then advised, "It remains now to consider on what authority these corrections of fact can be advanced without compromitting [compromising] the Executive. It would seem to be the best that the writer should assume the mask of a member of the Legislature."[63]

As documented by other scholars, Jefferson is known to have put on such masks himself, writing commentaries for publication but disguising his authorship. Cunningham's study of Jefferson's presidency provides two examples. The first concerns a commentary Jefferson wrote and sent to Levi Lincoln, who was to have the piece published in his home state of Massachusetts. In his letter to Lincoln, Jefferson indicated he had written the commentary "under the character of a Massachusetts citizen."[64] In the second, Jefferson sent his work to another newspaper editor and offered several options for disguising its real authorship; the piece could be published as "an anonymous communication, or with a feigned name, or as the editor's own observations."[65] Cunningham describes several other instances in which Jefferson, Madison, and other administration officials wrote material for publication in the *Intelligencer.*[66] Malone found a commentary in Jefferson's handwriting that was published in the *Philadelphia Aurora* in 1804, proclaiming that, with Jefferson's inauguration, the "arrogance of precedence in society" had been abolished in the nation's capital.[67]

Another time, now as a former president advising his successor, Jefferson again recommended the creation of an imaginary commentator. In a July 3, 1811, letter to Madison, Jefferson wrote of having "seen with very great concern the late Address of Mr. Smith to the public." Jefferson was referring to Robert Smith's *Address to the People of the United States.* The *Address* was a sensational attack on Madison by Smith, whom Madison had recently fired from his position as secretary of state. Smith had released the attack as a pamphlet, and his charges were being discussed by political leaders and published in newspapers around the country. Smith accused Madison of incompetence, pro-French and anti-English bias, and potentially criminal wrongdoing during his time as secretary of state under Jefferson. It was clear that a public response to the charges was needed.

Some of the charges concerned payments Madison had approved to an American legal representative in England, George Erving. In his letter, Jefferson asked Madison to refresh his memory about the "particulars" of the payments. Then, as expressed in the second quote at the beginning of this chapter, Jefferson succinctly conveyed his understanding of how political newspapers were used then. He said an explanation should be published and attributed to an invented persona, "some one personating the friend of Erving, some one apparently from the North."

As far as his Federalist opponents were concerned, Jefferson was definitely writing for the *National Intelligencer*. That claim came from the *Washington Federalist*, which began publication in the capital in 1801. As it described itself on July 31, 1802, the *Federalist* was the "only decisive federal newspaper at the seat of government." According to Bruce Ackerman, the *Federalist* was "the party's paper in the new capital" and was "voraciously devoured by politicos."[68] On November 13, 1801, in a long commentary entitled "Addressed to the Editor of the National Intelligencer," the *Federalist* described the *Intelligencer* as the "paper of the government," claiming that "it has been discerned from the stile of some of its paragraphs" that "the President himself" was writing for the paper.[69]

John B. Colvin, a newspaper editor and holder of a State Department patronage job in Jefferson's administration, wrote Jefferson a letter in 1811 that further supports the likelihood of Jefferson's frequent authorship of newspaper commentaries. Colvin had requested Jefferson's opinion on when a military officer could properly exceed his orders in the interest of a greater good, such as to prevent a widespread rebellion. Jefferson wrote Colvin a thoughtful reply, saying he had "indulged freer views on this question" in light of Colvin's assurances that they were for his eyes only and would "not get into the hands of newswriters." Colvin did not keep Jefferson's words to himself, however. He used them in his contribution to a book that James Wilkinson was writing about his involvement in putting down the Burr conspiracy of 1807 in New Orleans. Again in 1811, after Wilkinson's *Memoirs* had been published, Colvin wrote to Jefferson,

I presume that you have, by this time, read in your own words, the argument in favor of the proceedings at New Orleans against the conspirators. In truth, I copied those arguments, and gave them to Gen. Wilkinson, without the least intimation that they were from your pen: And thus, sir, you have contributed to do good without being seen in it—a thing which you, no doubt, have often done—and which, more than anything else, assimilates a man to his duty.[70]

As Jeremy Bailey concluded, Jefferson likely knew quite well from experience that his words would end up in print in this indirect form.[71]

Political elites on both sides of the aisle certainly regarded the *Intelligencer* as reflecting the views of Jefferson and his Republican allies. The testimonials are numerous. On May 12, 1801, the prominent Pennsylvanian Republican, close Jefferson ally, and longtime congressman William Findley wrote Jefferson a letter full of political news and advice. The letter concluded, "As I take Mr. Smith's [I]ntelligencer and always have taken his paper, I presume I receive correct information."[72] As discussed previously in chapter 1, when a Massachusetts Republican leader wrote Vice President Aaron Burr in October 1801 to inquire whether the paper could be considered a "reliable" guide for Jeffersonian Republicans, Burr wrote back that the *Intelligencer*'s content was based on information from the administration itself. James Bayard, the Federalist senator who played a key role in the maneuverings in the House of Representatives that resulted in Jefferson's selection as president, called the newspaper the "official administrative organ . . . unquestionably under the direction of Mr. Jefferson and his party."[73] (Bayard had family connections to the Smiths as well; he was Margaret's cousin and lived with her family after the death of his own parents.)[74] William Coleman, the editor of the *New York Evening Post*, referred to the *Intelligencer* as the "court journal of Jefferson" and labeled its editor "the little monkey."[75] Hearing rumors about the Louisiana Purchase when she was in New York in 1803, Margaret Bayard Smith wrote her husband, "I long to see your enunciation of this matter [in the *Intelligencer*] and to ascertain what is true. Everyone seems to rely on what you assert as the truth."[76]

A particularly impressive affirmation of the prestige and power of the *Intelligencer* came in 1804 from another high source, Supreme Court Justice Samuel Chase, then the target of impeachment proceedings by Republicans in Congress. After extensive debate, reported extensively in the *Intelligencer* and then many other newspapers, the House had resolved to impeach Chase. It had not, however, voted on the final articles of impeachment before the congressional session had ended in March. This meant there would be no impeachment trial of Chase in the Senate for many months, because Congress would not meet again until November. From Chase's perspective, he was left in the grossly unfair position of having the charges dangling in the public eye indefinitely, with no opportunity for rebuttal by him.

Chase's response, an early form of public relations damage control, showed the perceived power of the mass media even then in America. As is discussed in more detail in chapter 7, Chase wrote a long "Memorial" defending himself against all the charges. He sent it to "the editors of all the newspapers in the United States," asking them to publish it so that his side of the story could also be heard. In the Memorial, Chase said he especially wanted the *National Intelligencer* to publish it—which Smith did on April 4, 1804 under the title "IMPEACHMENT," capitalized and in larger font—because of the extraordinary influence the paper had due to its well-known connection with Jefferson and its national circulation.

> The recent publication of this testimony, in a Gazette understood to be the official organ of the government, and thence communicating an official character and sanction to whatever of this nature appears in it, is a circumstance calculated to increase, in a very great degree, the mischievous effects of the testimony itself. . . . From this Gazette, the publication will pass into others; and thus the most virulent misrepresentations of his conduct, and slanders on his character, sanctioned too, in some degree, will be spread throughout the United States; and will even extend to foreign countries; while the opportunity of refuting them, must, of necessity, be delayed for a considerable time.

In addition to these contemporaneous judgments about the *Intelligencer*, there is also commonsense inference. In 1801, Washington, DC, had a population of 3,210, and the national government there had in 1802 a total of 291 officials and other employees.[77] Most of the members of Congress lived in seven or eight boardinghouses when Congress was in session. Experienced politicians are well aware of everything going on in their worlds. This awareness would have included the knowledge that both the Washington and Adams administrations had employed a newspaper, the *Gazette of the United States*, as their semiofficial mouthpiece.[78] It would have been well known that Jefferson had arranged for Smith to establish the *National Intelligencer* in the capital as his media outlet;

that Smith was in close social and professional contact with Jefferson; that Smith's newspaper was under Jefferson's sponsorship, benefiting from favorable government printing work; and that the contents of the newspaper reflected the views of the Jefferson administration. Indeed, it could be said that Jefferson was just following in the footsteps of his great rival Alexander Hamilton, who had pioneered the idea of a pro-administration newspaper with the *Gazette of the United States*.

With such established political expectations and realities, Smith would hardly have dared to stray far editorially from the views of his sponsor—and everyone who was politically connected would have known that. Indeed, precisely that point was made in January 1801 by the *Intelligencer*'s rival, the *Washington Federalist*. During the crisis over the deadlock in the House of Representatives, the *Federalist* carried a response to commentaries in the *National Intelligencer* arguing that the House was obliged to choose Jefferson over Burr. Noting that the *Intelligencer* was being published in the capital "under the eye of Mr. Jefferson," a commentary in the January 13 issue of the *Federalist* attributed the *Intelligencer*'s position to Jefferson himself. After all, the commentary observed,

> With the known character of the Editor of that paper, is it to be supposed, that he would devote so many of its columns to this subject, contrary to the wishes of his political Idol? If the whole were not approved by Mr. Jefferson before publication, would not a slight intimation from him put an end to all such discussions in that paper?

Responding a few weeks later, on January 26, to *Intelligencer* commentaries threatening dissolution of the government if Jefferson were not named president, the *Federalist* mentioned Smith by name and sneered, "Do the great men behind the curtain, who pull the strings that direct these puppets, think to frighten the Federalists with this mummery[?]"

Later that year, the *Washington Federalist* made the ultimate explicit connection between Jefferson and the contents of the *National Intelligencer*. On November 13, 1801, the *Federalist* published a commentary by "Portencius" under the headline "Addressed to the Editor of the National Intelligencer." The commentary began by affirming that "liberty and good government" depend on frequent, free, and impartial discussions of government matters and that the "great body of the people . . . require only to be rightly informed to act rightly,"[79] However, the commentary charged, the *Intelligencer* was not acting impartially but, instead, only telling one side of the story, Jefferson's.[80] That slanted story was often coming from Jefferson himself, the *Federalist* asserted, saying that his authorship could be "discerned from the style of some of its [the *Intelligencer*'s] paragraphs." Rather than "condemning" this practice, the *Federalist* said, "we approve [it] in the President" because it showed Jefferson's willingness to provide information to the public about his actions. Having been "furnished with such information and explanation from such authority," all Americans would be better able to judge the "propriety" of the president's actions in two ways, the commentary said: both by what was provided in the *Intelligencer* and what was left out. This public review process was appropriate, the *Federalist* commentary asserted, because it was clearly the "method of defense" chosen by Jefferson "for his preservation."

This explicit linkage of Jefferson to the contents of the *Intelligencer* by his political opponents is highly significant from a scholarly point of view. It answers a challenge raised by Jeffrey Tulis to the argument, presented in my first book, that since readers of presidential newspapers understood that the newspapers were speaking for their presidential sponsors, the fact that the information was conveyed in this way, rather than through presidential speeches, messages, or proclamations, was essentially irrelevant. To that claim, Tulis responded,

> It is worth asking why presidents used the partisan press when they could easily have given speeches in their own name. . . . I think the answer lies in the connection of the form of communication to the constitutional doctrines of governance I describe in *The Rhetorical Presidency*. For example, the form of speech was conjoined with an understanding of the character of the office.
>
> Now it may be the case that the partisan press was the "functional equivalent" of popular leadership today. That is, presidents may have faced the same leadership prospects and pitfalls employing the indirect strategy as they do today through speeches. In order to show that through the partisan press earlier presidents were "popular leaders," one would have to demonstrate such an equivalence. For example, one might show that the public "blamed" presidents for controversial positions taken by their partisan organs in the way that the public "blames" presidents for misstatements or controversy on the stump today. That would, indeed, be hard to do, but if in future work Laracey can do it, he will have made an important contribution.[81]

This was precisely how the *Washington Federalist* viewed Jefferson's newspaper. It said the *Intelligencer* was the "method of defense" chosen by Jefferson "for his preservation," and that Jefferson intended the American public to judge the "propriety" of his actions from what appeared (or did not appear) in his newspaper. This certainly amounts to a contemporary, public declaration—by the mouthpiece of his Federalist opponents—that Jefferson could indeed be "blamed" for the contents of the *Intelligencer.* That declaration satisfies Tulis's challenge. As Stephen Skowronek interpreted that challenge, the empirical question is whether "indirect forms of popular communication," such as Jefferson's presidential newspaper, "actually did insulate the president from attributions of policy responsibility."[82] The answer as demonstrated here is clearly that it did not.

The commentary from the *Federalist* also addresses a related test posed by Terri Bimes. She wrote:

> But a more specific test would be to examine what the public knew about the president's relationship to the newspaper. That is, the hurdle should be to show that it was widely known that the president was placing editorials in the newspaper and nevertheless there was no public outcry against the presidents' actions.[83]

There certainly was no outcry here—quite the contrary. Rather than "condemning" Jefferson's use of the *Intelligencer* to communicate with the public, the *Federalist* said "we approve" it.

All high-level government officials in America—and, for that matter, in England and throughout Europe—knew that a common technique for high government officials was to speak to the public not directly but through a sponsored newspaper.[84] Indeed, governments on both sides of the Atlantic regularly used newspapers to send and receive signals on what was being intended or considered at the highest government levels.[85] Therefore, since the *Intelligencer* was known to be presenting the views of Jefferson and his allies, something that appeared in the newspaper would have been read not merely as Smith's opinions or thoughts but as reflecting those of the Jefferson administration. The *Intelligencer* would have had to consistently reflect that reality. After all, if it ever became unclear when the paper was speaking "officially" and when it was not, the usefulness of the paper as a communications tool would have been undermined, because the messages would have become of doubtful reliability.

US Senator William Plumer recorded in his diary an intriguing conversation he had with Jefferson regarding political newspapers. Plumer recounted that Jefferson had spoken disparagingly of most of the newspapers but had said that at least Smith's paper corrected its mistakes when it made them.[86] It is therefore noteworthy that Smith never published any retractions regarding the material that is presented in this book. The absence of retractions is further evidence of Jefferson's implicit approval of what the newspaper was saying. It is hard to believe he would have tolerated the publication of statements he did not agree with in a newspaper that was so closely identified with him.

On a deeper level, there is also the fascinating commentary in the July 12, 1802, *Intelligencer* to consider. That commentary responded to recent jabs by its rival in the capital, the *Washington Federalist*, condemning criticisms the *Intelligencer* had made of Napoleon's recent coup in France. Why should the *Federalist* care what the *Intelligencer* said about France? As the *Intelligencer* explained, the *Federalist* said the comments amounted to much more than ordinary newspaper commentary.

> It is said that as the National Intelligencer is the official paper, it is supposed generally to express the opinion and to coincide with the sentiments of the government; and it is asked if Bonaparte and the other officers of the French government will be expected to continue a friendly intercourse with a nation, whose government and citizens unite in holding them up to the abhorrence and execration of mankind?

The *Intelligencer*'s response took two tacks. The first simply denied that anything printed in the newspaper could be presumed to reflect any views of the Jefferson administration.

> [T]he sentiments, expressed in the National Intelligencer, may or may not be those of the executive government of the United States. Whether they are, or are not, is on this and all similar occasions, perfectly immaterial. Their appearance in the National Intelligencer, in the disconnected form in which they have been exhibited, is evidence neither one way or the other. It is only evidence that the Editor, or some writer, holds them, and recommends them to popular acceptance.

This denial is intriguingly worded. It actually does not deny that material published in the paper might well reflect views of the "executive

government," that is, Jefferson. It only says that because of the "discon-
nected form" in which material appears in the *Intelligencer*—without
attribution—the placement in the newspaper is "evidence neither one
way or the other" of whether a particular commentary comes from Jefferson or his administration.[87] The commentary then shifts, to say that when
material does appear in the newspaper, it *is* evidence that someone, the
editor or another writer, "recommends them to popular acceptance."
If one makes the simple assumption that Smith would never publish
material in his newspaper that he thought Jefferson would disapprove
of, then this means that the newspaper was indeed recommending "to
popular acceptance" things that Jefferson agreed with.

The deepest discussion of the Jeffersonian linkage between political newspapers and government responsiveness to public opinion
can be found in a series of commentaries on the topic of "Republican government" that were published as "Letters" in the *Intelligencer*
in September and October 1803. The commentaries may well have
been written by Madison, because they so closely reflect the theory of
governmental responsiveness to public opinion that, as discussed in
chapter 1, he had developed in the 1790s and expressed in newspaper
essays then.[88] The fifth letter, published on October 3, 1803, asserts
that in a republic, "all [governmental] power is conferred by public
opinion, and . . . constantly regulated by it." The process is robust:
"the virtuous or vicious conduct of rulers rouses perpetual enquiry"
and the "praise or censure is immediate and inevitable and just." The
monitoring is the "result of the freest enquiry and the impartial judgment of those who are enlightened by a knowledge of the prominent
measures of the government."

The letter maintains that unlike monarchies or aristocracies that
conceal the reasons for their actions, the motives of the government in
democratic republics are "avowed in the face of the nation," because
"the prevalence of public opinion is the vital principle, the life blood
of republics." In this public review of governmental actions, every citizen feels a "constant excitement," a "regular, habitual, animation in the
national feeling," because all "consider themselves as the ultimate judges
of its propriety or ability." In such a system, therefore, the public must be
"liberally supplied" with information about the workings of the government; secrecy should be rare and limited in scope and duration. As other
letters in the series argue, such a public process guarantees that unpopular government policies can never be maintained for long, because public opinion will force a change.

Occasional dissatisfaction there will undoubtedly be; but that cannot long exist where all power resides in the people, who appoint their legislators for short periods. There can be no impression of hostile interest between the people and their rulers. They are absolutely as to efficiency one and the same. (eighth letter, *Intelligencer*, October 12, 1803)

The people sit in perpetual judgment upon the action of their rulers. The rotatory principle, and the change of public favor, call a large number of citizens into the administration . . . by the talents of thousands of private men. (ninth letter, *Intelligencer*, October 17, 1803)

But how exactly could "thousands of private men" have enough information to be critically assessing every important measure of the government? Obviously, as Richard D. Brown observed, under this robust theory of popularly responsive government, "the need to be informed was constant, not episodic."[89] The solution, the fifth letter proclaimed, was Republican newspapers: "More than three hundred gazettes, devoted to political facts and enquiries, are published at short intervals, and carry a knowledge of the laws, the grounds on which they were enacted, and the manner in which they are executed, through the wide extent of the nation."

The letter then conjured a grand vision of America as a democratic school for the masses, led by elite Republican schoolmasters.

[W]hatever involves a knowledge of the true interests of our country, embracing an acquaintance with its topography, its natural productions, its manufactures and commerce, its physical wants, its relations, political or commercial, with other nations wherewith we are directly or indirectly connected; will become the objects of attention to every mind sufficiently expanded to receive it. The nation, in short, will become a great school, in which the most enlightened individuals will instruct, and the least informed be instructed in whatever regards political conduct; and every day's experience will exhibit examples of citizens rewarded for their observance, or punished for their violation of duty, by being elevated to places of distinction, or removed from them.

This was no "Utopean philosophy," the letter said. Right then, in the America of 1803, "[t]housands and tens of thousands are at this moment employed in discussing the wisdom of the measures of our rulers, and advising such measures as they think will best advance the national welfare."[90]

The vision sketched out here and throughout the related series of *Intelligencer* commentaries on Republican government closely matches Madison's concept of the creation of a national "commerce of ideas" that Colleen Sheehan found in her brilliant examination of his writings.

> Of course Madison noted the benefit of representatives from large electoral districts; he did not, however, look to representation as the panacea for popular injustice. (*James Madison and the Spirit of Republican Self-Government*, 92–93)

> Madison grounded his theory of public opinion in a new conception of the politics of communication. He envisioned a commerce of ideas in the extended republic that would not only refine the will of the majority *in the legislature* but, to the extent possible, would also modify and enlarge the will and views *of the majority (or society) itself.* (94)

> Madison's advocacy of the commerce of ideas and politics of public opinion was his sustained attempt to solve the problem of majority opinion in a manner fully consistent with the form *and spirit* of popular government. The spirit of free government cannot be attained by achieving the people's consent and then disassociating them from the acts of government. The spirit of republicanism is present only when it is embodied in the minds and mores of the citizens and sustained by the activity of political participation and communication throughout the land. The construction of public opinion involves a process of instructive dialogue and deliberation that permeates the whole society, from the influence of the literati, the statesmen, and the laws on the mores and views of the citizens, to the communication of ideas throughout the great body of the people, to the influence of the settled opinion of the community on the representatives in government. Accordingly, public opinion is both acted upon and is itself an active political agent upon which government depends for its direction. (105)

A remarkable example of this "process of instructive dialogue and deliberation" is a series of essays published in the *Intelligencer* from August to November 1801 and signed with the pseudonym "Solon," the name of a famed lawgiver in ancient Greece.[91] The first essay explained the purpose of the essays: to provide "the people a *correct* knowledge of their true interests" in connection with various disagreements that had already arisen over the interpretation of the US Constitution. Each essay examined one specific disagreement (such as whether the powers of the federal government under the Constitution should be construed broadly or narrowly), presenting a relatively evenhanded discussion of the issue.

Noting that the disagreements had in every case been grounded in "party feeling, or something very like it," the essays by "Solon" concluded that the only definite way to resolve the disagreements would be to amend the Constitution. That solution was unlikely in the moment, though, because, in every case, the "public mind" had not "settled down in[to] any firm uncontroverted positions." Fortunately, "Solon" said, the American system of government provided an alternative remedy: the "force of public opinion and rational inquiry, addressed to those who are at once the organs of the government and the representatives of the national will, if openly and persevering[ly] applied, . . . accommodate the provisions of the government to the wishes of the people."[92] In an intriguing, roundabout way, the populist-based solution "Solon" offered reflected Jefferson's conviction that popular self-government "requires that the people—and not the judges—have the last say on the meaning of the Constitution."[93] Readers of the essays would have been empowered to do just that, having been provided with a better understanding of even such complex issues as constitutional interpretation.

The *Intelligencer* was thus performing two important functions during Jefferson's presidency, one pragmatic, the other educational. Pragmatically, the newspaper was advocating politically on Jefferson's behalf—and therefore on behalf of the Jeffersonian wing of the Republican Party.[94] Educationally, the *Intelligencer* was presenting to the American public the information, ranging from the factual to the constitutional and even philosophical, that Jefferson and his allies thought would facilitate responsible popular control of the government, a bedrock principle of Jeffersonian Republicanism. Those functions reflect Pasley's description of the role played by political newspapers in nineteenth-century America: to provide their readers with "a common rhetoric, a common set of political ideas, and a common interpretation of current affairs."[95] In Stephen Howard Brown's vivid description, the *Intelligencer* was providing some of the key "rhetorical labor required to organize this new creature, 'public opinion,'" which, by the time of Jefferson's election, had become the keystone of American political culture.[96] What was said in Jefferson's presidential newspaper can therefore tell us much about his presidency and the information and principles that he and his allies thought needed to be presented to the people as part of their vision of democratic government in America. There is no better place to start than at the beginning: the election of 1800.

CHAPTER 3

The Extraordinary
Presidential Election of 1800

As the presidential election of 1800 approached, Thomas Jefferson and his Republican allies thought the election "might well be the last opportunity to save the Constitution and the union."[1] They faced a desperate Federalist opposition that seemingly would do anything, including prosecuting its political enemies for sedition, to stay in power. Federalists, likewise, thought the election was all that stood between the country and the horrors of the French Revolution.[2]

The election process was complicated, unfolding in different states in different ways over a span of several months—from May to December—in 1800.[3] When all the Electoral College votes were counted, the Republican ticket of Thomas Jefferson and Aaron Burr had won a majority of the votes over their Federalist opponents, John Adams and Charles Cotesworth Pinckney of South Carolina. There was a problem, though. Jefferson and Burr had each received the same number of Electoral College votes. Unlike their Federalist opponents, Republicans had failed to arrange the withholding of at least one electoral vote for their vice presidential candidate so as to secure the presidency for the party's acknowledged presidential candidate, Jefferson.[4]

In such cases, the Constitution provided that the House of Representatives would select the president and, further, that voting in the House would be by state, with each state having one vote. Unfortunately for

41

Republicans, they only controlled eight of the sixteen state House delegations in the outgoing, "lame-duck" Congress. Federalists controlled six delegations, and two others were divided equally. This situation opened up any number of options for Federalists, ranging from trying to select someone other than Jefferson as president (most obviously, Aaron Burr) to allowing the deadlock to persist until—and even beyond—the expiration of John Adams's term on March 3, 1801. Finally, though, on February 17, 1801, several Federalist representatives changed their votes to give Jefferson two more state delegations, thereby electing him president.[5]

The Strategic Uses of the National Intelligencer

How the *National Intelligencer* was used in 1800–1801 during the presidential campaign and subsequent electoral crisis provides fresh insights into the political thought and strategies of Thomas Jefferson and his Republican allies as they sought to promote his election and their politics. The paper was used during this period in three stages: campaigning and electioneering, electoral crisis management, and the promotion of victory, conciliation, and Republicanism. In the first stage, the *Intelligencer* promoted Jefferson and attacked his Federalist opponents. While the actual Electoral College voting was going on in the states, the newspaper reported the results as they trickled in and sought to persuade electors in states that had not yet held their Electoral College vote to choose Jefferson. In the second stage, when the election landed in the House of Representatives, the *Intelligencer* was used to explain why only Jefferson ought to be named president and to argue—stridently and ominously—against any other possible outcome. The third stage consisted of two aspects: conciliatory commentaries published in anticipation of a Jefferson victory and celebratory commentaries framing the actual victory as a national triumph of the ideals of Jefferson and Republicanism over the dark forces of Federalism.

Stage I: Campaigning and Electioneering

From its beginning, the *National Intelligencer* was used as a tool for promoting the election of Thomas Jefferson to the presidency. Its promotional activities took three forms: general attacks on Adams and the Federalist party, arguments that the Electoral College vote ought to favor Jefferson based on the results of the popular vote in state elections, and pro-Jefferson appeals directed to voters or presidential electors in particular states.

The very first issue of the paper, published on October 31, 1800, carried on its front page a biting critique of the Washington and Adams presidencies, signed "A Republican." The essence of the attack was that under their administrations, the constitutionally ordained separation of powers between the president and Congress had been destroyed, leaving the country with a government that could no longer be called "republican." Rather than being the "servant of the legislature," Washington and Adams had become "their master" by repeatedly pushing through Congress, "by a small majority," such measures as the Jay Treaty of 1795 with Great Britain and the Alien and Sedition Acts, which, "when first proposed," had been "rejected with disdain."[6] Under them, the commentary charged, the rule of conduct had been that the "will of one man is *everything*, and the will of the people and their immediate representatives is *nothing*."

The pseudonym "A Republican" would have conveyed two meanings to readers. Of course, it would have indicated that the author was aligned with the party opposing the reelection of Adams. It would also have implied that the criticisms of Adams and his party came from someone who understood the real meaning of the "republican" system of government as developed by the framers of the Constitution. As famously described by James Madison in Federalist Paper No. 10, a "republic" is a "government in which the scheme of representation takes place" via the legislature.[7] Accusing the first two presidents, both Federalists, of becoming the "master" of Congress was the equivalent of charging them and their party with having subverted a fundamental aspect of American constitutional government.

The *Intelligencer*'s first issue also carried long excerpts from a pamphlet published a few weeks earlier by Alexander Hamilton, arguing that Adams was unfit to be reelected to the presidency. Naturally, that extraordinary attack by the Federalists' most prominent leader against their own presidential candidate was seized on by Republicans and circulated widely. The *Intelligencer* prefaced the excerpts with a short, surprisingly mild note to its readers. Describing Hamilton's pamphlet as "replete with interesting political matter," the paper said it was publishing extracts "selected in such a manner as not only to excite but reward curiosity."

Later issues of the *Intelligencer* continued to attack Adams. The November 7, 1800, issue carried claims that his propensity for making entangling treaties would lead to the loss of peace and prosperity, as well as that he had once said that the United States would eventually be a hereditary government and that it would be no easier to govern the people of Europe by democracy than it would be to govern their cattle democratically. The November 28 issue reprinted a *Boston Chronicle* editorial arguing that Hamilton's anti-Adams pamphlet and a letter Noah Webster had written in defense of Adams had both demonstrated the unsuitability of Adams for the office of the presidency.[8]

By the time the *National Intelligencer* began publishing, Jefferson and his supporters must have realized they might have some difficulties in translating their apparent popular vote majorities in several states into actual Electoral College votes. Their unease is apparent in the first two issues of the paper. The October 31 issue carried an analysis of election results in recent voting for state legislators or members of Congress in Pennsylvania, New Jersey, Maryland, and Delaware. Even though only the Delaware results were complete, the analysis extrapolated from the partisan results to conclude that "the public spirit of those states, if fairly expressed," would give Jefferson three more Electoral College votes than Adams. Taking into account the likely voting in the other states, the analysis concluded that "in this event Mr. Jefferson would undoubtedly be President." Clearly, the paper was attempting to shape future state electoral outcomes as well as public response to them.

The November 3, 1800, issue elaborated on the theme that partisan popular voting results ought to be reflected in the Electoral College voting. Its front page carried a long commentary entitled "Interesting View" and signed "Lycurgus," arguing that Jefferson was entitled to the majority of electoral college votes because the "supreme law of a Republic is that the will of a majority should prevail.". Citing the results of the most recent elections in each state for state or federal offices, "Lycurgus" calculated that translating those results proportionately into Electoral College votes would give Jefferson an 81–41 victory over Adams. The commentary was an implicit acknowledgment that the actual voting in the Electoral College was not going to reflect this clear Republican advantage in popular support. The problem for Republicans was that the state selection processes for presidential electors often lagged behind current popular political tendencies, because many states left the selection of presidential electors up to their legislatures, which might have been elected as long as a year or more earlier under different political circumstances.[9]

After first stating that there did not appear to be the "least probability" of an Adams victory in the Electoral College, "Lycurgus" considered precisely that possibility. It could occur, he said, due to a combination of Eastern states giving no votes to Jefferson—despite the existence of "respectable Republican minorities" there—and Federalist minorities in other states being able to cast their votes for Adams. "Lycurgus" claimed that an Electoral College vote for Adams could not make Adams the "real representative of the people," because "the latest expression of the public mind is decidedly Republican." If Adams were nevertheless elected president, he would be confronted, "Lycurgus" argued, by a House of Representatives with a "vast majority" of Republican members and by a Senate, "hitherto anti-Republican," that would be "shaken in its attachment to Mr. Adams."

"Lycurgus" closed with a direct plea to those presidential electors who are "too honest to be the slaves of party." Even if they had previously supported Adams and his measures, they ought to acknowledge, he averred, that Adams has "lost the confidence of his constituents" and no longer merits their support. He warned that "one mistaken vote" could "hurry us into discord, plunge us into war, and despoil us of our freedom."

Republicans would invoke these populist and apocalyptic themes repeatedly during the crisis. At first, as illustrated in the "Lycurgus" essay, they employed these ideas in pleas to members of the Electoral College to choose Jefferson over Adams. Then, realizing that the actual problem was the tie between Jefferson and his running mate, Aaron Burr, in Electoral College votes, Republicans began arguing that the House of Representatives should for the good of the country recognize the obvious "will of the people" and name Jefferson president, rather than Burr (or anyone else).

The "Lycurgus" pseudonym was an apt choice for the author of the *Intelligencer* essay. It was the name of two noble Greek statesmen who would have been well known to anyone classically educated. A fourth-century Athenian orator named Lycurgus was famed for his selfless dedication to the welfare of the city of Athens and for his strong personal integrity.[10] A seventh-century Spartan lawgiver with that name was said to have gotten his laws from the Delphic Oracle.[11] Both Greeks were models of enlightened disinterestedness and good judgment, precisely how "Lycurgus" in the *Intelligencer* was urging the electors to act.

The *Intelligencer* also served as a means of communicating with the electorate in unusually contested states. In mid-1800, Alexander Hamilton had begun promoting a complicated presidential election strategy that involved urging Federalists to support their vice presidential candidate, Charles Cotesworth Pinckney, for the presidency, instead of Adams.[12] Maryland and South Carolina, two states with substantial Federalist support, were at the center of Hamilton's efforts. In an attempt to blunt the strategy, the November 7 and 12 issues of the *Intelligencer* carried lengthy pleas urging the voters of those states to not fall for Hamilton's plan. Were Pinckney to be elected president, the *Intelligencer* warned, he "will be the nominal President, Mr. Hamilton will be the real one."

If voters thought their only choice was between Pinckney and Jefferson, the *Intelligencer* argued, they ought to vote for Jefferson. His "good sense and moderation are best calculated to reconcile true Americans," claimed "Civis" in the November 7 issue, thus framing support for Jefferson as a matter of national unity. Moreover, "A Friend to Peace" contended on November 12, a president from one of the Eastern states might place too much emphasis on commerce, or, as the writer termed it, that "extravagant spirit of trade." This, he said, would produce "perpetual war, and war leads invariably to a loss of freedom." It would be better, "Friend" argued, to choose a president from a southern state, because such agricultural states "are generally undisturbed by this active passion."

The *Intelligencer* also weighed in on the developing electoral problem in Pennsylvania, where a Republican House of Representatives and a Federalist Senate were deadlocked over the method for choosing the state's presidential electors. Controlling the more numerous House of Representatives, the Republicans naturally preferred a joint House-Senate vote for the electors. An essay by "A Friend of the People," published on November 14, 1800, surveyed the various modes that had been employed in other states and concluded that Pennsylvania should use a joint vote of its two houses. Any other method, the essayist argued, would produce a result that "will either express no opinion at all, or an opinion at war with the existing sentiments of the people." The essay concluded with another warning about electing a president against the expressed wishes of a majority of the people: "A president of the United States who is the representative of the people will be respected, beloved and obeyed by the people. A president who is not the representative of the people may be despised, hated and opposed."

These words vividly illustrate the new, Republican view that explicitly connected the president to "the people" as their elected agent. This so-called plebiscitary view of the presidency was markedly different from the view held by the framers of the Constitution. As Terri Bimes explains,

The Framers' decision to leave the selection of presidential electors to the states by no means suggests that they intended the selection system to foster presidents who led, or were led by, the public. The concept of a plebiscitary presidency, or more generally, of a president heavily dependent on public opinion, would have run directly counter to their fears of public ignorance. Even the two main supporters of a popularly elected presidency, Gouverneur Morris and James Wilson, did not suggest that the president should reflect, let alone shape, public opinion.[13]

Yet just thirteen years after the adoption of the Constitution, the newspaper that was publicly affiliated with one of the two candidates for the presidency was making precisely the popular connection that the Founders had disavowed. Presidential elections, the commentary argued, were a way for "the people" to install their representative in the office to act on their behalf. Anyone placed in the office who lacked the legitimacy of having been chosen by the people would be "despised, hated, and opposed," to the obvious detriment of the nation. Therefore, the commentary implicitly asserted, the only way to be certain that the "will of the people" has been legitimately expressed in a presidential election is for presidential electors to simply ratify the results of the party-line popular vote in their state.

That was definitely not what the Constitution's framers envisioned in 1788. Yet just barely a decade later, this commentary argued that if Electors did not vote in accordance with the popular vote of their state, the constitutional process for electing a president would produce an illegitimate winner who would be unable to govern effectively. The simmering arguments over just how "democratic" the new republic should be, and how directly connected presidents were to "the people" and the "national will," had exploded into the open.[14]

The *Intelligencer* continued to follow and report on events in Pennsylvania as the struggle over the mode of selection continued there for two more weeks.[15] Eventually, the legislature brokered an arrangement in which the state's fifteen electoral votes were split, with Jefferson receiving eight and Adams seven. The newspaper also regularly reported the results of Electoral College voting in other states as they became known.[16] Based on those tallies, the front page of the December 12 *Intelligencer* proudly declared Thomas Jefferson the winner of the election.

We this morning published the following SPLENDID INTELLI-GENCE in an Extra to the National Intelligencer which we reinsert for the information of our distant subscribers. We have this moment received information from Columbia (S.C.) that the REPUBLICAN TICKET for Electors has been carried by a majority of from 13 to 18 votes. Mr. JEFFERSON may, therefore, be considered as our future President. Friday Morning, 9 o'clock.[17]

Three days later, the paper carried a triumphant essay, with vivid imagery, proclaiming that the presidential electoral "storm" was over; political parties had "tried their strengths," and Republicans had won. The election, it said, was a model to the world. While other "monarchical or aristocratical [nations] on similar occasions invariably appeal to the sword," America had accomplished a change in government peacefully, thereby modeling to "the old world" a "cure for all her evils."

The *Intelligencer* essay has a smug, self-congratulatory tone that also works in a rhetorical dig at the Federalists. It couples Republican elec-toral exhilaration with the assertion that the way Republicans had cap-tured power proved that a new America could be a model to older countries, rather than the other way around as thought by many Fed-eralists, including Hamilton and Adams. It thus combines celebration with subtle political propagandizing, foreshadowing themes in Jeffer-son's inaugural address.[18]

The essay then moves to a discussion of how the "enemies of Repub-licanism" were found in "two descriptions of individuals." The first description is "hostile" to the "spirit" of Republicanism, which stands for the diffusion of political power rather than its accumulation "in the hands of a few." The second description "consists of men of limited views and timid spirits, who make no allowance for the improved condition of the human race." The first sort of men, the writer explains, are "in general governed by their interests, while the second are subdued by their fears." Therefore, the writer asserts optimistically, the latter will quickly become supporters of Republicanism once they have witnessed a "decisive manifestation of her triumphs" under the new government. The essay concludes by urging Republicans to avoid "unworthy resent-ment" toward their vanquished opponents, thereby demonstrating that Republicans "are ready to respect virtue and talent, wherever found."

Parts of the *Intelligencer* essay read like early guidance to loyal parti-sans on the key elements of the Republicans' postelection strategy. The plan was to try to split the Federalist opposition, while assuring Federalists of "virtue and talent" that they had nothing to fear from a Republican takeover of the government. These themes also appear in Jefferson's inauguration speech, reflected in his famous statement of conciliation that even though during the election, "we have called by different names brethren of the same principle" in fact, "we are all republicans; we are all federalists."[19]

With so many parallels between the *Intelligencer* essay and Jefferson's inaugural address, the question naturally arises whether Jefferson himself might have been its author. An intriguing piece of evidence is a postinaugural letter from Jefferson to Joseph Priestley that uses similar phrasing and imagery. Explaining to Priestley the differences between Republicans and Federalists, Jefferson wrote that Federalists looked "backwards not forwards, for improvement," favoring education based on "the education of our ancestors." That language echoes the newspaper essay's description of many Federalists as "men of limited views and timid spirits, who make no allowance for the improved condition of the human race." Similarly, echoing the *Intelligencer*'s claim that the nonviolent transfer of power from one party to another in America had been "auspicious to the destinies of the world," Jefferson exulted to Priestley, "[W]e can no longer say there is nothing new under the sun. For this whole chapter in the history of man is new."[20] Even if Jefferson did not write the *Intelligencer* essay, these similar phrasings illustrate how closely the paper's commentaries reflected Jefferson's thinking.

Stage II: Electoral Crisis Management

The *National Intelligencer*'s first reports of Jefferson's election were of course premature, either by honest accident or, perhaps, in the hope that promoting a facade of victory might somehow contribute to a real one. Following the December 15 victory statement, the *Intelligencer* continued to carry a running tally of the known electoral votes. On December 17, the paper reported an incomplete tally showing Jefferson and Burr with sixty-six votes and Adams and Pinckney with fifty-one. More reports were published over the next two weeks, until the paper reported the last state return, from Kentucky, on December 29. Based on that information, the *Intelligencer* said, "we are enabled to announce the total result" as seventy-three votes for Jefferson and Burr, sixty-five for Adams, and sixty-four for Pinckney. Nothing was said about the tie vote indicated for the presidency.

Two days later, again without comment on the tie, the *Intelligencer* published an "Extract of a letter from Colonel Burr, to General Smith, dated New York, December 16, 1800." The text of Burr's statement follows:

> It is highly improbable that I shall have an equal number of votes with Mr. Jefferson; but if such should be the result, every man who knows me ought to know that I should utterly disclaim all competition. Be assured that the federal party can entertain no wish for such an exchange. As to my friends, they would dishonor my views, and insult my feelings by a suspicion that I could submit to be instrumental in counteracting the wishes and expectations of the United States—and I now constitute you my proxy, to declare these sentiments if the occasion shall require.[21]

As is well known, despite having issued this statement, Burr would subsequently allow the crisis to persist by never acting definitively to cut off efforts by Federalists to make him president.

Although the *Intelligencer*'s report on December 29 had not noted the apparent tie between Jefferson and Burr, the newspaper had already carried a commentary on just that possibility, on December 24, in the first of what would be five essays by "Aristides" on the presidential election. That first essay began by noting that under the Constitution, if there were a tie in Electoral College vote, the House of Representatives would determine the winner, with the vote of nine state delegations required to elect the president. The essay then stated bluntly, "If the voice of the people of America be at all regarded, Mr. Jefferson will be preferred to Mr. Burr." Clearly, "Aristides" argued, "the people and legislatures who chose the electors, as well as the electors themselves," all voted "either mediately or directly, for Mr. Jefferson as President, and for Mr. Burr as Vice-President."

Despite that indisputable fact, "Aristides" acknowledged what he could "scarcely believe": that some Federalist House members were "disposed to elevate Mr. Burr to the Presidency to the depression or exclusion of Mr. Jefferson." "Aristides" then considered why some Federalists might be tempted to vote for Burr over Jefferson, despite Jefferson's clear advantages in terms of "superior age," service, and political experience. Behind such Federalists' thinking, "Aristides" concluded, must be a cold political calculation.

> The genuine motive of such an act, if it be designed, is probably this: The Republicans have triumphed. The people are on their side. While

this remains the case, the federal party, hitherto the sole depositaries of power, must give way to their rivals. Though compelled to surrender their power for a time, their unceasing efforts will be to regain it. The greatest obstacle, perhaps that could be opposed to such a hope, would be the elevation of Mr. Jefferson to the Presidency. . . . He, then above all other men, is to be feared. Let us then, they exclaim, at every hazard keep *him* from the Presidency.

"Aristides" dismissed the strategy as a "Short sighted policy! Visionary dream!" Closing, he promised his next essay would expose the "consequences of such an attempt."

That essay appeared on the front page of the January 5, 1801, *Intelligencer*. It began by noting that the tie between Jefferson and Burr was now definite, so there was indeed the possibility of the House choosing Burr as president. "Aristides" said he would therefore discuss "some of the consequences likely to ensue from such a preference; I say *some* of them; for were I to enumerate the whole, I should portray a picture too gloomy for any eye to contemplate without horror." His first argument was that a vote by the House of Representatives to make Burr president instead of Jefferson would be a democratically illegitimate move. Burr as president could never "possess the confidence of the people," because his election would "not reflect the decided preference of the people, expressed in a constitutional form."

How could a vote of the House of Representatives, provided for in such a situation by the Constitution, be inappropriate? "Aristides" gave two reasons, both of which involved classic issues of democratic representational theory in America. The first was that the current House, "chosen two years ago" and on the "verge of political dissolution," was "not the Representative of the people at this time." Based on his projections of party affiliation of representatives in the new House that would take over on March 4, "Aristides" concluded that the new House would have a strong Republican majority and that the "*real representatives of the people hold opinions absolutely in collision with their present nominal representatives.*" His second reason was that in voting by state delegations to select the president, the House represented only the states and not the American people themselves. "Aristides" concluded by imploring Federalists not to "subvert the fair and decided expression of the national feeling."

In his third essay, published on January 7, "Aristides" discussed what might happen if neither candidate were able to muster the nine-state majority needed to win in the House. As noted previously, this was possible because the state delegations in the House were divided: eight for

Republicans and six for Federalists, with two delegations split evenly.[22] Stunningly, "Aristides" argued that if the deadlock continued after the end of John Adams's term on March 3, the federal government would most likely be dissolved. He asserted that, with no president or vice president in office, there would be no constitutionally "competent" process for passing laws because part of the legislative process was submission of legislation to the president. Furthermore, he maintained, without a president or competent legislative process, all other government officers would automatically be removed or, at least, be under no one's control. In that situation, the federal government would either be dissolved outright or "continued in the hands of certain subordinate public agents." In either event, the crisis would "destroy confidence, annihilate harmony, paralyze industry, and prepare the minds of men for desperate events." Americans would start to "apprehend evils of a darker hue" "Aristides" warned, paving the way to "convulsion and disunion."

In his fourth essay on January 21, "Aristides" mixed the apocalyptic with the plebiscitary. He first reiterated that the US government would be dissolved in the event of a deadlock in the House of Representatives over the presidency. Then he warned, "Until the Presidential election is passed, let every citizen realize that the country is in danger. Let him with prudence and firmness avow his opinions, that it may appear to the representatives of the people that the voice of the people is unequivocal, and that that voice shall not only be heard but obeyed." To dramatize the consequences of a constitutional dissolution, "Aristides" quoted at length from the *Federalist Papers* warning of the horrors of disunity among the states.[23]

Predicting that the country would descend into chaos if the House of Representatives did not choose a new president by March 4 was an obvious scare tactic. It would have resonated deeply, though, with many political elites. When they were arguing for the ratification of the new Constitution, many (most notably, John Jay in the *Federalist Papers*) had repeatedly predicted dire consequences and even disunion flowing from the absence of an effective national government.[24] Just thirteen years later, the argument that chaos and disunion could not be risked was being turned around on many of those who had made it in the first place.

The pseudonym "Aristides" would have again resonated with classically educated readers. The fifth-century Athenian politician Aristides was called "the Just" because of his impartial dedication to the good of the state. Ostracized for opposing his government's naval policies, he later returned triumphantly to command the Athenian army.[25] Attaching such an honorable name to these essays would have subtly communicated the idea that someone devoted solely to the survival of the new nation wrote them from a fair perspective. At the same time, many readers would have recognized that the pseudonym had also been used for numerous commentaries that had appeared in the Jeffersonians' *National Gazette* in 1791–93, when that paper was battling with the Federalists' *Gazette of the United States*.[26] Some readers may also have seen similarities between Aristides' triumphant return to Athens as the champion of the Athenian cause and Jefferson's return as the leader of the Republicans against the Federalist menace after resigning from Washington's cabinet and retiring to Monticello.

The "Aristides" essays were just one part of the effort directed from the pages of the *Intelligencer* to get the House of Representatives to select Jefferson president. The overall strategy seems to have been to force the House of Representatives to choose between Jefferson and Burr, to the exclusion of any other option. The part of the strategy manifested in these essays was to declare that the failure of the House of Representatives to choose between the two men would throw the country into chaos. Given the Federalists' "passion for order" and virtuous, deferential civic behavior in society, those dire predictions would have played on some of their worst fears.[27]

Another aspect of the strategy was promoting the Republican view of the constitutionally appropriate way for resolving the crisis. Once the possibility arose of the House deadlocking and being unable to select a new president by the end of the term of John Adams, questions naturally came up about what would happen then. Because the Constitution did not explicitly address the point, there was no agreed-upon answer. Not surprisingly, many Federalists began arguing that Congress, with its lame-duck Federalist majorities, should come up with a solution to the crisis. This was an obviously attractive option, because it might even result in naming someone other than Jefferson or Burr as president.

In the research for his now classic book on the crisis, *The Failure of the Founding Fathers*, Bruce Ackerman uncovered an essay by "Horatius" that appeared in two Federalist newspapers in the first week of January 1801. The essay presented an elegant, constitutionally based argument that Congress had the power to act in such a situation. Intriguingly, Ackerman speculates that John Marshall may have written the essay to promote his own selection as president to resolve the crisis. "Horatius" argued that Congress could pass legislation to deal with the problem under Article II, Section 1, of the Constitution, which allows Congress to provide for filling the presidency when both the presidential and vice presidential offices have become vacant due to "removal, death, resignation, or inability." The current crisis, "Horatius" argued, was the kind of situation this provision was intended to cover or, at least, should be interpreted to cover, given the similarity of this difficulty to those mentioned in the provision.[28]

Ackerman devoted more than a chapter of his book to the essay by "Horatius" but, surprisingly, makes no mention of the Republican response, which came promptly, on January 12, in an essay addressed "To the House of Representatives of the United States of America." Signed "An American," the response first argued that the provisions of the Constitution limited the House to choosing either Jefferson or Burr. "All other persons are not conscientiously in your contemplation," the writer informed the House, because the Constitution unambiguously directed the House to choose between the two top vote-getters in the case of a tie.

As to the argument that Congress could act under its constitutional authority to legislate regarding situations when the offices of the president and vice president had both become vacant, "American" argued that this authority only covered vacancies that occurred during the terms of a president and vice president. Thus, the writer reasoned, Congress was powerless to provide for filling a vacancy that occurred after the expiration of Adams's term.

Having asserted that the House was limited to choosing either Jefferson or Burr, "American" considered the consequences if it chose neither. In that case, he argued, there were two possibilities: either the union of the states would be dissolved completely, returning them to the status of independent sovereignties, or the states would again be under the Articles of Confederation, which had "never been expressly repealed." Clearly, either situation would be "deeply injurious to tranquility, order, and property." Rather than run the risk, members of the House needed to make a choice between Jefferson and Burr. Of those two, he argued, Jefferson should be preferred because he was clearly the choice of the people, "whose authority the President exercises." The "spirit of the constitution," he concluded, "requires the will of the people to be executed."

Just two days later, in another article in the *Intelligencer* again addressed to the House of Representatives, "An American" took on another proposal that had been made for dealing with the crisis. Under that proposal, which "American" said had been published recently in a Philadelphia newspaper under the pseudonym "Curtius," current vice president Jefferson should resign his position as president pro tempore of the Senate immediately, to allow the Senate to elect a new presiding officer.[29] That person could then become the new president under the existing presidential succession statute, if the House had not made a choice between Jefferson and Burr by March 4 when the office would become vacant. A legendary soldier-hero named Curtius saved Rome by leaping with his horse into a great chasm in the center of the Forum, which the priests had said would not close until the most precious thing in Rome had been cast into it.[30] The use of his name as a pseudonym thus would have been a clever way of suggesting to classically educated readers that Jefferson should sacrifice his own future prospects for the welfare of his country. Labeling the proposal an "unsound" but "ingenious attempt," "American" said the proposed solution was invalid under the Constitution. Congress only had legislative authority over matters of presidential succession, he said, when a president had actually taken office after being elected. Its legislation could not therefore cover a situation where no president had been elected at all, he argued.

"American" then reiterated the consequences of the House failing to select a president: "If the representatives neglect or refuse to elect one of the two, a national penalty results—*the disorganization of the government.*" It would be a "heavy penalty," he argued.

> Struggles for a new federal constitution will be commenced—The weakness of our government will invite foreign intrigue, its forms will render us the sport of factions, commerce will sicken, real estates will fall. . . . In short, the evils of 1784, 1785, and 1786, which impelled us to reform our government in 1787 will be all renewed.

The mention of "struggles for a new federal constitution" clearly refers to the possibility of a new constitutional convention being called to reconstitute the federal government. In letters to James Monroe and James Madison in February 1801, at the height of the crisis, Jefferson said Republicans were brandishing the threat of a new convention "openly and firmly." Finding no evidence that such a threat was ever made publicly, some historians have questioned whether it could have actually had any influence on Federalists.[31] The reference in the *Intelligencer* to struggles over a new constitution provides direct historical confirmation that the threat was indeed publicly raised by Republicans during the crisis and thus may have affected the outcome. "American" concluded on a strident note. Jefferson, he said, should not be expected to engage in a "criminal surrender of the chair of the Senate, in order to make room for *an unlawful usurping President.*" Instead, the House of Representatives should carry out the "prompt and faithful execution of the unqualified mandate of the people" and make Jefferson president.

On January 23, 1801, the *Intelligencer* carried a third essay by "An American." It was presented as his response to a "recent publication in Alexandria, under the signature of *Civilis.*" It appears that the "Civilis" essay was either the "Horatius" essay (published under a different pseudonym) or a very similar one. In his response, "American" essentially reiterated that Congress had no power to do anything to resolve the crisis except for the House to choose between Jefferson and Burr as president. The conclusion too was the same: should the House fail to act by March 4, "*it is plain* that the government of the United States will become dissolved on the fourth of March, 1801," and the powers of the presidency will "pass from the late incumbent *into the hands of his principals*—the People of the United States."

A fascinating essay published in the *Intelligencer* on January 21, 1801, provided an answer to the question of what could be done constitutionally to prevent the country from being left without a president on March 4. The answer was blunt: nothing. The essay, entitled "Letter from a respectable citizen to Members of Congress, on the ELECTION of a PRESIDENT," echoes the argument that Congress had only one option: for the House to choose a president from the top two vote-getters in the Electoral College. The problem with any other legislative solution to the problem, the writer argues, was that this "pretended necessity" could then become a common justification for the House to use "for appointing a President in a mode more pleasing to themselves, than that presented in the Constitution."

The writer asserted that since the crisis was due to a "defect in the constitution," Congress was powerless to do anything to avert it, because constitutional problems can only be fixed via the amendment process. He then asserted, though, that not even a constitutional amendment could solve this particular problem. The only remedy lay outside the Constitution itself: "But I am inclined to think that this is not a defect capable of a remedy; and that in this instance, as in many others, it was necessary to confide in the force of public opinion, for the execution of the constitution."

How could no constitutional remedy be possible? The writer asserted that, by their nature, some potential problems in government, such as the refusal of a group of states to elect senators, can only be deterred by the desire of responsible government leaders to avoid the "disgrace and danger of dissolving all the ligaments of society." The impasse in the House over the election of the president was precisely that kind of political crisis, a "dilemma" that was not capable of a constitutional solution. Just as nothing could be done under the Constitution to force a state to choose its US senators, neither could anything be done to require the House to choose a president. Rather, the failure of the House to choose a new president "would be a case proper for the tribunal of public opinion," which would either declare the action right or "reject the attempt." In the latter case, there would then "be in fact most clearly a case of revolution . . . followed by a degree of execration and punishment which constitute the only possible provision against vicious experiments."

Intriguingly, the invocation of the "tribunal of public opinion" echoed the reliance on the force of public opinion that Jefferson frequently invoked during his presidency. For example, after acknowledging to Senator John Breckenridge that authorizing the Louisiana Purchase without a constitutional amendment might be "stepping beyond the Constitution," Jefferson nevertheless urged the senator and his colleagues to "throw themselves on their country" and ratify the treaty with France. Only by approving the treaty, he said, could they avoid being "disavowed by the country."[32] The assertion in the *Intelligencer*'s commentary that public opinion was the ultimate arbiter in such crises also echoed Madison's assertion—first made in a commentary he wrote for the Republicans' *National Gazette* in 1791— that "public opinion sets bounds to every government, and is the real sovereign in every free one."[33]

Continuing the apocalyptic theme, the essay in the *Intelligencer* invoked another vivid depiction of what could happen in America once the "constitutional land marks between right and wrong are thrown down."

> Faction after faction will rise up. None can long retain the support of the people, because the power of all will be illegitimate. The despot of today may kneel tomorrow to a wretch whom he had consigned to a loathsome jail. Property will change as rapidly as power, and some warrior will finally become master of everything.

This specter would ultimately "rally up all virtuous men from the ensigns of party, under the standard of the constitution." In the next sentence, however, the commentary turned ominous. If an "enraged minority

should successfully oppose . . . the voice of the people, so audibly pronounced in favor of Mr. Jefferson, . . . it must then be a question of
revolution." The consequences would include the "destroying [of] all
property resting on credit, and of depriving Virginia and Maryland of
the Seat of Government." The writer concluded by asserting his hope
that because "all good men of both parties are inimical to a revolution,"
they would unite in support of Jefferson.

The choice of the pseudonym "Respectable Citizen" for this essay
seems intended to convey to readers the enormity of the threat to the
country if the deadlock was not resolved. If a "respectable citizen" could
lurch from the optimistic vision of "all virtuous men" rallying together
without regard to party affiliation for the sake of the Constitution to, in
the following sentence, images of "factions," "despots," and "warriors,"
the crisis must indeed be grave. The tone of the commentary illustrates
the "manic-depressive" side of political rhetoric at this time in America,
in which "images of the rising glory of America vied everywhere with
the prospect of utter dissolution."[34] Clever writers such as Thomas Paine
often employed this tone in their political writings, as a rhetorical device
to inflate the importance of what they were arguing for by juxtaposing
their solution with the alternate specter of national chaos and ruin.[35]

Attributing the essay to a "respectable citizen" may also have been
intended to appeal more particularly to Federalists, who, with their elitist pretensions, naturally considered themselves to be among the most
"respectable" of citizens.[36] The commentary could have been taken as a
special warning to Federalists of what they risked by continuing to promote a deadlock in the House of Representatives. As Jefferson advised
James Monroe four days into the House deadlock, Republicans were
pursuing the strategy of playing on the fears of Federalists, attempting
to scare them by using the threat that a new constitutional convention
would have to be called following the dissolution of the current government. "The very word convention gives [the Federalists] the horrors,"
Jefferson bragged, "as in the present democratical spirit of America they
fear they should lose some of the favorite morsels of the constitution."[37]
If Federalists, along with everyone else, were contemplating the need for
a new constitutional convention, they would undoubtedly also have been
susceptible to warnings about what might happen in that event. After all,
Federalists had barely been able to get the current US Constitution ratified over a spirited opposition whose adherents and tenets had largely
been absorbed into the Republican Party by 1800.[38]

On February 11, the Electoral College votes were certified in the

Senate, and the House began voting for president. Under the heading "ELECTION OF A PRESIDENT," the *Intelligencer* of February 13 carried an account of what had transpired, first in the counting of the electoral votes in the Senate and then as the voting began in the House. The article reported that severely ill Representative Joseph Hopper Nicholson from Maryland had been given a bed in a chamber just off the floor, to enable him to vote. Noting that, with the Nicholson vote, the Maryland delegation was now divided 4–4, the article pointedly observed that "with the accession to Mr. Jefferson of one federal vote from that state," Jefferson would become president.

With this note and the insistence in the pages of the *Intelligencer* that a House vote between Jefferson and Burr was the only constitutionally permissible way of resolving the crisis, the strategy chosen by the Jeffersonians—and promoted in the pages of the *Intelligencer*—was clear. They intended to hang tough, never break ranks, appeal to public opinion, put pressure on individual delegation members in closely divided states, and dare the Federalists to risk creating a constitutional crisis that might lead to revolution or civil war. That strategy was reflected repeatedly in the commentaries in the *Intelligencer*. Each side was probing the other for signs of weakness or potential willingness to compromise, and the constant drumbeat from the pages of the *Intelligencer* would have provided a useful backdrop for Republican leaders as they played out their hand in perhaps the greatest game of chicken ever played in American politics. Of course, with its known ties to Jefferson, the *Intelligencer* would also have provided public guidance, to friend and foe alike, regarding the current official position of Jefferson and his supporters. In the extraordinarily small, close-knit political community that existed in the new capital in 1800, each issue of the *Intelligencer* must have been the subject of much discussion.[39]

The next issue of the *Intelligencer*, published on February 16, employed at least four tactics: pressure on individual members, invocations of national disaster if the crisis was not resolved, public political posturing, and arguments that the only option constitutionally available to the House was to choose either Jefferson or Burr as president. The front page of the paper carried a letter to the editor, signed "An Old Inhabitant of Columbia." The writer argued, "[T]he representatives of Maryland, who persist in voting for Mr. Burr . . . are the betrayers of the will of the constituents." As the previous issue of the *Intelligencer* had noted, just one member changing his vote could break the 4–4 deadlock in the Maryland delegation. Singling out his Maryland district's congressman, John Chew Thomas, the writer affirmed, "I know not a man of respectability, derived either from wealth, talents, or virtue, that does not decidedly prefer Mr. Jefferson to Mr. Burr." Asserting that in continuing to vote with the Federalists, Thomas was risking the destruction of the union and the city of Washington, the writer concluded with the hope that "when convinced of the will of his constituents," Thomas would obey it.

The reference to "respectability" as derived from "wealth, talents, or virtue" was a classic Federalist formulation and must have been intended to convey the impression that the writer of the essay was a Federalist who had risen above party for the sake of country. The pseudonym "Old Inhabitant of Columbia" struck at least two chords. It evoked feelings of patriotism by its use of "Columbia," the venerable popular name for the United States in the eighteenth century. The description of the writer as an "old inhabitant" of the country also pleaded for deference to the wise voice of experience.

Next to the front-page letter from the "Old Inhabitant" was another commentary by "Aristides," reminding readers again how the potential for war between the "disunited" states had been described in the *Federalist Papers*. Also in the same issue was an unsigned analysis of the voting in the House after four days of balloting: "The Republican and Federal parties have remained immovable in their original vote for President." After asserting that Federalists had now given up any hope of "gaining over some Republican votes," the commentary asked, "What then will be the result?"

The commentary predicted, with the "most unlimited confidence," that the eight Republican-voting states would "remain immutable in their adherence to the public will." As for the six states currently voting for Burr, the commentator expected them to "yield," because the "unanimous and firm decision of the people throughout the US in favor of Mr. Jefferson will be irresistible." As evidence for such confidence, the commentator noted that there was "scarcely a dissenting voice" in Maryland in the public support for Jefferson over Burr.

The commentary then shifted to a tone of raw, pressure politics: "Let the representatives of the people know the will of the people, and *they will obey*." To facilitate the pressuring of representatives, the commentary included a state-by-state breakdown of how each representative had voted, so that "the people may know how the votes of their Representatives have been given."[40] Interestingly, those vote totals were supposed to have been kept secret during the voting.[41] The commentary also addressed again the plan being considered by Federalists to "make by law a *President pro tempore*" if neither Burr nor Jefferson were chosen president in the House voting. The commentary rejected the proposal in ominous language: "So hostile would the voice of America appear to be to this measure, that it is doubtful whether any man would propose it, and more doubtful whether any man would accept the station, if offered to him."

Fighting back, Federalists used their newspaper in the capital, the *Washington Federalist,* to respond to all of the Republicans' pronouncements in the *National Intelligencer.* The Federalists' public response took two main approaches. The first was to argue, in issue after issue, why Jefferson should not be named president. The general theme was that, as argued in the *Federalist* issue of February 12, for Federalists to give the presidency to Jefferson would be "dishonorable in the extreme" because of his known enmity to their party and policies.[42]

Such partisan-based appeals were often supplemented with mocking personal attacks on Jefferson. One, on February 4, reported that he had "for some weeks past become a constant attendant at church," appearing there "with the most edifying gravity and solemnity of countenance." The essay was titled "Voltaire the Second" and ended with praise for Jefferson as the "worthy disciple of such a Master!" On February 6, the paper continued the ridicule, attributing Jefferson's recent "religious turn of mind" to a "very serious shock" he had experienced while asleep and dreaming of an "intimate and indissoluble union between the pretty Miss Columbia, and her chaste French sister." Jefferson, the satire continued, had been suddenly jolted awake by the "ghost of Burr," holding a tablet bearing an image that "portrayed the *Sage* of Monticello just sinking into a yawning abyss," with a biblically-based quote reading, "Into the Pit which the wicked man did prepare for his righteous Neighbors, hath he himself fallen—It is the Lord's doing; and is marvelous in our Eyes."[43]

The Federalists' second approach was to match the bellicose threats of Republicans, in effect challenging Republicans to "bring it on." That theme was also trumpeted in multiple issues of the paper. Indeed, the *Federalist* had begun raising the specter of the election producing a revolution and a civil war in October 1800, just as the first hints of a possible Jefferson victory were emerging.[44]

This strategy culminated in the *Federalist*'s February 12 and 16 issues, when tensions over the continuing election stalemate were peaking. Saying, "*The Crisis* is momentous," the February 12 issue reported the proclamation of the "bold and impetuous partisans of Mr. Jefferson" that if anyone other than Jefferson were named president, "ten thousand republican *swords will instantly leap from their scabbards*, in defense of the violated rights of the *People!!!!*"[45] Could Republicans actually be "ripe for civil war," the paper asked, "and ready to imbue their hands in kindred blood?" If so, it said, then the conflict "could never be tried at a more favorable conjuncture!" Massachusetts alone had "*70,000 (regulars let us call them) in arms*," and the militias of New Hampshire and Connecticut, along with "half the number at least" of citizens in the other states, could be counted on to "fight under the federal banner in support of the Constitution." Against this array of force, the *Federalist* assured its readers, the untrained, lightly armed, and weakened militias of Pennsylvania and Virginia would be no match.

The threats continued on February 16, when the *Federalist* proclaimed that "if the enemies of our government are determined to have another insurrection—never was a more happy subject nor a more happy time!" The paper said that "from the circumstance of the *time*," Virginia was "as little to be feared as a rattlesnake with his fangs plucked out." This comment undoubtedly referred to the attempted slave rebellion in Virginia in August 1800, which had rattled elites there and, historians judge, left them feeling reluctant to use military force outside the state, out of fear that doing so might leave them vulnerable to more such threats.[46]

On February 17, 1801, after six days of voting and thirty-five ballots, Federalists finally capitulated.[47] The Federalists in four state delegations—Maryland, Delaware, Vermont, and South Carolina—changed their votes to allow Jefferson's election to the presidency.[48] In the decisive thirty-sixth ballot in the House, four Maryland representatives—one of whom was John Chew Thomas, who had previously voted for Burr—switched and cast blank ballots, thereby awarding Maryland's vote in the House proceedings to Jefferson.[49]

The Federalists' united front fractured when James A. Bayard, Delaware's only representative and a Federalist, announced that he would switch his support from Burr to Jefferson. Bayard's explanation indicates that he succumbed to precisely the sort of constitutional brinkmanship featured in the *National Intelligencer* since the beginning of the crisis. He finally gave up the fight, he wrote, when he became convinced that Federalists would have to "risk the Constitution and a civil war or take Mr. Jefferson."[50] Bayard's words are a good paraphrase of the main argument in many of the *Intelligencer* essays discussed in this chapter. Thus, the newspaper's hardline public rhetoric may well have played a significant role in the resolution of the crisis in favor of Jefferson and the Republicans.

Standing out from the commentaries in the *Intelligencer* is their absolutist approach coupled with an apocalyptic threat. Federalists had only one option, according to the commentaries: to elect Jefferson president. If they failed to do so, the commentaries argued, no alternatives were available under the Constitution. The country would be left without a chief executive, and the government would dissolve. As Jack Rakove has pointed out, political difficulties can prompt actors to turn to "constitutionalizing their disagreements," invoking whatever part(s) of the Constitution can be claimed to support their desired political outcome.[51] In this case, facing Federalist majorities in the lame-duck Congress, Republicans had to assert that anything those majorities might do to resolve the crisis, short of electing Jefferson president, would be unconstitutional. The Republicans' resolve would have been strengthened by the procedural rules the Federalist majority adopted for the balloting, which Republicans viewed as effectively precluding any outcome under the Constitution except the election of either Jefferson or Burr.[52]

But in arguing that Jefferson was the only constitutionally legitimate choice for president, Republicans were making some radical interpretive moves. They were asserting that the Constitution implicitly requires the will of the people to be paramount in matters such as presidential elections. This meant that Electors should just automatically follow the election results rather than determining on their own who would be the best leader for the country. Also, as Ackerman has shown, Republicans were declaring—again contra to what the Founders had envisioned—a direct plebiscitary link between presidents and "the people."[53] As Bimes puts it, this declaration that the job of presidents is to carry out "the will of the nation" was a constitutionally radical effort by Jefferson to stake out "new sources of presidential authority."[54]

On a more historical note, the *Intelligencer* commentaries and the responses to them in the *Washington Federalist* reveal just how *public* the crisis was. In contrast to evidence gathered from private correspondence among individuals during the crisis, the war of words between the newspapers demonstrates beyond doubt that everyone involved in the crisis would have been aware of the constitutionally apocalyptic commentaries that appeared in the *Intelligencer*. This contradicts the assertion by James E. Lewis Jr. that, although Jefferson had said it privately, there is "no evidence that the Republican solution of a new constitutional convention was made public at the time."[55] Republicans in fact were making it plain to all that reorganizing America under a new constitution was a likely outcome of deadlock in the House.

That commentaries in the *National Intelligencer* repeatedly invoked violent scenarios contradicts Ackerman's conclusion that there is "no indication" of Jefferson having threatened violence if Burr were named president.[56] Jefferson did just that, albeit in a more disguised fashion— through his newspaper—that would nevertheless have been clear to everyone involved in the crisis. Similarly, the heated responses that the *Washington Federalist* published to counter the *Intelligencer* threats contradict Michael A. Bellesiles's assertion that "most Federalists dismissed Republican threats of civil war should Jefferson be denied that office."[57] Indeed, in a letter to James Monroe on March 7, 1801, Jefferson said that the electoral crisis had ended when Federalists had chosen to capitulate "rather than risk anarchy."[58] What emerges from this study, then, is a much clearer picture of the political and rhetorical strategies that Republicans used during the electoral crisis of 1801 to finally get their man into office.

Stage III: Celebrating Victory, Conciliation, and Republicanism

On February 18, 1801, the day following the final House vote, the pages of the *National Intelligencer* were used to announce and frame the news of Jefferson's victory. The announcement began, "The voice of the People has prevailed, and THOMAS JEFFERSON is declared by the Representatives of the People to be duly elected President of the United States." The commentary extolled the manner in which Jefferson had been selected as having been a model to the world, pointing to "the proud example of a people of five millions, scattered over a wide extent of country, peaceably electing a chief magistrate, and the representatives of that people, constitutionally confirming the national will." Ignoring that the House process had been bitter, contentious, and threatening—feelings the paper itself had encouraged—the *Intelligencer* characterized the process as an "honorable regard to the public will, expressed with calmness and intrepidity." The lesson to be drawn, the paper proclaimed, was that "from this era all doubt of the fitness of a Republican system to answer every correct purpose of government [must] be dismissed!"

Like the premature victory statement published in the *Intelligencer* on December 15, this commentary had a self-congratulatory theme. The recent electoral experience in America, the commentary asserted, had proved that a democracy could indeed, despite the contrary predictions of both ancient and modern critics, peacefully govern itself and transfer power to new leaders. The commentary also introduced a new theme: the promotion of the Republican ideal of a popularly responsive government. As characterized by the commentary, the House of Representatives, in confirming Jefferson as president, had acknowledged the primacy of public opinion (the "voice of the people") in American government.

The main long-term goal of Jefferson and other Republican leaders was to educate the American people on the errors of their ways and instill in them the correct (Republican) principles of democratic government in America. As Stephen Skowronek has described it, Jefferson planned a massive reconstruction of "the terms and conditions of legitimate national government."[59] Once Americans understood those reclaimed ideals, Jefferson believed, almost all the people would find themselves in basic agreement on fundamental governmental issues, no matter what their personal and regional interests.[60] This coalescence of public opinion would, he hoped, ease the rumblings of disunion that, while always present even at that time in American history, had been heightened by the enmity that had arisen between the North-leaning Federalist Party and the South-leaning Republican Party.[61]

Occasionally during the four months that are the focus of this chapter, commentaries in the *Intelligencer* promoted such broad themes as national unity and the principles of Republicanism. It is surprising there were not more, given the national reach of the paper. Had Jefferson and his allies not been diverted, first by the unsure election results and then by the need to carry out the partisan public communications war to get him elected in the House of Representatives, it seems likely that more of this thematic material would have appeared in the paper prior to Jefferson's inauguration.

The most notable example of these efforts in the pre-inaugural period is a set of three essays signed "Timoleon" that ran in the *National Intelligencer* in November 1800. The main theme of the essays was that the American people were not really so divided politically after all. The first essay, published on November 10, began by asking, "Are the PEOPLE of the United States so divided in opinion, as would appear from the reiterated language of party?" "Timoleon" endeavored to show that Americans were not fundamentally divided, even by what he termed the most likely source of divisiveness, religion. Religious divisions are not a problem in America, he argued, because Americans are "in one point . . . universally agreed: and that is that religion ought to be kept distinct from politics." An "absolute silence," he said, had been imposed by "public opinion" on the few who might desire the establishment of religion in politics. That was good for America, "Timoleon" asserted, because "all the persecution, malevolence and wars, which bigotry has produced, have flown from an association between the church and the state." In America, he concluded, "no such association does exist, no such association can exist in this country."

The second "Timoleon" essay, published on November 17, 1800, asked, "Does any material difference exist among the PEOPLE from dissimilar or opposing interests?" Its author began by noting that the "great divisions of society" were into "agriculturalists, mechanics and merchants." Since these interests exist in all the states, there was no overriding difference that would "convulse the union" and lead to civil war as some in the country were arguing the presidential election might produce. Rather, "Timoleon" asserted, "It is all a *chimera*. . . . [T]he cry of separation, convulsion and civil war is raised to repress a free expression of opinions. Let then this great truth be proclaimed—THE PEOPLE ARE AGREED."

The final essay, published in the *Intelligencer* on November 19, asked, "If the PEOPLE of the United States are not divided, whence flows that spirit of hostility that rages through the union?" It is due, "Timoleon" argued, not from "any extensive, deep rooted division among the people" but from those who are trying to undermine the spirit of the Constitution by "pursuing schemes promotive of monarchic results." Those attempts were being "conducted with vigor and art, to change the nature of their political institutions, to divest them of many of their dearest rights, and in the end to enslave them."

There is certainly a strong element of electioneering in these essays, as well as some unrealism. Blaming the social divisiveness of an election season on the opposition is a classic political strategy that was employed by both Republicans and Federalists in the 1790s as partisan tensions rose.[62] But the assertion that all Americans were "universally agreed" that "religion ought to be kept distinct from politics" was as untrue then as it is now, although it obviously reflects Jefferson's own views on the subject.

The "Timolean" essays also reflect Jefferson's utopian belief that, outside of the dedicated Federalists, the "great body of our fellow citizens" shared the same basic principles.[63] Jefferson believed one of his great tasks was to bring back to their senses those Americans who had been deceived into supporting a party whose principles were essentially antidemocratic. What better way was there to set about accomplishing that task than to spread a message of reconciliation across America through the pages of the *National Intelligencer* and other friendly Republican newspapers?

Classically educated readers would have appreciated the choice of the pseudonym "Timoleon." The Timoleon memorialized by Plutarch was known as the "scourge of Tyrants." He achieved that fame by coming out of retirement to lead a small army in 344 BC, to free Corinth, the capital of Syracuse, from a dictator and replace the country's government with a democracy.[64] Timoleon's story nicely parallels the Republican saga of Jefferson coming out of retirement at Monticello to save the country from Federalism and restore it to its true republican nature. In fact, Jefferson used the pseudonym "Timoleon" himself for a newspaper essay he wrote that was published in the *Richmond Examiner* in 1803.[65]

Significantly, the *Intelligencer's* commentary on February 18, 1801, in the issue that announced the selection of Jefferson as president by the House, included an appeal to all Americans to support their national government. Proclaiming that any doubts as to the vitality of the "Republican system" should now "yield to the magnanimous policy of giving to that system all the support of undivided zeal and united talent," the commentary urged that the government become "the object of our invariable respect and regard." The commentary thus presaged Jefferson's appeal in his inaugural address for national unity and reconciliation.[66]

The story presented in this chapter ends with the inauguration of Thomas Jefferson on March 4, 1801. The first page of that day's issue of the *National Intelligencer* carried the text of Jefferson's speech which, as noted previously, he had provided to the newspaper in advance, so that it would be available to the public on the day of his inauguration. The first page also carried a short commentary (presented here in full) that suggested the role the *Intelligencer* would play in the new Republican era.

This day a new political era commences—the era of principle.

The people of the United States have done their duty; and it now devolves on those, to whom they have confided the guardianship of their rights, to do theirs. That they will discharge their duty with dignity, justice and impartiality, that while it shall reflect honor on themselves, will confer lasting benefits upon their country, we have every pledge, which experience can furnish, and every assurance that expectation can justify.

Men, selected for their virtues, no less than for their talents, are called to the highest stations under the government; men, whose field of observation and action have been enlarged; men who have devoted their earliest days to the establishment of our national independence, and to the formation of those political institutions which have been its strongest shield.

Under the administration of such men, who acknowledge their dependence upon, and accountability to the people, we may rationally expect the brightest concentration of talent and virtue. Freedom of thought and discussion, so far from being repressed, will be encouraged by the general conviction that truth will be received from any quarter. Under such a conviction, men of intelligence and information will contribute their stores to the common stock, and will powerfully contribute, by the correct ideas disseminated among our citizens, to produce that harmony of view and unity of action, that will at once impart mildness and energy to the government, and render it an object beloved by our citizens, and respected by foreign powers.

The commentary succinctly spells out the Republican view of democratic government in the United States. Through the recent election, the federal government was now in the hands of leaders who were explicitly dependent on and accountable to the people. They were of course expected to administer the government wisely in accordance with the wishes of the people. Significantly, though, there was to be an ongoing connection between the government and the people. Leaders would be regularly contributing their "stores" of "intelligence and information" so that "correct ideas" would be "disseminated among our citizens." The result would "impart mildness and energy to the government." In other words, "the people" could be safely and properly entrusted with the control of their government if they were employing "correct ideas" in their judgments. So guided, such a popularly based level of support would assure not only an energetic national government but also one that was compatible with democracy.[67] Obviously, a mass communication tool like the *Intelligencer* was a crucial part of the Republican plan; it was the only feasible way of distributing the correct "intelligence and information" that Republicans wanted all Americans to have.

The pages of the *National Intelligencer* during the four-month period examined in this chapter convey a vivid sense of the raw, popularly based brand of politics played by the Jeffersonian Republicans as they fought to wrest control of the national government from the Federalists. In the *Intelligencer*, Republicans argued unabashedly against the antidemocratic aspects of the Electoral College—despite its enshrinement in the US Constitution—and threatened dissolution of the union if the House of

Representatives did not confirm the result (in their view) of the most recent national popular vote, by selecting Jefferson president. This was pure democratic revolutionary rhetoric, trumpeted by the newspaper that was serving as the mouthpiece of the head challenger to the political status quo.

In arguing for Jefferson's election in 1800, the *Intelligencer's* columns articulated fundamental Republican principles of direct popular sovereignty. Commentaries in the paper advocated for such notions as the "will of the people" and the primacy of "public opinion," and promoted a direct popular (or plebiscitary) connection between the president and the American people. Those ideas would then have eventually circulated across the nation, providing a sort of official guide to Republicanism. In promoting them, the *National Intelligencer* played a key role in the Republican effort to transform American politics and make the election of 1800, in Jefferson's words, a "revolution in the principles of our government."[68] Like the pages of the *Intelligencer* itself, those principles endured long after the battle over the presidential election of 1800 had ended.

CHAPTER 4

Celebrating and Promoting Jefferson and Republicanism

Once in power, what would Jefferson and his allies do to secure their victory? How could they defend Jefferson and his administration from whatever attacks Federalists might make? Most fundamentally, how could they instill in Americans those proper constitutional understandings that would allow "the people" to perform their Jeffersonian (and Madisonian) function as the ultimate check to promote good government and deter future attempts at constitutional usurpations?

With the politics of controlling the federal government having been nationalized through the efforts of the Republicans and their Federalist rivals, the victors needed a way to promote their president, party, positions, and philosophies as effectively as possible. Given the technological limitations of mass communication at the time, the *National Intelligencer* would have been the obvious choice. It was based in the nation's capital, where Jefferson and his Republican allies could closely supervise it. In the small, close-knit community in Washington, it would have been easy to regularly provide the paper's editor, Samuel Smith, with guidance and material for him to publish. With the mailing of every issue of the paper to other newspaper publishers around the country, the *Intelligencer* would also have been the most effective way of rapidly circulating standardized, approved versions of Jefferson, his presidency, and Republican principles. This chapter focuses on the *Intelligencer*'s promotion of Jefferson and the extensive guidance on good Republican behavior it provided during the early part of his presidency.

Celebrating Jefferson

As noted previously, the March 4, 1801, issue of the *Intelligencer* had a celebratory aspect. It was a special issue, published early enough that those attending the inauguration ceremony would have advance copies of Jefferson's speech. This move compensated for Jefferson's weak speaking skills and his soft-spoken delivery of his speech that day. If true, Samuel Smith's report of the clamor for the special edition would have enhanced the sense of triumph and excitement that Republicans felt on that day and wanted to project.

The next issue of the newspaper, published on March 6, demonstrated vividly how the paper could be used to promote the intertwined subjects of Thomas Jefferson and Republicanism. It carried an effusive commentary on Jefferson's inaugural speech, calling it the "essential principles of our government, as received by the President." Jefferson's words, it said, amounted to a "political creed, in which all may unite in theory; and in which if all shall unite in practice, we shall truly be a free and united people."

The *Intelligencer* followed up this fawning commentary with its description of a "Pageant, exhibited in Virginia, on the election of Mr. Jefferson." The play was a dramatic depiction of Jefferson liberating America from the grasp of Federalism. The drama begins with an arresting image: "A beautiful virgin is seen in plain attire—her countenance benevolent and melancholy—tears are streaming from her eyes—[label]—'Behold Liberty at the point of Death.'" Liberty is surrounded by a cast of Federalist villains: a "fool magnificently dressed with a scepter"; a "fat and ruddy" person with a "mitre on his head," labeled "tythes"; an armed soldier "with his bayonet at the breast of Liberty"; and a "statesman," with the label "Energetic government," holding a "bundle of papers" on topics such as "banking, army, navy, sedition act, loaning, war, monarchy, hierarchy."

Against this backdrop, an "orator" arises and attempts to encourage a "multitude of spectators" to turn against Liberty. Pointing to Liberty, the orator calls her "a Jacobin—a disorganizer—a friend of France—an atheist." He promises the multitude that if they allow Liberty to be destroyed, they will "establish good order," "recommend [them]selves to God," and exchange their "absurd equality of rights, for the beautiful equality of balances." Also scurrying around are "busy figures" trying to bribe the people with "commissions, grants, contracts, warrants or accounts," all comprising a vast array of governmental privileges that "had been or would be invented, for raising and extending the public treasure to an incredible amount."

At the darkest hour, just as "the multitude are almost infatuated," a "trumpet is heard, a courier arrives." The courier announces, "Jefferson is President." At this news, Liberty revives and "assumes her wonted intrepidity." Seeing this, Liberty's attackers run to her for protection against the multitude, who are now chanting, "We are the votaries of liberty and will destroy her enemies." Liberty magnanimously "contents herself" with "breaking the scepter, trampling the crown and mitre to dust and ashes, disarming the soldier, tearing the papers of the statesman, and looking contemptuously upon the orator." The play ends with "sixteen beautiful women" appearing, each representing a state. They join hands in a circle and look adoringly up at the "guardian angel of America," who, while hovering above them, paints the word "Union" in "golden and capital letters."

This play is a particularly spectacular example of how, as David Waldstreicher has shown, the partisan press promoted a combination of national "rhetoric, ritual, and political action" in the early American republic by carrying accounts of such celebratory events.[1] It also illustrates the "emergence of a distinctive Jeffersonian culture" in the celebrations that, among other things, dramatized Jefferson's victory as a "new birth of liberty."[2] From the vivid descriptions of the characters in the play and their actions, the reader/viewer gets a dramatized version of the essentials of Republicanism and of its critiques of Federalism and even American society. One also sees Jefferson depicted as a classical, godlike hero whose election to the presidency miraculously awakens the people and sends their Federalist enemies scurrying away in disgrace. Significantly, the play's focus is solely on Jefferson as the nation's savior, even though Republicans had also captured both houses of Congress. Even at this early stage in American political development, presidents were becoming firmly established as the embodiment of the national government and the agents and protectors of its citizens.

Liberty herself is portrayed in the play as a "proud, militant, and strong woman," reflecting the more assertive depictions of the female figure of liberty that Democratic-Republican societies, inspired by French revolutionary iconography, began employing around 1795.[3]

The shocking turn of events in the play, in which an invigorated Liberty awakens the multitude who then turn on the elitist agents of Federalism, mirrors the Republican narrative of the political rescue and empowerment of the American people via the presidential election of 1800. The image of the common people as having been almost overcome ("infatuated") by the arts and threats of Federalist officials and their sympathizers dramatizes the highly individualistic ideal of Jeffersonian Republicanism: to free "the universal man hidden from himself by tyrants, priests, and overlords."[4]

Another way of looking at this aspect of the play's narrative is that it paradoxically reflects perhaps the greatest single anxiety of Republican leaders, which was that the people, even though they might be virtuous, could also be misled, by intrigue and clever oratory, into deserting their own fundamentally good principles.[5] That Liberty must then protect the villainous Federalists from the angry crowd introduces an important cautionary note into the play and reflects another element of this Republican education effort. All leaders of the early American Republic, Robert Ferguson has observed, "recognized a dangerous continuum from the people to faction, to the crowd, and finally into the mob."[6] One challenge for Jeffersonian Republicans as they set about consolidating their position in American politics was to be responsive to the will of the people while guarding against its excesses. As Jefferson put it in his inaugural address, "[T]hough the will of the majority is in all cases to prevail, that will, to be rightful, must be reasonable; . . . the minority possess their equal rights, which equal laws must protect, and to violate [them] would be oppression."[7]

As discussed previously, part of the Jeffersonians' task would be to ensure that public opinion would rest on the correct grounds, which would require "shaping an informed citizenry for a Republican future" through education and the subsidized spread of political information.[8] Americans would then have to be shown how to properly exercise their governing rights. Dramatically staged patriotic performances like the pageant reported in the *Intelligencer* played a key role in that educational process, using "public ceremony" to demonstrate proper "classical composure" in society.[9]

The appearance of America's guardian angel in the play has several levels of meaning. It conveys divine approval for the results of the election, thereby refuting Federalist charges that a Jefferson victory would mean the triumph of atheism.[10] The angel imagery also invokes the trope of the religious view of liberty, in which "each stage of America's uncertain struggle with England," as well as Jefferson's electoral triumph, was viewed as evidence of America's Manifest Destiny and the guiding hand of Divine Providence.[11] Finally, the image of the angel painting "Union" in golden letters above the actors conveys the divine will that the United States of America should remain united. That invocation of God's plan for a united America would have helped defuse the separatist sentiments that had been stirred during the presidential campaign and electoral crisis and that now needed tempering.

As in all good political advertising, the characters and staging in the play are so dramatic that they must have made a strong impression on everyone who saw or read it. All those so influenced would have become part of the "imagined community" of Americans who saw Jefferson and Republicanism as representing the best vision for government in America.[12] The play can thus be seen as the opening, dramatic salvo from the pages of the *National Intelligencer* in the long-term Jeffersonian project of the Republican reeducation—and reimagination—of America. The *Intelligencer* would repeatedly invoke the image of a slumbering republic, in danger of losing its liberties forever, then rousing itself, humbling its elitist enemies, and restoring its true principles of popular government through the election of Jefferson.[13]

In its next issue, on March 9, the *Intelligencer* printed an unsigned commentary, addressed to the "Citizens of the United States." It asserted that the recent federal elections had amounted to a double electoral mandate: a majority of the people had declared themselves in favor "not only of particular men" but also of particular "measures and principles." The leading features of the mandate included fiscal economy, avoidance of foreign entanglements, obedience to the law, and freedom of inquiry.

The July 22 issue recounted with pride how the *Intelligencer* had received a pamphlet printed in London that contained Jefferson's inaugural address and an essay praising the address. The *Intelligencer* reprinted the essay, which it took as evidence that a "large portion of Englishmen" were ready for the adoption of a republican government there. The equation of Jefferson with Republicanism was echoed in the *Intelligencer* months later, on December 7, 1801, in a commentary marking the beginning of the first session of the new Republican-dominated Congress. The commentary first presented the official Republican theory of government, which put Congress in the superior constitutional position.

As the Legislature is the most efficient, so it should ever be the most respected organ of power. Monarchies elevate one man to pre-eminent distinction; but it is the glory of republics, that their brightest honors are conferred on their immediate representatives, to whom are confided the enaction of laws. It is the Legislature that *creates*; the Executive only carries what has been previously willed into effect.

The commentary then contrasted that theory with what had happened during the Adams administration, when the "supineness of the legislature" had allowed the "executive department" to assume duties that were "legislative in their essence" and therefore not properly transferrable. An "evil of equal magnitude," noted the commentary, had been the "discretionary confidence vested in the executive branch."

The commentary claimed that through congressional abdication of its constitutional role, the Adams administration had taken actions and rammed through legislation that had produced a national crisis. Fortunately, though, Americans, motivated by "moral principle on a scale previously unequalled," had through the last national and state elections produced a "triumph of republicanism." Jefferson had been elected president, the House and Senate had become "decidedly republican," and Republicans now controlled twelve state legislatures, twice as many as they had before the elections.

Asserting that the state elections effectively constituted a sort of national referendum on Jefferson's presidency, the commentary asked,

Have the republicans, they who exclusively support the administration of the federal government—have they lost ground in a single state? Have they not, on the contrary, in the short period of one year, gained five states? And even when they have not succeeded, is not every election an evidence of their increasing strength?

Those who had claimed that "the President is on one side, and the nation on the other," had been proven wrong. Jefferson had come "to power as the man of the people" and had ever since demonstrated "a mind prompt to discern, and a heart warm in the pursuit of whatever promotes the public good." By voting in Jefferson and large Republican majorities in Congress, Americans had set the country on a new political course.

The nation believed that principles were entertained that unopposed would lead to monarchy. They saw measures pursued that confirmed their belief. The alien and sedition acts; the extension of diplomatic intercourse; the formation of pernicious treaties; the undignified reproaches of foreign nations; the rapid extension of warlike preparations; the imposition of heavy taxes, formed a mass of measures that menaced the republican structure.

On December 14, in a fawning commentary on Jefferson's annual message to Congress that he had delivered on December 8, the *Intelligencer* again applied the term "man of the people" to Jefferson, adding, "The title is the noblest that can be bestowed; nor will it cease to be continued, so long as his actions and principles remain truly republican."

Another depiction of the civic canonization of Jefferson appeared in the *Intelligencer* on January 20, 1802. The paper reprinted an article from the *Baltimore American* headlined, "THE GREATEST CHEESE IN AMERICA, FOR THE GREATEST MAN IN AMERICA." The article reported that on January 1, President Jefferson had been presented with "the Mammoth Cheese," which the article said weighed 1,235 pounds and had been made in Cheshire, Massachusetts, and then transported to the capital for presentation to Jefferson.[14] The address to the president by the citizen delegation from Cheshire said, in part,

> Notwithstanding we live remote from the seat of government. . . . Our attachment to the national constitution is strong and indissoluble. . . . But for several years past, our apprehension has been, that the genius of the government was not attended to in sundry cases; and that the administration bordered upon monarchy. Our joy of course must have been great, on your election to the first office of the nation; having good evidence, from your announced sentiments and uniform conduct that it would be your strife and glory to turn back the government to its virgin purity. The trust is great! The task is arduous! But we console ourselves, that the Supreme Ruler of the universe, who raises up men to achieve great events, has raised up a Jefferson for this critical day to defend republicanism and baffle all the arts of aristocracy.
>
> Sir, we have attempted to prove our love to our President, not in words alone, but in deeds and truth. With this address, we send you a cheese . . . as a pepper-corn of the esteem which we bear to our chief magistrate, and as a sacrifice to republicanism. . . .
>
> May God long preserve your life and health, for a blessing to the United States and the world at large.

There are striking parallels between the imagery in the Cheshire delegation's address and the play presented in the *Intelligencer* two days after Jefferson's inauguration. The play depicted Liberty as a beautiful virgin about to expire at the hands of various Federalist villains until she is saved by the election of Jefferson. In the address from the Cheshire citizens, Jefferson is similarly charged with the "arduous task" of restoring the government to its "virgin purity." In both cases, Jefferson's election evokes great popular joy in the country. Both tellings also portray Jefferson as God's gift to America. The Cheshire citizens say it in words, while the appearance of a hovering "guardian angel of America" at the end of the play says it in an image. Such manifestations of "oral speech on the printed page" were a new development in political rhetoric, stimulated by a dramatic increase in electoral participation that, in turn, required more popularly accessible political messages.[15] The images of a floundering country and the need to restore it to its original founding principles are, of course, a common trope employed by those seeking to unseat a dominant political regime.

Interestingly, in his brief reply to the delegation that was included in the *Intelligencer* article, Jefferson did not distance himself from any of the hyperbolic statements in their address. He simply stated his agreement with the constitutional principles expressed in it, and his "particular pleasure" at having received such a "testimony of good will" from "freeborn farmers, employed personally in the most useful labors of life."[16] The *Intelligencer* article said the delegation members had been "highly gratified with the *simple plainness* with which they have been received in the presenting of the *cheese*, which they conceive to be the *dignity of republicanism.*" While somewhat ambiguous, this statement could have referred to how Jefferson himself had conducted the presentation ceremony or perhaps even to how he was dressed. The mention of "simple plainness" reflects the "Republican style of behavior" that Jefferson was determined to cultivate as an antidote to what he perceived as the obnoxious ceremonies of deference that had sprung up under the Federalists.[17]

The end of the first session of the new Republican-dominated Congress, on May 3, 1802, prompted several commentaries in the *Intelligencer* about how closely connected Jefferson was to the people. A May 5 commentary asserted virtual unity. It acknowledged that Jefferson had "in some measure led public opinion"—as, it said, Washington had done. The commentary then claimed, "The truth, however, is that so perfect was and still is the identity between the public sentiment and that of the chief magistrate, that on most points, we in vain attempt to find the cause of the one in the other." Thus, when Jefferson had acted according to "the dictates of his own mind," his actions had equally been "in correspondence with the national wishes."

Republicans in Congress received similar praise for having passed legislation to address a number of problems in the country, including an unnecessarily large army, a bloated and distrusted federal judiciary, an immense debt, and oppressive internal taxes: "The people demanded, through the organ of elections, relief from these oppressions. Their voice has been heard. Their *Representatives* have done *their* duty." Federalist opposition had been "unprecedented in violence, to every measure proposed." Republicans had paid no attention to those "revilings of party," because they had "felt too strong a confidence in the intelligence of the people to doubt the correctness of their decision."

The *Intelligencer*'s issues of May 14 and May 17, 1802, carried a two-part review of the accomplishments of the last session of Congress. The review began by affirming, "It is the right and duty of the citizens of a free state to acquire and communicate correct knowledge of all the proceedings of its government, and as far as possible of the principles which produced its various acts." With that information, the people would then be able to "judge for themselves, [and] not from ill natured and bitter invectives, what is the true character of the administration." This was democracy in America, where "Government is instituted to secure and increase the happiness of the persons governed. It is the right and property of the public—not its administrators."

The commentary said that Congress had "united with the executive" to accomplish "great works of reformation and improvements." Rather than aggrandizing power, Jefferson had limited his own powers, reduced his "privileges," and exercised "every constitutional check to limit the executive will." The commentary presented a detailed explanation and justification of the important actions taken by the government, including the abolition of "sixteen useless offices" through the repeal of the Federalists' Judiciary Act of 1801, reductions in the armed forces, repeals of taxes, "reform" of the judicial system, revision of the naturalization laws, and a large reduction in government spending. The commentary concluded,

> Here is a just picture of the republican administration, which many have been taught to believe would destroy your civil and religious institutions, burn your temples, remove all distinctions between virtue and vice, rend asunder your conjugal ties, and substitute disorder and confusion for an obedience to law, and the due regulation of government.

Demonstrating how the *Intelligencer* was being used as a national communications tool, the two-part review was headlined with the request that "republican printers throughout the United States" give it "a place in their papers." They did just that, over and over again, as illustrated by the Boston-based *Republican Gazetteer*, which J. M. Dunham began publishing on May 26, 1802. Dunham reprinted the entire second part of the *Intelligencer* review on the first page of his first issue, then he reprinted the review's first part in his second issue, on May 29. In both cases, the reprinted commentaries filled up almost the whole first page of Dunham's paper. In his first issue, Dunham also published a commentary, signed "An Anti-Aristocrat," praising the Republicans for having repealed the Federalists' attempt to expand the federal judiciary. Sneering at the "midnight judges," the writer spoke of his outrage when reading the "speeches of these Congressional orators" who had opposed the repeal. As this episode shows, the *Intelligencer* was a multifaceted communications tool. The material it provided could be reprinted verbatim but also served to frame debates over policy issues and to energize other pro-Republican newspaper commentators.

The extent to which the *Republican Gazetteer* effectively served as a local conduit for the messages in Jefferson's national newspaper is impressive. On June 23, 1802, the *Intelligencer* carried the first installment of a voluminous series on "History of the Last Session of Congress." The series recounted the various proceedings of Congress by topic (taxes, the judiciary, spending on the military, etc.), mixing factual reporting and transcriptions of floor debates with pro-Republican and anti-Federalist commentary. The commentaries were an obvious effort to demonstrate that everything Republicans had done in the last Congress had been good, thus justifying voters' continued support for Republicans in the upcoming general election. For several months, almost every issue of the *Intelligencer* carried another installment of the series. Beginning on July 10 and continuing for the next six weeks, those commentaries were faithfully republished in Dunham's *Gazetteer*. Also in mid-1802, the *Intelligencer* published a series titled "Federal Misrepresentations," in which various "palpable violations of truth" that had appeared in Federalist newspapers were identified and rebutted.[18] The *Gazetteer* reprinted much of that series as well.

Promoting Correct Republican Behavior for Presidents and the People

Thomas Jefferson intended to give the American ship of state what he called a "republican tack," by "banishing Federalist formality" from presidential appearances and ceremonies.[19] In all his actions, he behaved in a "manner that advertised his republicanism."[20] His goal, in Joyce Appleby's phrase, was to instill the "psychology of democracy" in America. Jefferson realized, Appleby writes, that democracy "was as much about social interactions as political beliefs." Thus, behavioral changes were needed "as urgently as new convictions," and both would have to be modeled for Americans by Jefferson and other good Republicans. The aim was to create "social situations primed to promote egalitarian practices," such as simplicity in speech and dress and the abolition of socially or politically deferential behavior in public. Long before the advent of behavioral psychology, Jefferson had realized "that the body had to move out of the box before the brain could imagine different ways" of thinking and acting socially and politically.[21]

Thus, the March 6, 1801, issue of the *Intelligencer* reported that on his inaugural day, Jefferson's "dress was, as usual, that of a plain citizen, without any distinctive badge of office." The paper also reported that the manner in which Jefferson had delivered his address was "plain, dignified, and unostentatious." On March 9, it reported that "large assemblies of citizens" in several cities had gathered to celebrate the presidential election as a great "triumph of principle."

The Republicans' behavioral themes came together, in rather extreme form, in the *Intelligencer*'s treatment of citizen addresses to the newly elected president and vice president. It began on March 2, when the paper reported that Aaron Burr had been greeted by a "number of patriotic citizens" who had gathered to meet him on his arrival in Baltimore. The citizens' greeting occupied just a few printed sentences in the paper and praised Burr for his patriotism in having "disclaimed competition for the presidential chair," thereby "setting a just value upon the will of the people." Burr was said to have replied that the election had been a triumph not of two men but of "principle," and that he had never considered "stepping between the will and the wishes of the people in opposition to Mr. Jefferson."

According to the *Intelligencer*, however, Burr made these gracious comments only after first telling those greeting him that they should not have addressed him formally at all.[22] The paper said that Burr had expressed his "disapprobation of addresses of this kind" because, although they had originally been considered a "mere matter of form," they had "in our time" come to be "made use of as engines, and prostituted to particular purposes." In a commentary following the report, the *Intelligencer* praised Burr's remarks as having reflected the "principles of genuine republicanism." As the paper explained, "A servile spirit of adulation is at all times and in all countries disgraceful. Of this spirit personal addresses are too generally the vehicle." The commentary therefore urged the "enlightened friends of republicanism to cling *exclusively to principle* and to commend, not men but measures."

The sentiments expressed in this commentary reflected Jefferson's attitude precisely, according to Dumas Malone. Jefferson "strongly objected to any glorification of rulers. To him, public officials in a self-governing society were public servants and should appear as such. This was sound republican doctrine."[23] Appleby goes deeper in analyzing why Jefferson "hated the politics of deference." His attitude stemmed from his "awareness of the debilitating effect of a ranked society's deferential manners." Consequently, he was determined to eradicate the "time-honored hierarchies of authority" that Federalist leaders had been promoting since 1788.[24]

On March 13, 1801, an *Intelligencer* commentary signed "Temperance" asserted that "accumulating exaggerated praise" on any government official manifests a "degree of servility" that is unwarranted in a republican government. A March 18 commentary entitled "Thoughts on Addresses" reminded readers how offensively John Adams had behaved in receiving fawning addresses from citizen groups and then making public replies to them. That practice, the commentary said, had perverted the "constitutional power bestowed on the chief magistrate," by making "the President preeminently the legislator of national opinion." Such public posturing by Adams had been contrary to the "constitutional order," because, by only giving the president the power to recommend measures for the Congress to consider, the Constitution had "implicitly denied to him the right of appealing to the passions of the people, and inciting them to the adoption of favorite measures."

The most serious effect of such "adulatory and congratulatory productions," the commentary argued, was that they could have only one result: to "divide the citizens, whom it is the duty of the chief magistrate to unite." His opponents would still view with "jealousy" even a "prudent, modest, and dignified" presidential response to such addresses, and a "vain, arrogant, and undignified" response would antagonize and divide the country, possibly even hurrying the nation "into civil or external war," which had been the result under Adams. Republicans, the commentary said, "cannot forget what they have seen and heard; they have seen the peace of society hazarded; they have heard innocent, nay praise worthy sentiments denounced; they have heard patriots of unlimited virtue calumniated; they have heard threats encouraged and reciprocated."

To reinforce the condemnation of citizen addresses, the next issue of the *Intelligencer*, published on March 20, even claimed, rather implausibly, that "a considerable number of addresses to THOMAS JEFFERSON, President of the United States, had been withheld from presentment" to him, "on the advice of many of the most enlightened republicans in various parts of the United States." The problem with such addresses, the paper said, was that they were the "offspring of precipitate zeal, rather than the result of deliberate reflection." It was hoped that no more such "*complimentary* addresses" would be presented to Jefferson. "It is not on the *words*, but the *actions* of his fellow-citizens, that he is to place his firm reliance," the commentary explained, adding that "on *his* actions must depend the measure of support he shall receive."

To buttress its case, the March 25 *Intelligencer* published some of the replies Adams had made to citizen addresses, which showed how "humiliatingly" Adams had "committed his own personal dignity" and also how he had harmed the "character of the government and the peace of the nation." The newspaper cited statements that Adams made in 1798, when he had injected himself very publicly into the national debate over whether the United States should go to war with France. Federalists, who favored war, had organized citizen groups to send supportive letters to Adams, who not only replied to the letters but also released his replies to the public. After his replies were first published in two prominent newspapers in Philadelphia, 106 of the citizens' letters and 90 replies by Adams were published in a 360-page pamphlet.[25] Many of the replies contained thinly veiled attacks on his opponents and incensed Republicans, including Madison and Jefferson. Madison told Jefferson he thought that some of the statements by Adams were "the most abominable and degrading that could fall from the lips of the first magistrate of an independent people."[26] Jefferson monitored the letters as they were published in the newspapers and kept an annotated list of the most offensive statements.[27]

The *Intelligencer*'s curious focus on public communications to and from presidents becomes more understandable in light of Jefferson's determination to restore America to its true founding principles. As Jonathan J. Edwards has shown in his analysis of "resistance rhetoric" in the Fundamentalist religious movement in America, counterinsurgencies utilize both "negative ideographs" and "counter-symbols" in their efforts. Negative ideographs label certain behavior unacceptable, while "counter-symbols" go further, criticizing the behavior as a "betrayal of a common, prior unity between public and counter-public."[28]

One can see both of those counterinsurgency techniques at work in the *Intelligencer*'s condemnation of replies Adams made to pro-war citizen addresses he received in 1798. His confrontational responses had inflamed partisan passions and divided the nation.[29] Thus, the entire practice of citizen addresses to presidents had to be condemned to provide a concrete symbol of how things were to change under the Jeffersonian "countermovement."

On April 24, the *Intelligencer* carried on the attack, referring to two "complimentary addresses" that had been presented to the president by citizens of North and South Carolina. The paper noted pointedly that although the "addresses and the replies made to them" expressed "no other than the pure sentiments of republicanism," it was declining to publish them because such statements were "on *principle*, considered pernicious." These kinds of address, said the paper, "flow from a servile spirit" unbecoming the "citizens of a republic." Moreover, the "direct tendency" of such addresses is to "inflame the passions of contending parties." The commentary concluded by recommending that "the press neglect them."

In contrast, the *Intelligencer* regarded addresses from official legislative bodies as just fine to print. On December 9, 1801, the paper printed an address to Jefferson from the Vermont General Assembly. The address said the Assembly regarded the "Presidency with a cordial attachment and profound respect." As for Jefferson himself, they said, "We revere your talents, are assured of your patriotism, and rely on your fidelity—More than this, our hearts in unison with your own, reverberate the political opinions you have been pleased to announce in your inaugural speech." On March 15, 1802, the paper also printed both an address to Jefferson from the Georgia legislature and his reply.

The reason for the different approaches to publishing addresses had been provided earlier in the *Intelligencer*, on March 18, 1801, in a commentary titled "Thoughts On Addresses." Although addresses from informal citizen gatherings were condemned in that commentary, others of a different nature were not.

It may be necessary to observe, to prevent misconception, that these remarks do not apply to any expression of the sentiments or desires of any number or association of citizens on any particular or important

occasion, when such expression may be an act of high and indispensible duty; but *exclusively* to those adulatory and congratulatory productions, which have lately flourished so luxuriantly in this country.

Laudatory resolutions from state legislatures could clearly be denominated acts of "high and indispensible duty" not covered by the injunc-
tion. Jefferson made this point more directly on July 24, 1803, in a letter to William Duane, in which the president rejected the legitimacy of
communications from informal citizen groups as a part of the governance process. "The public opinion," Jefferson wrote, could be properly
expressed only through the institutions prescribed in the Constitution.[30]

That "official" adulatory addresses to the president were fine while
unofficial ones from citizens were not also seems to reflect the elite desire
(discussed previously in this chapter) to temper the wave of democratic
populism that had swept the country during the revolution, revived in
the 1790s, and resulted in the heated presidential elections of 1796 and
1800. As Jeffrey Selinger notes, such "deep partisan divisions, especially
insofar as they spread to the mass public, compromised the capacity
of elites to govern." Elites therefore "took steps to settle, neutralize, or
evade" anything that threatened to destabilize the fragile republic.[31]

Illustrating that approach is Jefferson's later handling of an unsigned
address from the Ward Committee of Philadelphia. The address concerned one of his appointments of an official in the city, so it was essentially the same in form as the address from the New Haven Merchants
that he had responded to with the famous defense of his policies on
appointments (discussed in chapter 5). With the Philadelphia address,
however, Jefferson took a different approach. In January 1806, he told
Uriah Tracy that he would not respond to it, because, unlike the New
Haven Merchants' address, it had not been signed. That omission made
the Philadelphia address "unknown by the Constitution," while the signing of the other address had made it "a part of the machinery of the
Constitution."[32]

Although it is possible to perceive, or at least construct, a logic in
the attitude manifested in the *Intelligencer* toward citizen addresses, Jefferson's Federalist opponents certainly did not see it. On two occasions
in 1801, the *Washington Federalist* even contrasted Burr's condemnation
of such addresses with Jefferson's responses to some of them. In its June
10 issue, the paper published Jefferson's one-paragraph reply to an
"address of sundry inhabitants" from York County, Pennsylvania. Referring to the "thankfulness and satisfaction" Jefferson had expressed to

the citizens for their address, the *Federalist* noted archly that "Mr. Burr seems of a different opinion, as he considers such addresses . . . merely complimentary, and often of bad effect." Similarly, on November 23, the *Federalist's* response to a claim by a Republican newspaper of contradictions in Federalist positions was to list contradictions in Republican positions. The first example listed, captioned "Burr vs. Jefferson," contrasted Burr's condemnation of the Baltimore citizens' address with the public expressions of thanks Jefferson had made to addresses from two church groups.

On December 10, 1801, the *Washington Federalist* said it finally had proof of the phoniness of Republican screeds against undue praise for elected officials. That proof was the glowing commentary that Samuel Harrison Smith had published in the December 7 *Intelligencer* regarding Jefferson's message to Congress. Noting that Smith had "professed himself an enemy . . . of servile adulation to men in power," the *Federalist* then quoted Smith's praise of Jefferson as a "chief magistrate equally distinguished by his *talents* and *virtues*." That adulation, the *Federalist* sneered (saying it did not know "whether to laugh or be angry"), was not only a lie but sheer "eulogium" and "flummery."

On the Proper Republican Way of Thinking and Behaving

Related to the *Intelligencer*'s emphasis on properly structured and restrained communications from citizens to the president was its frequent stress on correct individual behavior. Good Republicans needed to behave rationally and moderately in all their actions, thus modeling for other Americans the mode of behavior that was most conducive to a democratic republic. That guidance reflects, of course, the deep Jeffersonian-Republican commitment to an "Enlightenment faith in the rational, self-improving, independent individual," who could be counted on to realize their own true, best interests if only exposed to the correct information and education.[33] The emphasis also illustrates the strategy, of Jefferson and other Republican leaders, that Republicans could win over many of the reasonable Federalists through moderation in both Republican national policies and party rhetoric. Republicans ultimately hoped for the elimination of partisanship and partisan conflict, culminating in, as Jefferson put it, a "perfect consolidation" of all Americans under the same political mantra, Republicanism.[34]

Thus, on March 9, 1801, just a few days after Jefferson's inauguration, the *Intelligencer* carried an appeal to the "Citizens of the United States!" After listing the basic principles of a Jefferson presidency, the commentary acknowledged that different opinions might be held by some of "his late political opponents." "Instantaneous approbation" from them could not be expected, the paper conceded. The commentary hoped, though, that the president's opponents would remain "neutral" for a while. Doing that would "enable them coolly and deliberately to review opinions, to dismiss past prejudices, and to estimate relative weight of character." Where honest differences of opinion persisted, the commentary urged that they be discussed with "candor and truth . . . without manifesting the petulance of passion or the rancor of calumny." That approach could be the "harbinger of peace to contending classes of citizens," because it would "awaken and engage those powers of the mind on whose active exercise the public welfare essentially depends."

The emphasis on moderation and rationality even extended to the guidance the newspaper was dispensing to good Republicans on how to celebrate the Fourth of July. On July 3, 1801, the *Intelligencer* printed a front-page column entitled "FOURTH OF JULY!" Its commentary urged Americans to "celebrate this anniversary with a *rational* rather than *animal* joy" and counseled against "mingling in noisy scenes of riot and intoxication." It urged Americans to spend the day solemnly reflecting on their good fortune to be living freely in a peaceful, democratic nation while Europe was plagued with wars and foolish leaders. The piece concluded with the reminder that, however divided Americans might be politically, their "interests are all the same."[35]

The *Intelligencer* continued the themes of restrained celebration and rational reflection in its July 6 issue, where a commentary began by noting that the Fourth of July had been celebrated in the nation's capital with "patriotic and rational animation." Around noon on the Fourth, it said, the "first magistrate" had been greeted by numerous groups, including cabinet heads, military officers, foreign diplomats, "strangers of distinction," "most of the respectable citizens of Washington and George-Town," and even a delegation of Cherokee chiefs. The president was said to have received the "cordial felicitation" with "unfeigned satisfaction." The paper added that while there had been no "ostentatious homage to power," all present had been inspired with "patriotic gratitude" to be in the presence of the author of the Declaration of Independence himself. That "spirit of general amity [had] thrown a mantle of oblivion over past political differences." The celebration was reported to have continued for two hours, marked by band music, military processions, and abundant refreshments.[36] Later that day, the paper reported, most of the officers in the federal government and the military (but apparently not Jefferson, who was not mentioned) attended a dinner to celebrate the Fourth. At the dinner, there were toasts and songs, and the *Intelligencer* reprinted the lyrics of one song and the texts of several toasts.[37]

The commentary concluded by reiterating the themes of Republican rationality and moderation. "As we hoped," it said, the "festivity of the day was animated and rational." The celebrants' feelings had been "elevated by the sacredness of the anniversary," and "all disposition to intemperate gaiety" had been "repressed." The day had been a "precursor of that enlightened and philanthropic temper" that ought to "preside over every American mind!"

On July 13, the *Intelligencer* boasted that the Fourth had been celebrated across the Union with "more than usual demonstrations of joy" and that never since the adoption of the Constitution had "there been exhibited more unanimity and harmony." It was "most evident," the paper said, "that the animosity of party spirit is rapidly on the decline." The *Intelligencer*'s July 20 account of the Fourth of July celebration in Prince Georges County in Bladensburg, Maryland, was prefaced by more modeling of good Republican behavior: following a day spent in "harmony and conviviality," the celebrants had retired to their homes "in that sober and orderly manner which ought always to characterize Republicans."

Along the same lines is an *Intelligencer* commentary, published on November 16, in which the essayist "Moderation" counseled all Republican printers on how to do their jobs. "Moderation" began by congratulating them for having almost always responded properly to the attacks on Republicans over the past several years. "By stating facts with temperate commentaries," he said, those editors had "sought to enlighten the public, not by dictating to them what they should think, but by supplying them with the materials of self conviction." "Moderation" deemed the effects of the Republican victory in 1800 "great and glorious" already, noting that the "divisions of party rapidly subside." Soon the day would come, he argued, when the American people would be "re-united in principles and practice, as they always have been in interest."

"Moderation" did concede that a "few dissatisfied individuals" persisted in their opposition to Jefferson and that "many of the federal prints teem with misrepresentations of his actions and motives." In the face of this opposition, the writer counseled a new course of action: Republican editors should "suspend past animosities" and avoid ascribing "corrupt motives" to their political opponents. Lamenting that for every one dishonest politician, there are "a hundred who are misguided by error," "Moderation" advised printers to leave the door "open to such men": "Counsel them in the language of candor and temperance of their error, and they will generally join you as friends."

All of this advice strongly reflected Jefferson's moral sense of virtuous social behavior. He believed, as Jean Yarbrough showed, that "we are by nature social beings who depend for our happiness and well-being on the approval of others," which meant that the highest virtue, surpassing even justice, was the exercise of "benevolence," or goodwill toward others. As Yarbrough notes, Jefferson regarded the teachings of Christ as having been the "most perfect and sublime" moral guidance ever, because Christ had extended the moral obligation of benevolence and forgiveness "not only to kindred and friends, to neighbors and countrymen, but to all mankind."[38] Jeremy Engels points out that Jefferson was also strongly influenced by Adam Smith's *Theory of Moral Sentiments*, in which Smith outlined a moral theory of self-discipline that would lead to harmonious social relations in a community even in the absence of religion. The theory was based on the behaviorial ideal of always acting solicitously ("in sympathy") toward others, in ways that society finds "praiseworthy and deserving of approbation."[39] Malone's description of Jefferson's approach at the beginning of his administration echoes those principles: "His manners were conciliatory and his preferred methods those of gradualism and patience."[40]

In an "Address to Subscribers" on November 20, Samuel Harrison Smith advanced similar sentiments.[41] Declaring that all men would naturally only act virtuously were it not that "political fraud lead[s] them astray," he asserted that the "only irresistible weapons that rational agents can wield" against such fraud are "reason and truth." He assured readers that "the great mass of each party only requires a temperate and rational disclosure of its errors to abandon them." He therefore looked forward confidently to an era of "national harmony," when "the nation will be undivided in political opinion."

Smith reiterated the "All You Need Is Truth" theme in a note on April 21, 1802, rebutting claims in Federalist newspapers that the *Intelligencer*'s reports on governmental matters, such as congressional debates or presidential actions, were not always accurate or complete. Denying any deliberate misstatements in the paper, he said he always aimed for the truth, because those "who at present administer the federal government, require nothing but truth to triumph." The theme appeared again a week later, in an April 28 report gloating over recent elections in Rhode Island that had delivered massive Republican majorities. The report ended, "*Powerful is truth. It will prevail.*"

Almost all the themes discussed in this section were exhibited in the *Intelligencer* on January 13, 1802, in a commentary on the results of recent elections in New Jersey. Republicans had become the majority party, an understandable cause for celebration, but the commentary counseled moderation in the "language or the actions of our republican friends" as they savored victory. The strategy was to exhibit an "honorable spirit of conciliation. . . . Let this spirit be cherished and diffused, and we shall soon cease to be a divided people." This crucial time, the commentary proclaimed, had been brought about through education and the diffusion of information.

> A great political crisis has arrived. The tide has turned. Correct information pervades the union. Millions, perhaps, heretofore the unconscious victims of error, are ready to dismiss their prejudices, and with becoming honesty, to embrace truth.

For good measure, the commentary reiterated the condemnation of citizen addresses to government leaders. The problem was that "all *complimentary* addresses from private citizens to men in power" take the form of "adulation of our friends, and invective against our enemies," which can then discourage "the prevalence of that harmony, which might otherwise be produced." The commentary asserted with satisfaction that the state of Virginia, the enthusiastic supporter of Republicanism and the native home of the president, had (supposedly) not presented even one citizen address to Jefferson. This example "is a bright one," the commentary said, adding, "We offer it to the imitation of the union."

The guidance of the commentary can be boiled down into a basic set of precepts that Jefferson himself seems to have followed: In the political world, act carefully and deliberately. Do not allow passions, especially party passions, to color the rational analysis necessary to reach the best policy decisions possible. Behave reservedly in public, even at such obviously celebratory occasions as the Fourth of July, because that is the demeanor of a person who never lets emotion overcome reason and self-control. That behavior will convey the image of being someone who can be trusted as always speaking and acting carefully and thoughtfully. Therefore, when interacting with others (especially those of Federalist inclinations) in matters of politics, avoid rhetorical techniques that rely on emotion rather than rationality, such as personal attacks or partisan denigration.

Hasty actions were not conducive to Jefferson's approach, which is why he and his fellow Republicans condemned many citizen addresses, often generated quickly at boisterous meetings attended only by partisans. It is also why addresses from legislatures were considered appropriate: they had been produced through an official process that, at least in theory, required careful deliberation and was open to participation by representatives of the full partisan spectrum.

Why Jefferson Gave His Annual Messages to Congress in Writing, Rather Than in Speeches

The *Intelligencer* even provided an explanation of how Thomas Jefferson himself, as president, had behaved in a way that was consistent with all of this guidance. That explanation brings significant new evidence to bear on a question that generated a great deal of scholarly debate following the publication of *The Rhetorical Presidency* by Jeffrey Tulis in 1987. Tulis articulated a new interpretation of Jefferson's decision to send his annual messages to Congress in writing, to be read to Congress by a clerk, rather than delivering the messages himself in speeches as Washington and Adams had done.

The previous interpretation was based on the explanation that Jefferson himself gave in his first message. He said he had dispensed with a speech because it had spawned the practice, imitative of British parliamentary practice, of Congress then having to put together a formal response to the address.[42] He therefore had decided to relieve Congress "from the embarrassment of immediate answers, on objects not yet fully before them." Dispensing with the extravagant ceremony of the address was, according to Malone, a specific part of Jefferson's plan to eradicate all "ceremonial foolishness" that contributed to the "glorification of rulers."[43] Robert M. Johnstone Jr. similarly termed the decision a "calculated political act designed to underline the return to sound republican simplicity."[44] There had indeed been quite a bit of ceremony under Jefferson's predecessors; Adams, for example, had worn a ceremonial sword when he delivered his addresses.[45]

Tulis read Jefferson's action on a deeper level. He said it demonstrated Jefferson acting according to a fundamental constitutional principle: to avoid the dangers of demagoguery by presidents, presidential communications on policy matters should be done in writing rather than via speeches and be directed to Congress rather than to the people.[46] One obvious problem with this interpretation is that, as Stephen Lucas noted, Washington and Adams, who presumably knew as much about American constitutional principles as Jefferson, had acted differently.[47] Another problem is that Jefferson's own explanation in his first annual message made no reference to any such constitutional understanding.

New evidence on the question comes from a commentary in the *Intelligencer* on June 25, 1802, entitled "History of the Last Session of Congress." Before discussing Jefferson's annual message from the previous November in detail, the commentary quoted the president's own explanation for why he had presented it to the new Congress in written form rather than through a speech. Then the commentary elaborated on his decision. This is the full opening paragraph in the commentary:

> Hitherto the chief magistrate had delivered a speech to congress in session; and his personal attendance on the legislature had been considered as producing the necessity of a reply, which had been also presented to him by the members in person. Under this practice the two houses were called upon prematurely to discuss and decide on measures with which they could be but imperfectly acquainted. They were called upon, without information, to sanction whatever had been done by the President, and to pledge him their support. Hence the field of party was taken, and all its animosities kindled, to commemorate the triumph of party without the least pretension to public benefit. The practice had been copied from a monarchy, where the parliament are creatures of the crown; and to that monarchy it should have been confined. Republican magnanimity forbore to seize this occasion for unworthy triumph. Animated by a desire of conciliation, and by a determination *to do their duty,* the majority hesitated not a moment to substitute substantial acts in the room of [i.e., for] presidential eulogium.

The first reason given here for the message's form, that Jefferson wished to spare Congress from having to act without complete information, essentially parallels the explanation Jefferson gave in his message to Congress: that he had not wanted to force Congress into "the embarrassment of immediate answers, on objects not yet fully before them." It also matches up with a letter Jefferson wrote to Benjamin Rush on December 20, 1801, in which Jefferson reported,

Our winter campaign has opened with more good humor than I expected. [B]y sending a message, instead of making a speech at the opening of the session, I have prevented the bloody conflicts to which the making an answer would have committed them. [T]hey consequently were able to set in to real business at once, without losing 10 or 12 days in combating an answer. . . . [H]itherto there has been no disagreeable altercations.[48]

As Robert Johnstone pointed out, the process followed in the Washington and Adams administrations regarding the annual message was indeed time-consuming and often fraught politically. After the president's address, "Congress in turn prepared, debated, voted, and delivered a reply to the address, and the president, in his turn, delivered a formal reply to the reply!"[49]

The explanation in the *Intelligencer* commentary's first paragraph mentioned two other reasons for the written message: Republicans desired to promote partisan reconciliation and were determined "*to do their duty.*" Regarding the former reason, the commentary explained that under the old practice followed by Washington and Adams, "the field of party was taken, and all its animosities kindled." When their turn had come, Republicans, "animated by a desire of conciliation," had chosen to avoid such an unnecessary partisan provocation. That Republicans hoped partisan differences might eventually fade away was exemplified by the conciliatory declaration in Jefferson's first inaugural speech that "we are all federalists, we are all republicans." Similarly, in his first annual message, Jefferson had expressed the hope to Congress that "the prudence and temperance of your discussions will promote within your own walls, that conciliation which so much befriends rational conclusion; and by its example, will encourage among our constituents that progress of opinion which is tending to unite them in object and in will."[50]

The newspaper's explanation characterized Jefferson's action as having been a determination by Republicans, rather than by Jefferson himself. As Johnstone found, the decision actually "came after extensive discussions with Republican leaders and seems to have been reached as early as seven months before the delivery of the address, precisely to reduce the 'relics' left by the Federalists."[51] Characterizing the act as a group Republican decision would thus have modeled the conciliatory approach to Federalists that the *Intelligencer* had said all Republicans should follow.

The commentary's reference to Republicans wanting "*to do their duty*" was followed by the assertion that Republicans had chosen to "substitute substantial acts" for empty partisan praise of Jefferson ("presidential eulogium"). As discussed previously, the *Intelligencer* had carried several commentaries in the first year of Jefferson's presidency—several in the first month—that had discouraged citizen addresses to the president, because they were directed to the "man" rather than to "principle" and were thus "un-Republican." The explanation given in this later commentary was a way of saying the same thing: rather than wasting their time putting together a response to the president's annual message, the new Republican majority in Congress, led by Jefferson, wanted to "substitute substantial acts" of real legislative effort.

The commentary actually made this point several paragraphs later, asserting that another advantage to Jefferson delivering the message in writing was that he had been able to include with it much more additional information than could have been provided in a speech. Under the prior system, the commentary claimed, after the annual message speech Congress had been left waiting for weeks for more detailed information from the executive branch about the state of the government's affairs. The delay, it said, had rendered Congress dependent "on the opinions of the President or the heads of department," inverting the "constitutional and rational order of things by making the legislature the instrument instead of the director of the executive." The legislature, the commentary proclaimed, "ought to be above all dependence except the people." (Of course, the obvious flaw in this argument is that Jefferson could have delivered his message as a speech and still supplemented it right away with more detailed, written information.)

In a deeper sense, Jefferson's decision to deliver his address to Congress in writing was also portrayed in his presidential newspaper as having modeled for the nation the correct form of behavior in the new American democracy. The will of the people was to be followed, but the carrying out of that will in Congress, through the people's elected representatives, had to be done with full information and in a way that prevented irrational factors, such as emotion and partisanship, from influencing rational discourse and deliberation. The commentary made just that point in its last paragraph. To "put an end to this evil" of Congress having to act while still uninformed,

> the President, at the time he delivered his message, accompanied it with full details of whatever had been done by the executive, and of whatever elucidated the probable measures of the legislature. He, who

considered information as the vital principle of a republic, and as the only safe substitute for confidence, dangerous even when reposed in the best of men, rejoiced to see copious stores of knowledge unfolded; which would enable the legislature to exercise with effect its salutary control on the executive department; and which would enable the people to exercise their still more salutary control on both.

Still missing is any statement by Jefferson—or anyone else, including his newspaper—that his action had been taken out of deference to some sort of constitutional norm. On this point, the leading opposition Federalist newspapers of the time, the *Washington Federalist* and the *New York Evening Post*, offer no help. Both had heard in advance of Jefferson's plan to deliver his message in writing, but neither invoked any constitutionally based reservations in reporting that news. In its first mention of Jefferson's upcoming message, the *Federalist* issue of December 4, 1801, coupled its reference to Jefferson's professed wish to avoid imitating "British proceedings" with the sarcastic claim that Jefferson was really just trying to avoid contradicting himself in a speech.

> It is suggested that the President will not next week deliver a speech, as is usual on such occasions. We think there is much probability in this suggestion. Not that we imagine there is the least likelihood, of the President's fearing that the delivery of such customary speech would be an approximation to the forms of British proceedings, but, the fear of his being unable to say aught that shall not contradict his former contradictory contradictions.

On December 11, the *New York Evening Post*, which had recently been established by Alexander Hamilton to serve as the Federalists' media outlet there, simply published a brief note received from a "gentleman in Washington" that said, "We are to have no *Speech*—only a simple Message."

On December 16, after Jefferson had delivered his message in writing, the *Federalist* said,

> It is well known to have been heretofore customary for the President, at the commencement of every session of Congress to deliver his speech *personally.* This by some has been said to be an imitation of British precedent, an assimilation to monarchy, in opposition to true republicanism. But of this we believe Gen. Washington to have been

as good a judge as Mr. Jefferson, and far more of a republican. The President's neglect of a personal address appears rather than otherwise an innovation intended to catch some childish applause. What were those "circumstances" that rendered his presence in the Capitol "inconvenient"?

On December 17, the *New York Evening Post* published a long commentary on the annual message that began by deriding the mode of its delivery.

Instead of delivering a *speech* to the House of Congress, at the opening of the present session, the President has thought fit to transmit a *Message*. Whether this has proceeded from pride or from humility, from a temperate love of reform, or from a wild spirit of innovation, is submitted to the conjecture of the curious. A single observation shall be indulged—since all agree, that he is unlike his predecessors in essential points, it is a mark of consistency to differ from them in matters of form.

The commentary was signed "Lucius Crassus," an intriguing pseudonym because the real Lucius Crassus was a famed Roman orator.[52] A Connecticut Federalist congressman, Roger Griswold, similarly mocked the significance of the change.

Under this administration nothing is to remain as it was. Every minutiae is to be changed. When Mr. Adams was President, the door of the president's House opened to the East. Mr. Jefferson has closed that door and opened a new door to the West. General Washington and Mr. Adams opened every Session of Congress with a speech. Mr. Jefferson delivers no speech, but makes his communication by a written message. I fear that you Aristocrats of New England will think these important changes unnecessary and be apt to say that they are made with a view only to change, but you ought to recollect that you are neither Philosophers or skilled in the mysteries of Democratic policy.[53]

On January 11, 1802, the *Federalist* published a brief commentary that found only political expediency in Jefferson's action. Jefferson had refrained from addressing Congress in person out of "fear of submitting his recent conduct to the scrutinizing investigation of the minority of Congress."[54]

On January 15, the *Federalist* published a three-column critique, signed "Republicanus," of the reasons Jefferson had given in his message for not delivering it in person. In response to Jefferson's claim to have done it for the "convenience" of Congress, the commentary said that if Jefferson was referring to the previous custom of members "waiting in a body on the president, at his house, to present an address in answer to his speech," there would have been no inconvenience at all. Members could either have walked the mile and a quarter "along an excellent paved footway" or taken an inexpensive carriage ride "along an excellent street."[55]

Responding to Jefferson's mention of the "economy" of the members' time and his desire to relieve Congress of the "embarrassment of immediate answers on matters not fully before them," the commentary made two points. First, if Jefferson had been referring to the time members would have spent listening to his speech, then of course they had spent just as much time listening to it being read to them by a clerk. Second and more important to the present analysis, the commentary disputed Jefferson's claim to have spared the members of Congress from a partisan battle over their response to his message. The commentary asserted that, although there had sometimes been contentious debates over how to answer the annual messages of Washington and Adams, Congress had finally settled on a different practice. Both parties had agreed that it "was proper to avoid, in these addresses every thing that might be likely to excite opposition and party heat, or to pledge the house to particular opinions or measures." Consequently, according to the *Federalist*, the more recent practice had been for a committee to develop a mildly worded declaration of "some general opinions and principles concurred in by all, some complimentary expressions of respect to the president," followed with the promise that the "serious matters recommended or mentioned in the speech, should receive the early and attentive consideration of Congress." The whole affair had only consumed a few hours of work and, in the meantime, "the ordinary business of the house went on." This had been the practice, it said, during the last three years of the Adams presidency.

The commentary then addressed the view, held by "many," that under Washington and Adams the delivery of the president's annual message as a speech to Congress had been nothing more than "an idle ceremony." It answered by asserting that Washington would never have done anything "not founded on some good reason," and that the "interchange of civilities" promoted by the ceremony was good institutionally and for the nation. Noting that the prior practice had been "uniformly obtained for 12 years," the commentary asserted that "it is the part of a prudent man to respect ancient traditions, even in matters apparently indifferent, and to change nothing without strong and solid reasons."

More than three years later, on March 29, 1805, the *Evening Post* republished a sarcastic commentary entitled "*Republican Simplicity*," from another Federalist newspaper, the *United States Gazette for the Country*.[56] The commentary began by recounting that during the presidencies of Washington and Adams, Republicans had complained strenuously about the "court of customs" that had been established, such as evening presidential public receptions known as "levees." Republican newspapers, the commentary reported, were "filled with lamentations on the subject, and we were taught to believe that nothing but a revolution in the administrations could save us from all the horrors of monarchy and despotism."

With the "revolution" supposedly having been accomplished via the election of Jefferson, the commentary said, "it would now be amusing" to see how our "genuine republicans" had managed "on the score of forms and parades."[57] It then asserted that "at the opening of a late session of Congress," Republicans had planned to herald the delivery of Jefferson's annual message to Congress by having a "grand fire of artillery at the naval yard," with a number of men posted "day after day," waiting for the signal to fire.[58] However, the article said, the Senate had been unable to form a quorum for almost two weeks, "by which time these preparations had excited so many sneers and sarcasms, that the administration shrunk from their purpose." When Jefferson's message had at last been read to Congress, it had been received with "such perfect quietness in both houses, that not a soul . . . could have distinguished it from one of the pompous communications of the tory Washington or one of the courtly messages of the monarchical Adams." This interruption of Jefferson's plan, the commentary sarcastically predicted, might well have set a precedent.

> The consequence of that one accident may be, that through all future time every democratic President will think himself obliged to deliver his message in the same homely, humdrum style as was practiced by the aristocrats in the reign of terrour [*sic*], without the discharge of cannon or any other military display to demonstrate his attachment to *republican simplicity*.

Ironically, the paper's prediction came true. Every president—not just "democratic" ones—followed Jefferson's practice for more than a century before Woodrow Wilson returned to the old practice of delivering his annual messages to Congress in person.

Still missing is anything in the historical record to support the idea that Jefferson's decision to deliver his annual message in writing rather than as a speech was a recognition of any constitutionally based norm regarding the form of presidential communications. In his public statements and private correspondence, Jefferson never mentioned such a norm, nor did his newspaper in explaining his decision. Federalists, too, never saw anything of constitutional significance in the change. Indeed, they even wondered how Jefferson had managed to uncover a constitutional truth missed by George Washington and John Adams. Regarding "true republicanism," the *Washington Federalist* archly stated, "[W]e believe Gen. Washington to have been as good a judge as Mr. Jefferson."[59] The other commentary it published on Jefferson's departure from the prior practice for annual messages objected faintly that "ancient traditions, even in matters apparently indifferent," ought not to be changed. Still without any support in the historical record, the alluring idea of a constitutional principle lurking behind Jefferson's decision to deliver his annual message to Congress in writing must be viewed skeptically at best.

Furthermore, the statement in the *Intelligencer* explaining the reasons for Jefferson's action actually provides positive evidence *against* the claim that presidential discussion of policy matters should be directed to Congress and not the people. That statement said Jefferson considered "information" to be the only "safe substitute" for "confidence" in a country's representatives, which is "dangerous even when reposed in the best of men." It went on to say that he therefore "rejoiced" to see "copious stores of knowledge" provided to Congress, because doing so would ultimately enable the people to exercise their "control" over both Congress and the president. Logically, the only way that process could work would be for the people to have access to all the information given to Congress. Without it, the people would be left in the position of having to trust their representatives, which the commentary said was "dangerous." Thus, the commentary envisions a process through which all information regarding the government is promptly and directly communicated to the people, rather than filtered through Congress. Certainly, under that understanding of democratic governance, nothing would be wrong with presidents directly communicating with the public on policy matters.

CHAPTER 5

Defending Jefferson's Policies on Appointments and Removals

One of the most pressing challenges faced by Jefferson after becoming president was how to deal with the 316 upper-level federal offices whose occupants he could remove or appoint. As is well known, he resolved not to honor, where possible, the numerous "midnight appointments" that Adams and the Federalists had pushed through the outgoing, lame-duck Congress.[1] As is also well known, although Jefferson first tried to follow a measured approach of not terminating incumbents except in cases of malfeasance or extreme partisan behavior, he essentially moved, within a few months, to a policy of filling the offices with Republicans. Two years into his presidency, he calculated that only 130 of the 316 offices under his control were still occupied by Federalists.[2]

Not surprisingly, Federalists protested vigorously, and Jefferson had to be defended. The *National Intelligencer* was the perfect vehicle to do that. Historians seem to have missed the defenses there, which, if not actually authored by him, surely would have reflected Jefferson's positions on the sensitive political topic. For example, Dumas Malone's account of Jefferson's famous reply to the Remonstrance of the New Haven Merchants in late July 1801 regards the reply as particularly significant because "the 'principles' of the new President with respect to removals had not yet been made public."[3] As this chapter shows to the contrary, those "principles" had been quite clearly articulated in the *Intelligencer* by the time Jefferson wrote that reply.

The first explanation of Jefferson's motivations in removing or refusing to appoint Federalist-leaning officials came in an unsigned commentary in the March 23 *Intelligencer*, less than three weeks after his inauguration.[4] The commentary began in a moderate tone, noting that about two-thirds of the appointments Jefferson had made to justice of the peace positions in Washington, DC, had originally been nominees of John Adams. The commentary claimed this was "indisputable evidence" that Jefferson had resolved to make "no other changes than those which a regard to the equal claims of different classes of citizens prescribe."

The commentary then veered in a much more aggressive direction. "Even after his successor was appointed," it charged, President Adams had appointed to office a "long list [of] men opposed in political opinion to the national will." That will, the commentary asserted, had been "unequivocally declared" by the presidential election, in which Adams had been replaced by a "successor of different sentiments."[5] Adams had made two kinds of appointments, and those to the judiciary were obviously "beyond the reach of nullification." All the other appointments, however, were to offices that are "organs of the president" and serve "at his pleasure." For those officeholders, it was a "sensible necessity that they enjoy his confidence."

Regarding the latter class, the commentary then focused on the Federalist-appointed US marshals and district attorneys who had been removed by Jefferson for what it called "misconduct," especially in the selection of jurors for trials and grand juries, which had politicized the "impartial administration of justice." Jefferson's new appointments, it said, would correct the problem. Because "almost all the judges are men of certain political tenets," the commentary explained, there was a risk of "undue influence of their political opinions upon the exercise of their judicial functions." Such influence could be prevented, "to a degree," with the appointment of attorneys and marshals of "different political principles." Each group would then be a "check on the partialities of the other," with the result that "both descriptions of citizens will be protected."

The commentary was a remarkably candid acknowledgment of the role that partisanship had come to play at such an early time in the federal judicial system. US attorneys or grand jury members who were Republicans could serve as a check on the Federalist judiciary by declining (either on their own or at the direction of the president) to initiate particular prosecutions. New marshals could provide another line of defense, because an important part of their job then was selecting members of juries and grand juries. As Lawrence M. Friedman has observed, Federalist judges "often harangued grand juries in a most partisan way."[6] Moreover, at this time in American legal history, there was much more leeway for jurors to determine "the law" independently of whatever the presiding judge might say.[7]

Thus, buried in the somewhat opaque language of the *Intelligencer* commentary was the idea that Jefferson was using the only tools he had, US attorneys and marshals, to counteract the Federalist judicial phalanx in the national government.[8] This public pronouncement reflected what Jefferson was saying privately. In a letter written to William Giles the same day as the publication of the commentary, Jefferson said, "the courts being so decidedly federal, & irremovable, it is believed that republican Attornies & Marshals, being the doors of entrance into the courts, are indispensably necessary as a shield to the republican part of our fellow citizens."[9] A few days later, in a March 29 letter to Elbridge Gerry, Jefferson said he planned to remove "officers who have been guilty of gross abuse of office, such as Marshals packing juries, &c."[10] Even more significant was the commentary's public assertion, for the first time, on Jefferson's behalf, that among the officeholders who were "organs" of the president, the president would be choosing men who enjoyed his "confidence" and whose appointment would advance his goal of providing representation to "both classes of citizens."

Less than two weeks into his presidency, Jefferson encountered the very problem alluded to in the *Intelligencer* commentary. On March 16, 1801, he pardoned and ordered remission of a $200 fine for James Callender, who had been convicted of sedition for his fiery newspaper attacks on Federalists. (Callender was in jail when Jefferson was elected.) However, the US marshal at the time, David M. Randolph, a Federalist, refused to refund the fine. Jefferson promptly dismissed Randolph on March 24. For reasons that are unclear, the refund of the fine was delayed for almost three more months. According to Noble E. Cunningham, the delay created a situation "which became increasingly intolerable to Callender and embarrassing to the administration."[11] Callender began demanding money and a post office position from Jefferson but was rebuffed. Enraged, he turned against Jefferson and began publishing embarrassing material about the president, including Jefferson's relationship with Sally Hemings.

The *Intelligencer*'s next articulation of Jefferson's approach to appointments came on April 3, in a response to a letter that had appeared in a Federalist newspaper, the *Philadelphia Gazette*. The letter had criticized

Jefferson for withholding the judicial commissions that would eventually become the subject of the *Marbury v. Madison* litigation. Anticipating an argument the Supreme Court would consider and reject in *Marbury*, the *Intelligencer*'s response first argued that the commissions had no legal validity because, due to Jefferson's intervention, they had never been delivered to the appointees. The commentary then argued that because the "happiness of the community depends essentially on the wisdom and integrity of its officers," it was the president's "solemn obligation" to have "proper persons placed in office." Therefore, if a president became aware of "new facts, or information of old ones," that, in his judgment, raised questions about the suitability of an appointee for a position, he was duty bound to withhold the appointment, no matter how close the appointment had been to completion.[12]

On June 12, the *Intelligencer* published a remarkable full front-page commentary entitled "Appointments by the President" and signed "A Friend to Impartial Justice." The commentary directly confronted the "murmurs" it said were being heard concerning "the appointment of particular men to offices previously held by different citizens. Why, it is asked, are officers who have faithfully discharged their duties, dismissed from places, on the tenure of which depends their personal comfort?" The answer was simple: Jefferson was demonstrating to his supporters that "while he respected the virtue and talents of a federalist, he would not be indifferent to the equal virtues and talents of a republican."

The commentary then launched into a lengthy discussion of the "grounds on which certain marshals and attorneys have been removed." It began by discussing the Sedition Act, and arguing that the most recent national election had effectively been a referendum on the constitutionality of the law. As the commentary put it, with a majority of citizens having voted for a change in "men and measures," they "constitute the nation" and thus had "declared no less in their actions than in their words, this law to be unconstitutional."

What did this claim have to do with Jefferson's appointments policies? According to the commentary, the prosecutions under the Sedition Act during the Adams administration had revealed a problem. The judiciary, which the framers of the Constitution had intended to be a "barrier" against the government exercising "undue power," had instead been converted, by sanctioning and spearheading prosecutions under the law, into the government's "most efficient instrument" of oppression. By "executing unconstitutional laws," the judges had destroyed "all freedom of opinion." There had been no way to resist that judicial tyranny.

Federal judges, having "wisely" been given life tenure by the Framers to resist becoming "instruments of political intolerance," had also, in the process, been "removed, as far as civil institutions can remove them, from all influence, either popular or governmental." When the unintended had happened, and the judges had turned from their expected independence from the government into its tools of oppression, the American people had been left defenseless in their civil liberties.

The commentary asserted, though, that the Founders had wisely, "as the result of mature reflection and deliberate design," anticipated this problem and provided a remedy. To prevent the judges' constitutional "irresponsibility" from leading to the oppression of the people, "the rights and property of the citizen are protected by trial by jury." Whatever might be the "designs or measures of the judge," jurors are "invested with legal authority to guard the citizen." Juries, "formed immediately from the great body of citizens," were thus intended to "translate into the administration of justice *popular* feelings and *common sense* ideas."

This is where the marshals figured in the Founders' plan, because they would select jurors. Marshals were not given life tenure under the Constitution, but rather "hold their offices only during the pleasure of the President." Unlike federal judges, they could not be "rendered independent of the people," because they would always be subject to the direction, and correction, of the popularly elected president. When there was a "change of public opinion," as had occurred in the last national election, new marshals appointed by the new president would reflect that new public opinion and select jurors who also held the same views. Thus, federal marshals were intended to play a crucial role in connecting the "will of the people"—that "grand impulsive power" of the American political system—to the administration of justice in the country. In effect, this was an avenue for popular control—exercised on behalf of the people by the president—over the otherwise insulated federal judiciary.[13]

Under Adams, the *Intelligencer* commentary continued, the system had failed to work as the Founders envisioned. Federalists had abused the "liberal confidence of the constitution" that judges would be appointed for their "impartiality and talents and not their politics." The US marshals, the only possible "wholesome check" on the judiciary under this Jeffersonian vision of nonpartisan justice in America, had also been Federalists. Upon assuming the presidency, Jefferson found an unchecked, oppressive Federalist judiciary, supported by "an active, and even an enthusiastic devotion of attorneys, marshals, and juries, to the views of the courts." "Under such circumstances," the commentary concluded, for Jefferson "to have hesitated would have been criminal."

Republicans had indeed considered the political bias of jurors a huge problem during the Adams presidency. Federalist marshals would appoint grand juries or, with the cooperation of Federalist judges, trial juries composed of all Federalists. Those packed juries would then issue indictments for prosecutions or verdicts in trials under the supervision and guidance of those same Federalist judges—who usually believed it was also part of their job to tell the jurors, in strongly partisan instructions, what to do, including what verdict to render.[14]

For similar reasons, US prosecuting attorneys were, according to the *Intelligencer* commentary, also intended under the Constitution to be "peculiarly the agents of the President." Citing Jefferson's order, when he assumed the presidency, that all pending prosecutions under the Sedition Act be dismissed, the commentary noted that US attorneys are "bound by his directions in the institution and progress of prosecutions," meaning that the president "can control, as he actually has controlled, them, according to his own judgment." Yet Jefferson had found that the attorneys had "different understandings of the Constitution," as demonstrated by their prosecutions under the Sedition Act. It would have been naive of Jefferson, the commentary argued, to expect the current US attorneys to change their core beliefs and become "republican today" after having been "federal yesterday."[15]

Jeremy Bailey has characterized Jefferson's overall approach to appointments as demonstrating that Jefferson thought he should be a "kind of custodian of public opinion." Jefferson believed, he writes, that the proportion of offices awarded to each of the "natural parties" in a society "should reflect the public will, as determined by the national elections, especially the presidential election."[16] At least with regard to federal officials involved in policy decisions, the reference to "proportion" seems inapt.[17] Rather, the *Intelligencer* commentary indicates Jefferson's belief that, when making such appointments, presidents were obligated to act solely in accordance with the most recently expressed national public opinion as manifested in their election. To infuse that opinion into the workings of government, presidents should, in truly plebiscitary fashion, appoint only officials who could be counted on to act in accordance with that opinion—always subject, of course, to direction from the president to ensure they did just that.[18]

In *The Contested Removal Power, 1789–2010*, Alvis, Bailey, and Taylor incorrectly say that "the details of Jefferson's removals are difficult to mark with precision."[19] To the contrary, the key detail the *Intelligencer* commentary makes clear is that when it came to policy, Jefferson wanted to have people who would think and do just what he wanted. And if they could not be relied upon to do that, he would replace them.

Furthermore, the *Intelligencer* essays seem to erase the difference these authors say existed between Jefferson's and Madison's views on presidential appointments within the executive branch. They say Jefferson thought such appointments should reflect the partisan makeup of the nation, while Madison thought they were a necessary part of making the president accountable to his supporters in the execution of policy.[20] The essays discussed here invoke both considerations. Via presidential appointments, Republican views should now be given representation in the government to begin to counteract the previously overwhelming and now electorally discredited Federalist presence in the government. Since presidents were elected to carry out those Republican views, they had an obligation to their supporters to appoint other government officials who would do the same.

Jefferson himself seems the most likely author of the June 12 essay. Its argument certainly reflected his thinking. In a letter to William Giles on March 23, 1801, he explained that with the judges beyond reach, his only option to influence the judiciary had been to aggressively replace US attorneys and marshals, because they were, as he put it, "the doors of entrance into the courts."[21] In a letter to Edward Livingston on November 1, 1801, he asserted, "The President is to have the laws executed. He may order an offence then to be prosecuted. If he sees a prosecution put into a train which is not lawful, he may order it to be discontinued and put into legal train. . . . There appears to me to be no weak part in any of these positions or inferences."[22]

Another possibility for the essay's authorship is James Madison, who made a similar argument in Congress during the "Great Debate of 1789," over whether presidents had the absolute right to remove officials in the executive branch. That right, Madison explained, logically flowed from the connection between the president and "the people."

> If the President alone should possess the power of removal from office, those who are employed in the execution of the law will be in their proper situation, and the chain of dependence be preserved; the lowest officers, the middle grade, and the highest will depend, as they ought, on the President, and the President on the community. The chain of dependence therefore terminates in the supreme body,

namely, in the people; who will possess, besides, in aid of their original power, the decisive engine of impeachment.[23]

That same year, in a letter to Edmund Pendleton, Madison described the president as the "most responsible member of the Government" in terms of being held accountable, via election and impeachment, for the course of the government.[24]

With regard to the selection of jurors by marshals, Jefferson and Madison actually made a similar proposal to the Virginia legislature a few years earlier. In October 1798, searching for a way to protect Republicans from prosecutions under the newly adopted Sedition Act, they petitioned the House of Delegates to pass a law to provide for the popular election of jurors and abolish the current practice of federal marshals selecting them. Their plan, according to Adrienne Koch, was that "the activities of Federalist-dominated courts would be effectively hamstrung" by the election of Republicans as jurors.[25]

Printed at the top of the front page of the next issue of the *Intelligencer*, published on June 15, was a Shakespeare quotation obviously intended to be a commentary on the appointments controversy: "[H]ow wretched is that poor man, that hang's on princes' favours! . . . [W]hen he falls he falls like Lucifer, never to hope again." Following the quotation was an "Extract from Rousseau's Emilius," in which the philosopher advised that even children of royalty should be taught a trade, because that training would invest the child "with a title that cannot be taken from him." The royal parents who do not do so, counsels Rousseau, unwisely "place a dependence on the actual order of society, without thinking that order subject to unavoidable revolutions." Taken together, the Shakespeare and Rousseau quotes were a wry commentary on the fact that Federalists, whom Republicans often disparaged as members of the "Party of Aristocracy or Monarchy," were suddenly confronting the possibility of losing positions in the national government that, like royalty, they had come to assume were lifetime appointments.[26]

Federalists were clearly not amused at what they were reading in the *Intelligencer*. On July 1, 1801, the paper's editor and publisher, Samuel H. Smith, advised his readers that he had been compelled to appear before the DC Circuit Court on the previous day, to "answer a charge of libel on the Judiciary of the United States" based on his having published the June 12 "Friend to Impartial Justice" commentary.[27] He said he could not say more because he knew of a recent contempt punishment that had been levied by a court ("without the concurrence of a jury," he noted) against another newspaper editor who had commented on a pending prosecution. The two judges who had initiated the libel proceedings against Smith were Federalists; the third judge who opposed the action was a recently appointed Republican. Weeks later, after the district attorney refused to prosecute the case and after a grand jury refused to indict Smith, the action was dropped.[28]

Ironically, Smith must have been saved from prosecution for precisely the reasons stated in the commentary that had prompted the legal action against him. Thanks to Jefferson's appointments, Smith had acquired several levels of protection. One of the three judges on the panel was now a Republican, as was the US district attorney; and the grand jury that would not indict him was probably also Republican, having been selected by the new Republican US marshal.[29] Indeed, it is hard to imagine a more offensive judicially instigated contempt proceeding to Republicans than this one, brought against the editor of Jefferson's own presidential newspaper for having dared to publish a commentary—perhaps written by Jefferson himself—accusing the Federalist judiciary of having been blatantly anti-Republican for years.

Federalists knew what was going on and portrayed it in the *Washington Federalist* as practically incestuous.[30] On July 10, the paper said it was "whispered" that the US district attorney had actually been the author of the anonymous *Intelligencer* commentary that had gotten Smith in trouble. The paper wondered how, if that were so, "the business will be prosecuted." One thing seemed likely: "We shall see whether there be a *packed* jury, of which the democrats have so much complained. The tables are turned."

On August 7, 1801, the *Federalist* reprinted an essay from the *Charlestown Gazette*. Addressed to the "President of the United States" in response to the *Intelligencer*'s June 12 "Friend to Impartial Justice" commentary, it lamented the "serious charges of corruption exhibited against our national judges" and hoped the publisher would "be punished, and the author detected." The essay even speculated ("it is said") that James Madison had written the essay.

Finally, in another commentary on November 6, the *Federalist* sarcastically complimented Republicans on how well they had used their newly acquired control over the composition of the federal grand jury in Washington. All had turned out as Federalists had expected: the new Republican federal marshal "would be careful to select a democratic jury, who would very honestly say *ignoramus*. Have not our expectations been realized?" In a separate note that day, the *Federalist* claimed that the same technique had been used to end the prosecution of Republican newspaper firebrand William Duane for sedition. Jefferson, it said, had first halted Duane's prosecution and then later resumed it, when he could be sure that the new, now reliably Republican grand jury would "say *ignoramus* or *sumus ignorami.*" The note's clever wordplay coupled the traditional grand jury finding of *ignoramus* (meaning "we take no notice of / do not know [this charge]"), when declining to authorize a prosecution, with the mash-up phrase *sumus ignorami* ("we are ignorant").[31]

Wordplay aside, the *Federalist*'s description of what Jefferson had done was essentially correct. In a letter he wrote to Edward Livingston on November 1, 1801, Jefferson said he had ordered the dismissal of the Senate libel charge against Duane because it had been brought under the Sedition Act, which he regarded as unconstitutional. He had then ordered the commencement of a new proceeding against Duane, "founded on whatsoever other law might be in existence against the offence." That proceeding ended, he said, when the grand jury (now almost surely composed of good Republicans) found "no other law against it."[32]

Presumably, the grand jury that refused to indict Duane for any new crime after the dismissal of the charge against him under the Sedition Act was the same as (or similarly composed to) the one that had refused to indict Samuel Harrison Smith for "libel on the Judiciary of the United States." Since the Sedition Act had, by its terms, expired on the last day of the Adams term, the only possible basis for charges against either Smith or Duane would have been a hotly contested one: that they could be prosecuted for the nonstatutory, common-law crime of libel against the federal government. Federalists generally supported the idea that there could be common-law federal crimes, because the doctrine obviously gave judges the power to declare the existence of a prosecutable crime in virtually any situation (which is what the two federalist judges who initiated the prosecution against Samuel Harrison Smith had done, by asserting he should be indicted for libeling the federal judiciary). Republicans naturally rejected the idea, because it placed more potentially oppressive power in the hands of unelected judges.[33] Jefferson called the doctrine an "audacious, barefaced, and sweeping pretension to a system of law for the U.S. without the adoption of [the] legislature and so infinitely beyond their power to adopt."[34] Therefore, the grand jury refusals to indict Smith or Duane would have been welcome early opportunities for Jefferson and his allies on the jury to strike a blow against the doctrine.[35] The occasions would have been even sweeter because they were rejections of attempts by Federalists to punish two Republican newspaper critics in this way.

Together, these actions and the essays in the *Intelligencer* manifest an early robust articulation of the "unitary executive" theory of the presidency that still resonates today. Advocates of the principle assert, "As the only elected executive officer, the president must be accountable for all that his subordinates do and must therefore be able to direct what they do and how they do it."[36] Opponents of the principle point out that while it does flow logically from the idea that presidents should be held politically responsible for the actions of other officials in the executive branch, applying it to federal law enforcement potentially wipes out the basic legal norm that enforcement should be carried out impartially, without regard to political considerations.[37]

Indeed, Federalists would make this point repeatedly in their newspaper attacks on Jefferson's actions. They charged that in directing law enforcement actions such as the discontinuance of pending prosecutions under the Sedition Act, most notoriously that of Duane, Jefferson was acting unconstitutionally, because such actions made him the ultimate arbiter of what was legal in the United States, in blatant disregard for the rule of law. On September 14, 1801, in an essay reprinted in the *Federalist* from the *Gazette of the United States*, the commentator "Juris Consultus" railed that in ordering the end to Duane's prosecution, Jefferson had "*broken the constitution!*" and for that should be impeached as a "*usurper*" of the "constitution and liberties of our country." In the next issue, the same commentator pointed out that the prosecution of Duane had been "directed by a resolution of the Senate" after a "most flagitious and daring libel" on that body. On what basis, asked the commentator, did Jefferson have to intervene and stop the prosecution: "Pray who made the President a judge of that? Does not that belong to the Judiciary to decide?"

In its own commentary on October 21, 1801, the *Federalist* asserted that while the Constitution gave the pardon power to presidents, it "certainly does not give him the power of *stopping an action* like that the Senate instituted against Duane." In doing so, it said, Jefferson had degraded the dignity of his office and insulted the Senate and "common justice." For these (and many other offenses), the commentary asserted that Jefferson deserved impeachment. On December 14, the *Federalist* renewed the attack, publishing a pseudonymous essay arguing that by ordering the dismissal of Duane's prosecution, Jefferson had "usurped a power not delegated by the constitution" and "violated the oath which bound him to be faithful to it."[38] A commentary on May 26, 1802, referred to Jefferson's "despotic stopping of a prosecution."

The New York *Evening Post* literally echoed the *Federalist* criticisms. On December 22, 1801, it reprinted from the *Federalist* a commentary condemning the "stopping of prosecutions" by Jefferson.[39] On December 30, it republished another commentary from the *Federalist* charging that the president had "assumed" a power not "merely to pardon offence," but to protect "partizans of the President, from investigation and inquiry, by arresting prosecutions against the offenders."

Many scholars have skipped over the controversial nature of Jefferson's action discontinuing Duane's prosecution. Malone, for example, devotes only two sentences to it, characterizing it as one of several actions Jefferson took early in his presidency to "relieve those persons who were still suffering under the Sedition Act or threatened by it."[40] The other actions Jefferson took, however, were pardons to two other Republican newspaper editors. For a president to stop an ongoing prosecution is arguably a different situation, as Federalists asserted, because it raises the possibility of a president exerting essentially unchecked control over the enforcement of federal laws. Legal scholars are divided on the issue, even though Washington, Adams, and Jefferson all ordered either the initiation or dismissal of federal prosecutions and, in Washington's case, both.[41]

On July 29, 1801, the *Intelligencer* printed the well-known "Remonstrance" that merchants in New Haven, Connecticut, had sent to the president to protest his replacement of the Federalist port collector there with a Republican. It also printed his reply to the merchants. Jefferson first dismissed the argument that the appointee, who was seventy-seven years old, was not up to the job physically. He then proceeded to justify, in general terms, his plan to replace some Federalist officeholders with men from whom he could expect a more "cordial cooperation." His reply echoed points already made in the *Intelligencer*, saying they were in furtherance of the "will of the nation, [as] manifested by their various elections." The results of those elections, he said, demanded "an administration of government according with the opinions of those elected," which meant that his removal of some Federalist officials and the replacement of them with Republicans was thoroughly justified.[42]

At least some Federalists viewed the issue of Executive Branch appointments and removals in a radically different way—one that restricted removals only to instances of official misconduct. According to the previously discussed commentary that was published in the August

7, 1801, *Washington Federalist*, marshals, attorneys, and other federal officials acquired when they were appointed to office a "life estate, dependent on the contingency of good behavior." Therefore, the commentary asserted, "*rightful* Presidential control" required that the occupants be retained in office as long as they deported themselves with "integrity, fidelity, ability, and industry."[43]

On August 14, the *Intelligencer* published a long essay, signed by "Justice," entitled "Appointments by the President." Although this essay employed a slightly different pseudonym, it clearly was a follow-up to the June 12 "A Friend to Impartial Justice" commentary because the author bragged first on having satisfactorily shown why the replacement of marshals and attorneys had been justified. That justification was again grounded in a plebiscitary conception of the presidency: "My preceding remarks must have convinced the reader, that the change of Marshals and Attorneys . . . was [en]joined by principle, and that the public mood absolutely required it."

The essay then focused on Jefferson's removal of nineteen customs officers around the country. It argued that all the removals were justified on one or more of the following grounds: failure to perform the job properly, "gross immorality of character," "incompetency," "negligent attention," and "settled hostility and active enmity to republican principles." Regarding removals based on "hostility to republican principles," the essay first noted that government officials often have "great influence." It then asked, "If this influence is employed in depreciating republican principles, . . . has not a republican government, itself the guardian of republican principles, a moral right to displace him? Would it not be accessory to a political crime, if it did not displace him?" Based on his "personal knowledge," "Justice" asserted, those were the grounds on which "most, if not all, of the recent removals have been made."

On August 21, the *Intelligencer* reprinted a *Boston Chronicle* essay by "Old South" entitled "On the CONSTITUTIONAL and APPROPRIATE Executive Appointments." The essay argued that in replacing appointees for political reasons, Jefferson was just doing what John Adams had done in his original appointments, and that Jefferson therefore had as much right to do so as Adams had. "Old South" then argued that, as president, Jefferson "must have officers who are friendly to his operations," adding that the president "must have republican materials if he is to effect republican purposes."[44] His concluding argument was that "rotation is rather a republican principle" and that "no man has such a claim on government as to demand a constant support from it." Therefore, he asserted, no one has any reason to be offended if "some other citizens are provided for, equally as deserving as themselves." Down to its use of the term *rotation*, the "Old South" commentary previews, by decades, the approach toward appointments that would be taken by a Jeffersonian successor, Andrew Jackson.[45]

The *Washington Federalist* responded to the *Intelligencer* on August 24 in a piece entitled "A Rattle for Children." The commentary dripped with sarcasm: "The National Intelligencer whines out a doleful eulogy on the measure [Jefferson's removal of the nineteen customs officers]; and, if notes of admiration are *arguments*, proves the President, and the Secretary of the Treasure [*sic*] a couple of the best men in the world." Of the reasons given in the *Intelligencer* for the removals, the *Federalist* said the "most ridiculous" one was for claimed "hostility and active enmity to republican principles." The term *republican*, it said, encompassed nothing more than a "due mixture [of] monarchy, aristocracy, and democracy" that was "most conducive" to the "good of the whole." In that sense, Federalists were just as "republican" as Republicans. The claimed savings would be offset, the commentary said, by other expenses needlessly incurred by the Jefferson administration. In conclusion, the *Federalist* mocked, if the arguments of the *Intelligencer* commentary were reduced "to a *point*, we know it would be a *mathematical one*, which has neither *parts* nor *extension*."

An August 31 *Intelligencer* commentary on the New Haven appointments controversy rebutted some of the merchants' specific complaints and turned Jefferson's public reply into an interesting positive assertion about his relationship to the American people. Previously, the commentary said, executive power had "almost always [been] exercised without an exposure of its reasons." Officials had been relieved of office with no explanation, even when they asked for one. In explaining to the merchants the reasons for his action, Jefferson had dispelled "the clouds which too generally involve executive acts." He could have acted as his predecessors had, but he had pursued a "wiser course" instead, because "[i]t is his opinion that the people ought to be informed, and he has informed them of the motives of their rulers."

The commentary recognized that prejudiced, die-hard Federalists could never be persuaded. (Of them, it said, "A predisposition to censure never wants fuel, for if it cannot find it elsewhere, it will find it in the stars.") Fortunately, though, "thanks to education and the freedom of the press, there is a large class of citizens who, having no interests at variance with the public, preserve their judgments unperverted." It was their support that "an honest government will chiefly value," and it was to them he had addressed his explanation.

The *Intelligencer* commentary on the New Haven appointments illustrates how it could be used in several ways to project and amplify the justifications for Jefferson's actions. First, before Jefferson wrote his reply to the New Haven Merchants, the newspaper had published several commentaries that previewed publicly his argument that presidential appointments ought to "accord with the opinions of the elected." Second, by publishing his reply to the merchants, the paper ensured that the reply would be circulated nationally, thereby informing all interested parties of Jefferson's position and the reasons for it. Third, in its commentaries that followed Jefferson's public letter, the *Intelligencer* could defend and elaborate on Jefferson's policy.

Finally, sometimes those justifications could go beyond the actual removal policy and turn into something even grander. As characterized in this commentary, Jefferson's letter demonstrated that he was a new kind of president, one who felt the obligation to publicly explain his acts so that all Americans could judge for themselves the correctness of those actions, just as Jeffersonian democratic theory proclaimed. That theory was indeed a radical departure from Federalist democratic theory, which held that the place of the people in government was limited to their participation in electing their representatives and nothing more.[46]

Throughout 1801, Federalists kept up a steady drumbeat of protests against Jefferson's appointment actions. A few examples will suffice. The June 10 issue of the *Washington Federalist* printed Jefferson's one-paragraph reply to a citizens' group in Pennsylvania, in which he said that his dearest object was to "heal the wounded confidence of society." The only confidence that had been wounded, the *Federalist* said, was that of many Americans in Jefferson, due to his "wanton display of power in the discharge of old, faithful and able officers, without any apparent cause." On September 18, 1801, the *Federalist* carried a commentary, signed "A Virginian," criticizing Jefferson's actions in "dismissing honorable and faithful men from offices" as a "scene of flagrant injustice and persecution commenced under the full tide of presidential power." On September 28, the paper carried a commentary from "L. J. Brutus" that used excerpts from the Federalist Papers to show the wrongfulness of Jefferson's actions. On November 23, the paper quoted Madison's statement, in a congressional debate, that it would be an "abuse of power" for a president "wantonly to dismiss a meritorious and virtuous officer," and then contrasted that claim with Jefferson's statement to the New Haven

Merchants that removing some Federalist officials and replacing them with Republicans was a "painful . . . duty" in his presidency because few vacancies could be "obtained" otherwise.

The partisan skirmishing over Jefferson's appointments continued into 1802, with occasional *Intelligencer* essays presenting statistical arguments about the claimed reasonableness of Jefferson's overall approach to appointments in the executive branch.[47] It would eventually fade, as other issues arose and the controversy became essentially a fait accompli, with Jefferson having made great strides toward his goal of moving Republicans into many of the federal offices.[48] Federalists, undoubtedly hampered by having pursued the same policy on behalf of their own partisans during the Adams administration, had been unable to do anything about Jefferson's action except complain and criticize, to which the *Intelligencer* had ably responded.

Significant about the *Intelligencer*'s defenses is the way they were framed. Their argument was not just simply that the president needed his "own people" or that Republicans deserved a "share of the spoils." Those arguments were made, but so were two deeper ones. The first was grounded in classic Jeffersonian democratic, or plebiscitary, theory: the recent federal election had amounted to a national change in popular opinion, which ought to be reflected as much as possible in the officials working in the executive branch of the government. The other deeper argument was grounded in what, to modern ears, is a much more radical idea. Federal prosecutors, marshals, and even the jury system could be used to resist, "to a degree," the potential problem that lifetime judicial tenure can present to a democracy. Equally intriguing is the *Intelligencer*'s claim this avenue of resistance as part of the Framers' grand constitutional plan.

While it is hardly "news" that the *Intelligencer* vigorously defended Jefferson's actions in appointing and removing government officials during his presidency, some of the bases for those defenses have been underappreciated at best. Taking into account that the defenses were publicized nationally through his newspaper, Jefferson's policy regarding his officeholder appointments seems, at least in the ways it was justified to the American public, to have been more extreme than it has often been characterized. The *Intelligencer* commentaries also provide a new level of historical support for the argument that presidents, as heads of the nation's entire apparatus for law enforcement, have absolute authority over federal prosecutorial actions. Previously, scholars looking for evidence of the attitudes of our earliest presidents on this issue found it in the actions and (except in perhaps one case) the private messages of those presidents.[49] The authors of some of the leading works in this field (Prakash; Calabresi and Yoo; Andrias; and Roiphe and Green)[50] were able to point to many such examples. In contrast, the research presented in this chapter reveals public messages in a nationally circulated newspaper that was widely understood to be speaking on Jefferson's behalf. What Jefferson thought about the issue as president, as well as what he wanted everyone else to understand too, now seems beyond question.[51]

Perhaps the most important finding from the research presented here, though, is that there actually was some strong, public opposition to Jefferson's actions. Previously, one scholarly argument has been that since "no one complained" when the earliest presidents ordered prosecutions to be dropped or initiated, there must have been an implicit common acknowledgment that doing so was just fine constitutionally.[52] As shown in this chapter, however, Federalists did complain about Jefferson terminating prosecutions. They did so loudly and publicly, in their flagship newspaper in the nation's capital.

Not much has changed. In 1801, Thomas Jefferson through his newspaper was asserting a robust version of the Unitary Executive, extending even to the claim that a president had to have absolute control over federal prosecuting attorneys. In response, Federalists pushed back, asserting that partisanship should not be the sole consideration in Executive Branch appointments and that unrestrained presidential control over criminal prosecutions would undermine the rule of law by allowing presidents to be the ultimate arbiters of which laws should be enforced. That both sides made good points is demonstrated by their continuing to be made today.

CHAPTER 6

Attacking Judges, Part 1

Judicial Review

Battles involving the federal judiciary were a major story during Thomas Jefferson's first presidential term. They included the Republicans' repeal in 1802 of the 1801 Judiciary Act (which Federalists had rammed through at the end of the Adams administration), the Supreme Court's decision in *Marbury v. Madison*, and the impeachment of Supreme Court Justice Samuel Chase. Despite the immense amount of scholarship on the subject, scholars disagree regarding the specific attitudes and strategies that Jefferson and his Republican allies had toward the judicial branch of the US government during his first term in office.

Regarding the Jeffersonian Republicans' attitude toward judicial review, the scholarship has fallen into three sometimes overlapping camps. The first, invoking many of Jefferson's well-known negative statements about the doctrine, asserts that he was very hostile to it. Dumas Malone, for example, writes that for Jefferson, "the doctrine of absolute judicial supremacy was . . . another name for tyranny."[1] The second camp argues that Jefferson was not opposed to judicial review per se but objected to it when, in his view, the wrong kind of judges were doing it. Thus, Stephen Engel asserts that the Jeffersonians' hostility to the judicial branch stemmed from their belief that the political philosophy of the judges needed to be consistent with that of the American people as a whole. If it were, then even the judicial branch would reflect the concept of "popular sovereignty." If it were not, as was the case with the totally Federalist judiciary at the beginning of Jefferson's administration, then judicial review by such politically out-of-touch officials was essentially illegitimate.[2] The third camp, exemplified in the work of Keith Whittington and Bruce Ackerman, asserts that while the original Republican attitude toward judicial review may have been hostile, Jefferson and his allies soon realized that favorable judicial review of the constitutionality of their actions could serve as a useful tool of political legitimization.[3]

Deciding who is "right" on the question is challenging and complicated, since everyone's conclusions depend on often debatable interpretations, inference, or sometimes even forms of rational choice analysis. This chapter and the following one bring to bear on the question a previously unexamined source of information: how such judicial controversies were treated in Jefferson's presidential newspaper, the *National Intelligencer*. This chapter focuses on the Supreme Court's decision in *Marbury v. Madison* and its two decisions on the legal challenges to the Republicans' Judiciary Act of 1802, *Stuart v. Laird* and *United States v. More*. In each instance, how the *Intelligencer* addressed the controversies provides new perspectives on Jefferson's attitude toward judicial review.

Marbury v. Madison

The decision in *Marbury v. Madison* is widely considered one of the Supreme Court's greatest, because it established the principle of judicial review. Some of the most authoritative examinations of the decision, however, minimize the extent to which Jeffersonian Republicans perceived the Court's affirmation of that principle as controversial at the time. In his discussion of the controversy, Ackerman asserts that Jefferson and the Chief Justice, John Marshall, "shared the same basic constitutional understandings."[4] Richard E. Ellis made a similar assertion.

When Marshall's opinion was announced, it received very little criticism from even the most partisan of the Republican newspapers. The little hostility that did exist, moreover, was directed not at the Court's right to decide on the constitutionality of a law, but at the Chief Justice's stigmatization of the President as a violator of the laws he was sworn to uphold. The indications are that few Republicans were prepared to deny the right of the Supreme Court to review for itself an act of Congress.[5]

What was said about judicial review in the *National Intelligencer* before and after the *Marbury* decision provides a more nuanced view.[6] On January 19, 1803, less than a month before the beginning of the Supreme Court's long-delayed new term on February 10, when the Court would at last be able to issue its decision in the *Marbury* case, the front page of the *Intelligencer* carried a polemic against judicial review. Titled "On the Judiciary" and signed "Publicola," the commentary framed the issue contentiously.

> It is now boldly and openly maintained, that the judiciary are the judges of the constitution itself; that under this authority, they have a right to declare a law enacted by the legislature null and void . . . not only without the consent of the people, but in direct opposition to their express will, as declared by their representatives.

The commentary labeled the argument in support of judicial review a "preposterous . . . opinion." Jeering that "the talismanic powers of a written constitution are now to preserve us from national misfortune," the commentary said the claim was "in fact . . . altogether a puerile idea, more worthy of the sixth than the nineteenth century—of an age of savage ignorance, when the substantial benefit of clergy was attached to the rare faculty of reading or writing."

On February 2, the *Intelligencer* carried another commentary indicating the hostility of Republicans in Congress toward the *Marbury* lawsuit.[7] The commentary expressed Republicans' resentment over the Adams administration's "midnight appointments" that had led to the lawsuit, as well as the Republicans' belief that the Supreme Court should not have gotten involved in Marbury's case at all. Of the appointments, the commentary said, "if they did not violate the letter, [they] certainly did violate the spirit and the end of the Constitution."[8] Arguing that Marbury's suit had been brought by persons "fired with party vengeance," the commentary asserted that the Supreme Court—which it sarcastically referred to in parentheses and italics as "that *paramount* tribunal"—ought to have "refused any instrumentality into the meditated, and we may add, party invasion of Executive functions."

The commentary then described a controversy over evidence in the *Marbury* case that had been brought before the US Senate. Because Marbury did not have his commission (Jefferson had refused to allow its delivery after assuming the presidency and finding a stack of undelivered commissions in the vacated office of the secretary of state),[9] he had a proof problem. How could he prove he really had been commissioned by Adams to be a new justice of the peace in the District of Columbia? One way would be to obtain a copy of the Senate journal in which the Senate's approval of his nomination would have been recorded. Marbury's lawyers tried to do that, only to be rebuffed, as the commentary of February 2 reported. The commentary described the request as one for an "authenticated transcript" from the Senate's "*secret Executive Journals.*" The commentary reported the reasons for the Senate's vote to deny the request.

> This memorial was taken up on Monday, and rejected, Ayes 15—Noes 12—on the ground that the measure was a party measure; that it was meant as the basis of Executive crimination; that it claimed an act from the Senate, who were the great constitutional Judges of the Executive in case of impeachment, that might indelicately and improperly commit them; that it sanctioned a right of the Judiciary to which they had no legal pretensions; and that it totally abrogated that rule of the Senate which injoined that the Executive Journal should be kept secret.

According to Malone, debate on the proposal was on "strict party lines," as this commentary suggests.[10] By asserting that in considering Marbury's lawsuit, the judiciary was claiming a "right to which they had no legal pretensions," the commentary was clearly declaring that Republicans in the Senate rejected the propriety of judicial involvement in the dispute.

That statement in the commentary could be interpreted to mean merely that the Supreme Court had no right to involve itself in presidential affairs. However, that point had already been mentioned via the reference to "Executive crimination."[11] As Ellis points out, although the parties in the congressional debates over the repeal of the 1801 Judiciary Act had initially viewed the mandamus question in *Marbury* "simply as a contest between the judiciary and the executive," the case had soon taken on the larger significance of involving the legitimacy of judicial review itself.[12] This suggests that the reference in the *Intelligencer* commentary was indeed a reiteration of the Republicans' objections to the principle of judicial review. According to Malone, that was the tenor of the entire Senate debate over the transcript request from Marbury's lawyers, with Republicans arguing that the request was part of an attempt to enable the Supreme Court to assume "unheard of and unbounded power."[13]

In light of the January 19 commentary, it is clear that Republican opposition to the idea of judicial review had been clearly announced on the front page of Jefferson's presidential newspaper just weeks before the *Marbury* decision was released. Its publication obviously undermines some scholars' assertions that by this time there was little Republican opposition to the principle.[14] Depending on how the second commentary is interpreted, the opposition was being portrayed as reflecting not only Jefferson's position but also the united position of the Republican majority in the US Senate.

Just a month before the Court would be announcing its decision in the *Marbury* case, Chief Justice Marshall and the rest of the Supreme Court justices were being reminded of the official position of Jefferson and his party regarding judicial review. For good measure, the justices were also reminded that they should not have gotten involved in the case at all: in the words of the commentary, they "ought to have refused any instrumentality into the meditated, and we may add, party invasion of Executive functions." Chief Justice Marshall was thus warned again how politically charged the lawsuit was and how difficult it would be to craft an opinion that could both assert the principle of judicial review—a principle Federalists would have seen as their last bulwark against radical Republicanism—and avoid an immediate fight with Jefferson and his Republican Congress over the principle. As is generally agreed, Marshall did so brilliantly, by first affirming the principle of judicial review and then using that very principle to find that the Supreme Court did not have the power to order any relief on Marbury's behalf (thus avoiding that fight with the Republicans), because the law under which Marbury had sought relief was unconstitutional.[15]

The *Intelligencer* statement that the majority in the Senate regarded the Supreme Court as having asserted in the *Marbury* litigation "a right of the Judiciary to which they had no legal pretensions" explains why Jefferson and his administration consistently refused to participate in any way in the case, even when it was argued before the Supreme Court. Since the Republicans were publicly asserting that the case involved a "right" the Supreme Court either did not possess or, at least, was being improperly exercised in the case before it, they could not afford to cooperate with the proceedings in any way. If they had, the very act of their participation might have been cited as a tacit admission of the legitimacy of the proceeding. Indeed, as is discussed later in this chapter, Republicans used this logic to argue that, when Federalist judges (including the justices of the Supreme Court) and ex-judges had participated in federal court proceedings after the passage by Republicans of the Judiciary Act of 1802, they had implicitly conceded the constitutionality of the act.

The February 2 commentary in the *Intelligencer* ended with a curiously worded tirade against "judicial power" in general.

> It would seem, from the recent attempts to disturb the harmony of the legislature, that as much effect is calculated upon from the *ghost* of judicial power, as from the *reality* of it. On the annihilation of the latter, the former appears to have risen from the tomb of the Capulets, and to have stalked into either House, alternately crying "*vengeance, vengeance*"—"*money, money.*"

The phrase, "recent attempts to disturb the harmony of the legislature," would have referred not only to the Senate proceedings regarding the *Marbury* case but also to a controversy that had roiled the House a few days earlier. It concerned a petition ("memorial") submitted to Congress by the US Circuit Court judges who had been appointed by Adams under the Judiciary Act of 1801 but then lost their offices when the 1802 Judiciary Act abolished the positions. In their memorial, the judges asked Congress to request Jefferson, through the attorney general, to begin a legal proceeding on their behalf to determine whether their lifetime tenured positions could have been eliminated constitutionally. The House, in a contentious party-line vote, rejected the petition the same day it had been submitted.[16] The mention of an "annihilation" must refer to those lost positions, as well as those lost by others such as Marbury. The derisive reference to the "ghost of judicial power" sounds like a dig at the judges who, although their positions were "dead," were still trying to contest their loss. It could also have been a reference to the vagueness of powers claimed by judges at the time, which included not only judicial review but also their right to determine unwritten "common-law crimes." Both powers were frequent targets of Republican ire.[17]

The commentary's reference to "vengeance" from the "ghost of judicial power" would have been an expression of the Republican fear that the Federalist judges would use their powers to make the Republicans pay for all their actions. The reference to cries for "money, money" obviously referred to the claim by the newly disenfranchised judges that, as they put it in their memorial to Congress, they had a "right" to "their compensations . . . secured by the constitution." Finally, calling "judicial power" a "ghost" that was stalking the halls of Congress certainly conveys the idea that the federal judiciary was a menace to the nation's popularly chosen legislative body. To say the least, Republicans were hardly saying complimentary things about the judicial branch of the US government.

Federalists were feeling the heat. A satirical piece published in the *Washington Federalist* on February 18, 1803, told a tale of a stagecoach carrying elite Republicans getting stuck just a mile outside the capital. The piece mocked Republicans in several ways, including their animosity to the federal judges. If only the carriage incident could be "fixed upon the Judiciary," it sarcastically observed, Republicans would then have the "fortunate opportunity to rid our country of that aristocratical junto—as congress being now in session, might immediately *impeach* them."

Five days later, Samuel Harrison Smith reprinted the article in the *Intelligencer*, labeling it an "unsuccessful attempt at wit." He said he was presenting it as "a specimen of the *paper edited by the Clerk of the Supreme Court of the United States.*"[18] Smith probably published the piece mainly to show the tenor of the pro-judiciary and anti-Republican material being published in the opposition's flagship newspaper. However, by identifying the paper—in italics—as being edited by the clerk of the US Supreme Court, it seems Smith was disparaging the justices themselves just as they were on the verge of rendering their decision in *Marbury*. As this skirmish suggests, tensions must indeed have been high.

The next mention of the *Marbury* case in the *Intelligencer* came on February 14, 1803, when the paper carried a straightforward report of the argument of the case before the Supreme Court. The report said the plaintiffs' attorney had spoken "at considerable length"; that the attorney general had told the Court he "had received no instructions to appear"; and that following the plaintiffs' argument, the Court had "observed that they would attend to the observations of any person who was disposed to offer his sentiments." The *Intelligencer* reported that the Court had made no decision.

Two weeks later, the *Intelligencer*, under the heading "Mandamus," reported the Court's decision, in a brief three-paragraph summary apparently prepared by the Court's clerk. The summary stated that the Court had considered three questions: whether Marbury had a right to the commission, whether he had a remedy under the law for being denied the commission, and whether the Court could order the president to deliver Marbury's commission to him. The *Intelligencer* reported that the Court had found Marbury entitled to the commission but that "the act of Congress giving the power to the Supreme Court, to issue a writ of Mandamus in such a case, was unconstitutional, and consequently void."

Almost three weeks later, on March 18, 1803, the *Marbury* decision figuratively burst into the attention of *Intelligencer* readers. The paper devoted its first page and a half to a summary, apparently by the Court's reporter, of the proceedings on February 4 when the Court had considered the case. The paper then printed the first part of the Court's opinion, indicating that the rest would be published later. More was published in the March 21 issue, with the rest appearing in the March 25 issue. That the paper devoted a good third or more of three of its issues to printing the opinion indicates the Republicans' high level of interest in the decision.

Another indicator of that interest and of the apprehensions it must have raised in Republican minds was the publication of the following note in the same March 21 issue that published the second part of the *Marbury* decision:

> An act has passed the legislature of New York, changing certain provisions of the incorporation of the city of New York: The most important alteration is that, which in correspondence with our political institutions, extends the right of suffrage for aldermen and members of the common council. . . .
>
> *Judge Kent,* a member of the council of revision, and a *firm* federalist, *has declared these alterations UNCONSTITUTIONAL*; and has attempted to establish the absolute inviolability of charters!

Coming on the heels of the *Marbury* decision, this note must have been intended to highlight for readers of the *Intelligencer* the damage that judicial review could do in the wrong (i.e., Federalist) hands. The judge's reported declaration of unconstitutionality struck at two core principles of Republicanism: expanding the right to vote to include all freemen and allowing popularly elected representatives to legislate as they saw fit.

The *Intelligencer* did not publish any other negative commentary in 1803 on the specific idea of judicial review, nor did other Republican newspapers.[19] The explanation for that silence may be, as has been often suggested, that Jefferson and the Republicans had little to complain about: Marbury had, after all, lost the appeal.[20] However, an essay that appeared in the April 13 *Intelligencer* suggests another possibility: that Republicans had realized judicial review could help them politically. That issue carried the first installment of a series of essays under the pseudonym "Algernon Sidney," the name of the seventeenth-century English patriot who was executed for his opposition to the king. The

essays, entitled "A Vindication of the Measures of the Present Administration," were reprinted in Republican newspapers across the country
after being first published in the *Intelligencer*. The author of the essays was
Gideon Granger, Jefferson's Postmaster General and a leading political
figure and lawyer in Connecticut.[21]

The first issue addressed in the April 13 essay was the repeal of the
Judiciary Act of 1801 by the Republicans' Act of 1802, which, the essayist said, Federalists had warned would "loosen the bands of civil society, destroy the constitution of our country, and defeat the operations
of justice." None of those things had happened. Instead, "the judges of
the supreme court have sanctioned the law—and justice is fully administered as heretofore. All the purposes of society are answered [and] an
important constitutional principle settled."

A key provision in the 1802 act was the abolition of the new federal judgeships that the 1801 act had created. As has been discussed by
Ackerman in *The Failure of the Founding Fathers*, the constitutionality of
abolishing those lifetime tenured positions was a difficult problem for
Republicans. Thus, as the "Sidney" commentary suggests, Republicans
must have welcomed the Supreme Court's decision to uphold the constitutionality of the 1802 act in *Stuart v. Laird*, just one week after the
Marbury decision. Once they realized that judicial review, however dis-
tasteful it was as a matter of democratic theory, could aid them politically
when the decision went their way, Jefferson and other Republicans may
have decided to mute their public criticisms of the doctrine. After all,
they could hardly criticize the Supreme Court for having acted illegiti-
mately in overturning a law passed by Congress and then later trumpet
a positive decision by the Court on a different law as having "settled" its
constitutionality. On April 27, the *Intelligencer* advised its readers that the
"Sidney" essays were now available in book form. The note included a
warm endorsement: "We recommend this able performance to our readers as worthy of perusal and preservation."

The interpretation that Republicans had suddenly found themselves in a position of liking judicial review, because it could be a tool of
political legitimization, undermines some scholarly interpretations. The
most common interpretation is that there was nothing for Republicans
to object to, since Marshall had ordered nothing. A similar interpretation, also grounded on the rationale that the Republicans had no reason
to object, is that the *Marbury* case only required the Court to interpret
"legislation involving its own judicial sphere." No objections would have
been appropriate, because the Court's action would have been consis-

tent with Jefferson's expressed attitude that each branch of the government could make its own determinations regarding the constitutionality of matters before it.[22]

The idea that Jeffersonians backed off on their public objections to judicial review once they saw that it could help them politically fits perfectly, however, with Keith Whittington's thesis in *The Political Foundations of Judicial Supremacy*. As he shows, sometimes politicians welcome a judicial decision if it supports their efforts to change constitutional understandings. Employing Stephen Skowronek's conceptual framework, Whittington calls this process "regime elaboration and enforcement."[23] Similarly, Ackerman labels the decision in *Stuart v. Laird* a "moment of judicial accommodation" that resulted in the "legitimation of the new constitutional order."[24]

It is therefore significant that the first and only commentary on the *Marbury* decision to appear in the *Intelligencer* in 1803 did not criticize the principle of judicial review. In its May 11 and 13 issues, the *Intelligencer* republished (from the *Virginia Argus*) seven letters addressed "To the Chief Justice of the United States" regarding the "mandamus in the supreme court." The letters were signed "Littleton." In the fifth, the writer called the *Marbury* decision an attempt by the Supreme Court to "intrude into the cabinet, and to intermeddle with the prerogative of the executive." Overall, he had harsh words for the Court's decision and its author. Criticizing Marshall as having delivered "an extra judicial opinion, upon an ex parte hearing," "Littleton" urged the Chief Justice to disavow the "hideous monster" of a decision. "Littleton" likened Marshall to a "demon" judge from the Inquisition and lamented the disgrace that follows when the "heart of a judge becomes corrupt."

The specific critiques "Littleton" aimed at the decision were a mass of technical legal arguments, involving such arcane issues as when a court can order injunctive relief and when judicial commissions become effective. Rather than criticizing judicial review, though, "Littleton" asserted an interesting behavioral form of it, by pointing out, in his fourth commentary, that Marshall, like the other members of the Supreme Court, had resumed his circuit court duties in 1802 as the new Judiciary Act had required.[25] That resumption was constitutionally significant, "Littleton" said, because if the Judiciary Act of 1802 really was unconstitutional as many Federalists had claimed, then the Supreme Court justices should not have resumed their circuit court functions, because they could not "constitutionally occupy seats that had never been constitutionally vacated."[26] Therefore, "Littleton" concluded (with capitals for emphasis), "the act of the whole bench of justices of the Supreme Court in taking their circuit seats" in conformance with the 1802 act had "tacitly, though solemnly, with the Congress decided THE REPEALING ACT TO BE CONSTITUTIONAL."

The "Littleton" series was not the first time the courtroom conduct of Federalists had been trumpeted in Jefferson's newspaper as being an implicit concession of the constitutionality of the 1802 Judiciary Act. On December 17, 1802, the *Intelligencer* reprinted a commentary from the *Hartford Bee* that cited not only the actions of the presiding judges but also the actions of litigants in proceedings before the "new" circuit courts. The commentary noted first that when the new term for the federal court in Hartford had begun in September, Supreme Court Justice Bushrod Washington had arrived and "opened the court in the usual manner." That behavior, the commentary asserted, meant that "the judges of the supreme court, who are distinguished for their federalism, [had] admitted the constitutional existence of the court" as it had been reconfigured, which amounted to conceding the constitutionality of the new Judiciary Act.

The *Bee* commentary identified two other ways in which Federalists acting in the newly reconfigured courts had implicitly recognized the constitutionality of the changes. The first, as Ackerman has discussed, was that several Federalist attorneys in their pleadings challenged the constitutionality of the new federal trial courts but then withdrew the challenges. The attorneys seemed to be making a rhetorical point about the law, demonstrating that they were well aware of a legal argument that could be made about its constitutionality, but then always withdrawing the challenges for reasons that are unclear.[27] The second way, not mentioned by Ackerman, involved the actions of two former circuit court judges whose judgeships had been abolished by the 1802 act. Those now former federal judges had participated in a court case, one as the defendant in the case and the other as his attorney, in one of the new federal trial courts that had been established by the 1802 act. Their actions showed, according to the commentary, that "the alarms and foreboding of these federal declaimers are false, and that all the attempts to assail the present administration will be equally unsuccessful."

All of this focus on the actions of those involved in these controversies manifests the idea that constitutional understandings can be developed in ways outside the usual judicial decision-making process. Jefferson's refusal to cooperate with the litigation process in the *Marbury* lawsuit seems to be an implicit recognition of the point that just the behavior of political elites can have constitutional ramifications. This can even apply to the behavior of judges. The Justices' "acquiescence . . . for a period of several years" to sitting as circuit court judges before the passage of the 1801 Judiciary Act was cited by Justice Paterson in his opinion in *Stuart v. Laird* as being a "contemporary interpretation of the most forcible nature."[28] The episodes discussed here—all occurring in the space of just six months, from late 1802 to mid-1803—are interesting early examples of what has been labeled "popular constitutionalism," in which constitutional understandings can informally develop from the "sensibilities of the nation's people and political elites" and not just via formal judicial opinions.[29]

United States v. Benjamin More:
The Forgotten Case of the DC Justice of the Peace

In 1803, the *Intelligencer* called attention to a pending lower court case, *US v. More*, that would not even reach the Supreme Court for two more years. Although the case has now been relegated to scholarly obscurity, Republicans must have regarded it as highly significant at the time. On August 5, the *Intelligencer* carried a report of the decision, headlined "LAW CASE" with essentially the same prominence that had been afforded the *Marbury* decision by the Supreme Court. Why the attention? In a 2–1 decision, the appeals court had held a portion of the Judiciary Act of 1802 unconstitutional. The decision would obviously have alarmed Republicans. Their alarm would have been heightened because the rationale for the decision was based on a strong argument—that the pay of federal judges could not be diminished during their tenure—that was not an issue and thus not considered by the Supreme Court in its four-paragraph *Stuart v. Laird* decision.

US v. More was a strange case. It was a common law criminal prosecution. The defendant, Benjamin More, was a justice of the peace in the District of Columbia, and his supposed "crime" was that he had continued to collect court fees that had been authorized under a provision of the Judiciary Act of 1801 but then repealed by the Judiciary Act of 1802. The issue would have been a serious matter to More and his judicial brethren, because those fees constituted their sole source of compensation. The grand jury that indicted him included five other justices of the peace.[30] The case was therefore almost surely a test case, brought to produce a definitive court ruling on the issue, rather than a serious prosecution of More for criminal wrongdoing.

More's "defense" to his "prosecution" echoed the main argument Federalists had made against the constitutionality of the 1802 act's elimination of the circuit court positions that had been created by the 1801 act. Federalists had then argued that eliminating the positions violated the constitutional guarantees to judges of life tenure and no diminishment of their compensation while in office. More argued similarly that the fee provision could not be abolished constitutionally because DC justices of the peace were federal judges and, therefore, also constitutionally protected from having their compensation reduced.[31]

As reported by the *Intelligencer*, the lower court did find the repeal of the fees provision to have been "unconstitutional and void" because More was a "*judicial officer* of the United States." That rationale was the only one mentioned in the *Intelligencer*'s report of the case, so the ruling would have reignited Republican concerns that Federalists might still be able to use the argument to undermine the 1802 act. Judging from its featured placement in the *Intelligencer*, the ruling must have been considered important. The report of it filled an entire column and was featured as the first item in the paper's regular political commentary, "Washington City."

When the case reached the Supreme Court two years later, the opinion by Chief Justice Marshall dodged the issue of the constitutionality of the repeal of the fee. More's argument that he was an Article III federal judge and thereby constitutionally protected from having his pay diminished during his time in office was certainly plausible, because judges are only mentioned in that article of the Constitution. It was the same argument made by circuit judge Richard Bassett in 1802 in his public protest against the abolition of the circuit court positions by the new Judiciary Act. As Ackerman suggests, Bassett's reasoning could have been employed to render a different decision in *Stuart v. Laird*—if the Court been willing to do battle with Congress over the 1802 act.[32] Arguably, that reasoning could have been used to rule in More's favor as well.

Had the justices done so, however, they could have run into the same problem that they had obviously decided to avoid two years earlier, in their *Stuart v. Laird* decision: getting into a dispute with Jefferson and his strong Republican majority in Congress over the validity of any part of the act. Instead, in a move that echoed his tactic in *Marbury*, Marshall found that the Court had no jurisdiction over the case because the congressional grant of jurisdiction relied on by More in his appeal did not extend to criminal cases. But unlike what he had done in *Marbury*,

Marshall stopped there and did not address the merits of More's suit. By dismissing the suit on jurisdictional grounds, Marshall and his colleagues were able to avoid expressing any opinion on the argument that the 1802 Judiciary Act had unconstitutionally diminished the pay of sitting federal judges. That approach is in marked contrast to the approach taken in the *Marbury* opinion, where Marshall, despite finding that the Court had no jurisdiction in the case, had addressed Marbury's basic contention. Thus, *US v. More* seems to be another example of Marshall and the Supreme Court, post-*Marbury*, strategically retreating from a confrontation with the Jefferson administration over judicial review.[33]

Apparently recognizing that there was nothing in the Supreme Court's decision worth reacting to, the *Intelligencer* never said anything about it.[34] Ironically and perhaps significantly, the decision was announced on March 2, 1805. That was just one day after the acquittal of Supreme Court Justice Samuel Chase in his Senate impeachment trial[35] and two days before Jefferson's inauguration for a second term.

John Taylor's "Curtius" Essay

The *Intelligencer* would not carry any more negative commentary about the idea of judicial review until late 1804, when new commentary on the subject came in one of the essays that John Taylor wrote, under the pseudonym "Curtius," as justifications for Jefferson's reelection. The plaque that marks Taylor's homestead in Caroline County, Virginia, identifies him as Thomas Jefferson's "chief political lieutenant." In 1820, Jefferson said of Taylor: "Col. Taylor and myself have rarely, if ever, differed in any political principle of importance. Every act of his life, & every word he ever wrote, satisfies me of this. . . . I know them both to be of principles as truly republican as any men living."[36] Taylor authored several well-known works of American government and political philosophy, including *An Inquiry into the Principles and Policy of the Government of the United States*, which historian Charles A. Beard described as one of the "two or three really historic contributions to political science that have been produced in the United States."[37]

Taylor's fourth essay, published in the *Intelligencer* on September 24, 1804, directed a classically Jeffersonian attack on the twin ideas of "judicial independence" and "judicial review."[38] Of the idea that judges were somehow "independent" of the rest of the federal government, Taylor pointed out that the term "is not to be found in the Constitution."

Rather than making any part of the government independent, Taylor argued, the "wise system" of the Constitution had "provided the most efficient checks to make them all dependent."

Regarding judicial review, Taylor's discussion was more extensive and ended with a sophisticated twist. He first presented the populist critique of judicial review.

> We all know that the judges have assumed the power of pronouncing laws unconstitutional, and of refusing to execute them. . . . A great majority of Congress, the President and the people, may consider them constitutional; the judges alone may pronounce them unconstitutional. It is as probable, nay more probable that the judges should err on this point, than the legislature, elected for the special purpose of passing laws. Their decision, supported by that of another department of the government and by the people, greatly multiplies the probabilities on their side. Still the judiciary put their veto upon the laws, and thereby jeopardize life and property, and the peace of the country.

This characterization of judicial review is the opposite of how the courts are viewed today, when judicial review is commonly thought of as a means of preventing the government from jeopardizing "life and property." It demonstrates the hostility that many Republicans must have felt toward the federal judiciary.

Taylor's essay continued by questioning the authority of the judiciary to declare a popular law unconstitutional: "Are the legislature, in this case, to submit? Are they to give an absolute control over the laws to the judiciary?" His answer was blunt: "This absolute authority is opposed to the whole theory of our government, and opposes all responsibility to public opinion." Taylor then argued that constitutional errors made by judges had unacceptably long-lasting consequences.

> Grant the legislature to be in error. The opinion they express is that of the people most directly expressed, and if incorrect, the people themselves will experience the evils resulting from it. Unless supported by the enlightened and permanent impressions of the people, it will be short lived; it will not be likely to endure for more than two years. But an error of the judges, if paramount, will be of great duration, and will admit of no remedy until the existing judges die and new ones are appointed. Before this shall occur, the liberties of the people may be destroyed.

The concluding paragraph of Taylor's essay contains an intriguing plebiscitary-based argument for the constitutionality of the 1802 Judiciary Act. Taylor's argument, which he said ought to be "conclusive" on the question, was based on the results of the 1802 midterm congressional elections: "A lively appeal has been made to public opinion; and the people have been called upon to displace those who supported the measure. In every instance, except one, they have re-elected those who supported it, and in numerous instances they have ejected its opponents." The question of constitutionality, Taylor therefore maintained, had been decided by "public opinion, . . . the highest and the only competent tribunal, in litigated cases." He added that, because more than two-thirds of the US House and Senate and three-fourths of the state legislatures were now Republican, the elections had produced Republican majorities "adequate to effect, if necessary, a correspondent alteration in the constitution, had that been necessary." Taylor's argument that the constitutionality of a law could be decided by the national vote in congressional elections was far more consistent with Jeffersonian democratic theory than the idea of judicial review, which leaves such decisions in the hands of insulated and unelected judges.

Conclusion

The pages of Thomas Jefferson's newspaper provide helpful additional possible perspectives on Jefferson's attitudes toward judicial review. When threatening cases like *Marbury* and *More* were pending, the *Intelligencer* conveyed that his administration was concerned about them. But following the *Marbury* decision, while there was hostility to the decision on other grounds, the principle of judicial review was implicitly supported rather than criticized. Then, when the Supreme Court affirmed the constitutionality of the 1802 Judiciary Act in *Stuart v. Laird*, the decision was cited in the *Intelligencer* as conclusive proof on that point. Finally, when the Supreme Court again avoided a conflict over the 1802 Judiciary Act in the *More* case, its decision is not mentioned in the *Intelligencer*, even though the potentially threatening lower court decision in the case had been noted alarmingly in the newspaper. Indeed, not until the fall of 1804 did Jefferson's mouthpiece carry any negative commentary about the idea of judicial review, when it published John Taylor's vigorous attack.[39] Coming so long after the *Marbury* decision, though, and known at the time as having come from Taylor rather than Jefferson himself, that attack seems almost like a "for the record" statement of the principled Jeffersonian position on judicial review rather than a call for official resistance to it. Overall, the coverage and commentary in Jefferson's presidential newspaper supports the conclusion that Jefferson, early in his presidency, adopted the "regime legitimization" approach toward judicial review. So famously complex in his thinking and actions, Jefferson probably had little difficulty accepting that one of his great theoretical nemeses, judicial review, could also, depending on the circumstances, be a great ally when it came to actually governing.

CHAPTER 7

Attacking Judges, Part 2

The Impeachment of
Supreme Court Justice Samuel Chase

One of the most dramatic episodes in Jefferson's presidency was the effort by Republicans to remove Justice Samuel Chase from the Supreme Court through the impeachment process. Examining how the *Intelligencer* "reported" that controversy presents new insights into the thinking and strategies of Jefferson and his allies as the process unfolded. It also reveals that the effort to remove Chase produced a vicious public counterattack from Chase that is shocking by modern standards of judicial behavior. Chase publicly accused the president and his Republican allies in Congress not only of acting out of base partisan and personal motives but also of attempting to undermine the integrity and independence of the judicial branch of the US government. Viewed through the perspective of Jefferson's presidential newspaper, the Chase battle represents one of the greatest public fights of one government branch against the other two in the history of the nation.[1]

The basic story of the Republican effort to remove Chase from the US Supreme Court is well known.[2] In the estimation of one historian, Samuel Chase was hated by Republicans "more than any other man in America" with the possible exception of Alexander Hamilton.[3] Chase had demonstrated open bias against Republicans on trial for sedition and tax protest during the Adams administration and had imposed heavy penalties on them following their convictions, including a death sentence in one case. In the presidential election of 1800, he even openly campaigned for John Adams (thus forcing the Supreme Court to delay the opening of its term for lack of a quorum).[4] Jefferson's election and the Republicans' growing strength at the congressional and state levels seemed to inflame Chase even more, as evidenced by what he wrote to a friend in early 1803.

> There is but one event (which will probably never happen) in which I will interfere with politics. I mean the establishment of a *new* Government. I believe nothing can save the *present* one from dissolution. Some Events, such as a War with France, may delay it for a few years. The Seeds are sown, they ripen daily. Men without *Sense* and without *property* are to be our *Rulers*, there can be no Union between the Heads of the two Parties. Confidence is destroyed; if attempted they will be branded as *Deserters*, and lose all Influence. Things must take their natural Course, from *bad* to *worse*.[5]

Finally, when word reached Jefferson, later in 1803, that Chase had raged about Republicanism and impending "mobocracy" in his charge to a grand jury in Baltimore, the president essentially ordered Republicans in Congress to begin impeachment proceedings against the justice.[6]

The Republican case against Chase was initially laid out in a broadside published in the *Intelligencer* issue of May 20, 1803. The commentary, entitled "JUDGE CHASE'S CHARGE," provided what it said was a "fair summary" of the charge Chase had made to the Baltimore grand jury on May 2. The commentary said the *Intelligencer* had delayed publishing the summary in the hope that "the whole Charge would appear" in the press. It said the summary was "taken by a person present" and added, "In some emphatic sentences the words are nearly such as he used; though, for the most part, greater regard has been paid to the ideas than the language."[7] (As will be seen, the summary had actually been made by Samuel H. Smith himself.)

Chase's charge amounted to a scathing Federalist critique of the core elements of Republican ideology. As reported in the *Intelligencer*, Chase ridiculed the idea that "all men had equal rights derived from nature," asserted that a monarchy could protect personal liberty as well as a republic, said that the "great bulwark of an independent judiciary has been broken down by the legislature of the United States," and strongly criticized a proposal in the Maryland legislature to expand suffrage to all white males even if they owned no property. If measures like these were allowed to stand, Chase had said, "[i]nstead of being ruled by a regular and respectable government, we shall be governed by an ignorant mobocracy."

Chase's comments were first reported in a Baltimore newspaper. All prior accounts of the story of Chase's impeachment have stated that Jefferson learned of the comments from that newspaper report. It appears, however, that Jefferson would have heard about them directly from the editor of his presidential newspaper, Samuel H. Smith, who had attended the hearing. On March 16, 1804, Smith published the testimony he had given in the House impeachment proceedings against Chase regarding the record he had made of Chase's charge to the Baltimore grand jury and then published in the *Intelligencer*. (As discussed later, Smith's publication of his testimony was part of the stream of "evidence" he was publishing in 1804 that had been presented in the House against Chase.)

Smith testified he had attended the hearing because he had been called as a witness before the grand jury. He said he had found Chase's charge to the jury so extraordinary that "it impressed me with the opinion that it ought to be made public." He had written down his account of it that evening, he said, after unsuccessfully trying to obtain the original from Chase and the grand jury members. Smith added that when he made his request to the jurors, he had been told "that the grand jury (although they agreed in political sentiment with Mr. Chase) thought the charge a very imprudent one, and would not, probably, assent to be instrumental in making it public."

Given the close relationship between Smith and Jefferson, it seems highly likely that Jefferson would have quickly learned about the episode from Smith firsthand rather than through a newspaper report. On May 13, 1803, Jefferson wrote to Republican congressman Joseph Nicholson about Chase's charge, hinting pointedly, "Ought the seditious and official attack on the principles of our Constitution and of a State to go unpublished?"[8] Although it would take almost a year for the House of Representatives to vote articles of impeachment against Chase, the attack on Chase in the *Intelligencer* began just one week later.

The paper's May 20 commentary labeled Chase's charge "the most extraordinary that the violence of federalism has yet produced." Chase had clearly violated his judicial oath to administer justice fairly and "agreeably to the constitution and laws of the United States." Of his criticism of the expansion of suffrage in Maryland, the commentary said the change was, on the contrary, a salutary move, because it would make the state "more republican than it previously was." Of Chase's claim that liberty can exist under any form of government, the commentary said, "This remark is very absurd. But it merits attention, not so much for its absurdity, as for its evidence of a rooted attachment to monarchy."

The Chase matter was next mentioned in the *Intelligencer* on August 5, 1803, when the paper reprinted, without commentary, the part of Chase's charge to the Baltimore grand jury that had been published in the Baltimore *Anti-Democrat* on June 25. The excerpt from the charge was prefaced by a statement from Chase himself, explaining that he had "with great reluctance" provided a copy of his charge because it had been "misunderstood by some editors, and shamefully misrepresented by others." Chase added that he believed a judge can "neither explain nor justify his judicial opinions" and "must therefore remain silent, although he is misunderstood or misrepresented."

On August 10, in its first item under the regular column "Washington City," the *Intelligencer* attacked Chase again. The attack began by quoting from the Declaration of Independence that all men are created equal. The commentary observed that it was becoming "too common" to hear public denunciations of the sentiments expressed in the Declaration. There were now many men who "affect to despise republican government, ridicule the idea of equal rights as visionary, abhor democracy, and leave no occasion unimproved of recommending the energies and splendors of monarchies and aristocracies." The commentary then quoted extensively from Chase's charge to the Baltimore jury, in which he had, as noted, derided the idea of equal rights in society. Pointing out that Chase had been one of the men who had signed the Declaration of Independence, the commentary acknowledged that men can change their minds in the honest pursuit of truth. However, in an apparent reference to Chase's recent statement that, as a judge, he was obligated to remain silent even when his opinions were questioned, the commentary asserted that Chase and all those other old revolutionaries who "now think with him" were hypocritically invoking nonpartisanship to make themselves look better: "Their *honest and disinterested* motives will elevate them above the reproach of being swayed by party spirit, by the love of power, the thirst of lucre, or any of those ignoble passions that in other times have covered with the mantle of infamy the proudest names."

The attack closed with the promise to demonstrate later the "novelty and weakness" of Chase's claim that there can be "no rights of man in a state of nature." The next issue, on August 12, did just that, in an essay entitled "Natural Rights." The essay quoted provisions from eight state constitutions in which "the possession of natural and unalienable rights is solemnly asserted." It said that in comparison to those statements and the sentiments expressed by so many great statesmen during the Revolution, Chase's grand jury comments could only be described as "ill-timed, misapplied, undignified, and untrue." For good measure, the commentary quoted from Locke and other English political philosophers on the subject of natural rights.

The August 12 commentary concluded with a vivid explanation of why Chase's charge to the grand jury was so offensive to Republicans.

> So much would not have been said on this point, but for the insidious tendency of the opinion that man, having no natural rights, derives all the rights he possesses from government. It is far, very far, from being a mere abstract question. Once establish the dogma of Judge Chase, and governments become omnipotent. Man looks to them for all he possesses. Neither the laws of God nor the ordinances of nature are entitled to his respect. The despot, who lives on the misery of his subjects, becomes the object of exclusive homage. However governments may abuse powers given to them for the advancement of the public good, however they may oppress those they were formed to protect, the oppressed has no tribunal to appeal to, no established principles, engraven on the hearts of all men, to invoke, around which the affections of a nation may rally; and a sacred regard for which may unite them in their defense. If there be a doctrine, which may emphatically be denominated that of tyrants, it is this doctrine.

The eloquent wording of the commentary certainly suggests that Jefferson himself could have written it. In any event, the assertion that Chase's views represent the doctrine of "tyrants" indicates clearly the main motivation for Republicans seeking his removal from the Supreme Court. It was a difference in basic political philosophy. Chase had publicly denounced a core principle of Republicanism first expressed in the Declaration of Independence. In his position as a Supreme Court justice, he had thus become a major institutional and doctrinal threat to the Republican vision of democracy in America.[9]

In January 1804, the House proceedings against Chase began. After days of debate, the House formed a committee to consider impeaching Chase. The committee recommended impeachment; after more debate, the committee report was approved by a vote of the whole House, seventy-three to thirty-two. The *Intelligencer* noted the formation of the committee in its January 11 issue and, in several later issues that month, published accounts of the House debate regarding the formation of the committee. On March 9, 1804, the paper filled its first two pages with documents that had been included with the report of the House impeachment committee. Those documents included several affidavits by the defense lawyers for John Fries (the Pennsylvania tax rebel whose trial for treason Chase had conducted in what Republicans had regarded as a seriously biased manner) and answers to interrogatories by others involved in the trial. In several subsequent issues (on March 12, 14, and 16), the paper published more documents, including testimony from others who had attended the Baltimore trial, filling more than a page of each issue with them.

The March 14 issue also presented two happy news events for Republicans that had occurred on March 12. The first was the conviction of federal district judge John Pickering on his impeachment charges by the Senate. As Sean Wilentz puts it, that proceeding had been the "warm-up case" for the Republicans' planned assault on the Federalist judiciary. Pickering's descent into alcoholism and bouts of insanity had made him an attractive first target for Republicans.[10] The second happy event reported on March 14 was the vote, by the full House, to begin impeachment proceedings against Chase. Under the headline "Judge Chase Impeached" (technically inaccurate, since the House had not yet approved any specific charges), the paper presented a summary of the floor debate on the motion to proceed with Chase's impeachment.

On March 26, the *Intelligencer* printed the speech of Vermont representative James Elliot in the March 12 House floor debate on impeaching Chase. Interestingly, Elliot asserted that although various charges had been made against Chase, the only one he thought amounted to an impeachable offense was Chase's conduct of the trial of James Callender, a Republican newspaper editor. Chase, he concluded, had denied Callender the right to call witnesses and to be tried by an impartial jury. Whether Chase's actions had been "the consequence of passion, prepossession, or party spirit," noted Elliot, to "allow judges to disregard the constitution . . . would be giving them a dangerous latitude indeed." Despite his strong condemnation of Chase's conduct in the Callender trial, Elliot's rejection of the other charges against the judge foreshadowed the difficulties Republicans would eventually encounter in trying to get the two-thirds vote needed in the Senate to convict Chase.[11]

On March 26, John Randolph introduced seven articles of impeachment against Chase. He did it just one day before the end of the House session, which meant that the House would adjourn without acting on them. The March 28 *Intelligencer* then published Randolph's draft articles of impeachment. They were full of highly charged language. One accused Chase of "manifest injustice, partiality, and intemperance" in the trial of John Fries. Another condemned his "intemperate and inflammatory political harangue" to the Baltimore grand jury as an attempt to incite the "odium" of the "good people of Maryland against the government of the United States." Chase's jury charge was further described as "highly indecent, extra judicial, and tending to prostitute the high judicial character with which he was invested to the low purpose of an electioneering partisan."

In his classic study of Chase's impeachment, Richard E. Ellis says that until his Senate impeachment trial, Chase remained "publicly silent" in the face of the proceedings against him.[12] But rather than remaining silent, Chase fought back strongly and in the most public way possible. As Congress was coming to the end of its session in March, he wrote a "Memorial" to the House of Representatives, protesting the fairness of the proceedings against him. Then, when he had been unable to deliver his protest to the House formally in the closing days of the session, Chase sent the memorial and an accompanying letter to newspaper editors around the country, including the *National Intelligencer*, asking them to publish both.

As Chase explained in his memorial, he believed he had been the victim of an extremely unfair process. He complained that the House had made no specific charges against him before it had adjourned. It had only received a committee report, buttressed with statements and depositions of fourteen witnesses, recommending his impeachment for undefined "high crimes and misdemeanors." Randolph's proposed articles of impeachment had then come at practically the last minute.

All of this, Chase noted, had been published in the *National Intelligencer*, thus giving it "an official character and sanction" due to the newspaper being widely "understood to be the official organ of the government." Once published in that newspaper, all of the evidence and charges against him would be "spread throughout the United States" and "even extend to foreign countries." For months, he said, he would have no opportunity to defend his reputation, because Congress would not meet again until November of 1804. Unrebutted, the material in the House report would, he charged, "become a very powerful engine in the hands of calumniators and party zealots."[13] Indeed, it appears this may have been precisely the Republicans' plan. In her study of the impeachment effort, Jane Elsmere concluded that Randolph deliberately delayed the beginning of the House's impeachment inquiry until late in its session so that its adjournment of nearly a year would give Republican newspapers "more time to exploit" the evidence and charges "as propaganda against Chase."[14]

Asking newspaper editors around the country to publish his memorial to the House of Representatives was Chase's bold move to defend himself in the public eye. As he put it, "I deem it proper now to make it public, as an appeal to my country, to the world, and to posterity." Chase was essentially conducting a public relations campaign, carried out in the only way possible then: through the nation's newspapers. By modern standards, in which federal judges, especially Supreme Court Justices, behave circumspectly even in the face of criticism, what Chase did is extraordinary. Never since has a Supreme Court Justice acted in such a public, aggressive manner against a president and his congressional allies.

The *Intelligencer* granted Chase's request and published his memorial and accompanying cover letter in its April 4, 1804 edition.[15] In an introductory note, Smith explained why he was publishing them. Since Chase had asked the editors of "all the newspapers in the United States" to do so, for the *Intelligencer* to refuse "would be denounced as partial or pusillanimous."

Chase's memorial was a stunningly direct attack on Thomas Jefferson. He charged that the impeachment process had been driven by partisan and personal motives traceable to the president himself. He made the charges via insinuation, saying he "trembled for the honor of his country, and for the success of republican government in this her last and fairest experiment," that a time might "ever arrive"

> when a majority of Congress, inflamed by party spirit, and seeking the destruction of its opponent, shall desire to criminate a judge, in order to heap odium on the party with which he is connected; when a President, at the head of this majority, and guiding its passions, shall desire, from motives of private resentment, the ruin of any judge; when the schemes of the dominant party or of its leaders, may require the removal of all firm upright and independent judges, and substitution of others more complying or more timid.

As further proof of the partisan nature of the proceedings against him, Chase noted that most of the complaints were for judicial actions he had taken years ago. Only now, he charged, when Republicans were confident of majorities in both houses of Congress, had those complaints been revived to provide the basis for his impeachment and removal.

In the same issue, the *Intelligencer* followed Chase's letters with its critique of them. Pulling no punches, it said that Chase's letter to the House of Representatives was a "mass of misrepresentation . . . never, perhaps, equaled by a high official character." Because the "long and inflammatory remarks" could not all be dealt with individually without trying the "patience of the reader," they were dismissed generally as "inapposite, untrue, or illogical." The commentary did respond to some of Chase's points specifically, however. As to his claim that the impeachment effort was blatantly partisan, the commentary argued that of the fourteen called witnesses whose partisan affiliations were known, "is it not a little extraordinary that *seven* are *federal,* and *seven republican.*" It then condemned as "envenomed" the "insinuation that attempts insidiously to instill into the public mind charges against the executive and legislative departments of our government, which it dares not openly avow." Saying it was "honored by Judge Chase with being denominated the official organ of the government," the *Intelligencer* employed classic Republican democratic theory in defending its publication of the House report, witness testimony, and the proposed articles of impeachment. Publication was necessary so that "the people" could judge for themselves what Congress should do regarding Chase: "The representatives of the people are responsible to their constituents. If they err, the people ought not to be left in the dark. If they act right, the people, whose interests they guard, ought not to be ignorant of their motives of action."

Surprisingly, Chase's public defense of himself and the *Intelligencer*'s partisan-tinged reply have largely escaped scholarly attention. As noted previously, Ellis wrongly says that Chase remained "publicly silent" after the House adjourned in early 1804 without voting on the proposed articles of impeachment against him. Similarly, Keith Whittington's extensive examination of the political and doctrinal aspects of Chase's impeachment makes no mention of Chase's public defense of himself.[16] Dumas Malone briefly discussed Chase's memorial but curiously characterized it as an attack on the Republican Party and the House of Representatives, with no mention of what Chase had said about Jefferson or the status of the *Intelligencer* as the recognized voice of his administration.[17]

Though noting that Chase wrote and circulated a defense, Bruce Ackerman did not analyze its contents.[18] In his brief discussion of Chase's action, he noted only that all of the publicity would have helped dramatize the partisan nature of the struggle as Americans began voting for the next Congress.[19] That point, though surely true, shortchanges the seriousness and ferocity of Chase's charges. As framed by Chase, his impeachment represented an institutional struggle, with the Supreme Court on one side and the president and his compliant, Republican-dominated Congress on the other. According to Chase, the struggle was a clear threat to the integrity and independence of the judicial branch. In contrast to this high-minded, constitutionally based charge, Chase also painted Jefferson as nothing more than a vicious partisan schemer, claiming that Jefferson was acting "from motives of private resentment" and "guiding" the "passions" of a Congress that was "inflamed by party spirit and seeking the destruction of its opponents."

Many scholars, including Ellis and Robert McCloskey, have concluded that Jefferson eventually became disinterested in the effort to impeach and remove Chase.[20] This would not have been evident to readers of the *Intelligencer*. Just a few days after publishing and critiquing Chase's defense of himself and after Congress had adjourned, the *Intelligencer* took a sudden interest in the impeachment proceedings the Senate had conducted against federal judge John Pickering. On April 5, it published the Senate's report to the House stating its readiness to proceed with the trial. The report included the text of a petition from the judge's son that he be allowed to show that Pickering had been insane for two years, as well as a summary of the Senate's consideration and rejection of the petition and its vote to proceed with the trial. In a brief note, the *Intelligencer* explained its sudden attention to the matter: the newspaper was going to "commence a detailed statement" of Pickering's trial "to present an antidote to the flagrant misrepresentation" that was "circulating in the Eastern quarter of the union" about it. The paper then carried descriptions of the Senate proceedings against Pickering for weeks.

Once Congress was back in session in November, the Republican-dominated House did not take long to act on Chase's impeachment. On December 5, 7, and 10, the *Intelligencer* carried accounts of the House proceedings, a few days earlier, that had culminated in the approval of eight articles of impeachment against him. Coverage continued in the December 12 issue, with a note that the Senate had scheduled Chase's trial to begin on January 2, 1805. The front page of the next issue, on December 14, published the procedural rules that the special Senate committee had approved for the trial.

On January 4, the paper printed an account of the January 2 opening of the trial in the Senate. Chase was reported to have requested, "in consideration of age and infirmity," a chair to sit in, which had been "immediately furnished" to him. Federalists promptly contradicted this innocuous account, however. On January 5, the *Washington Federalist* printed its own account of the incident.

> About the time that Judge Chase was expected in the Senate Chamber, it was observed, that a chair was placed somewhere about the middle of the room, and every person (from the unusual situation of the chair) supposed that it was placed there for Judge Chase; and so it indeed was. But to the astonishment of all who observed it, just before the Senators took their seats, this chair was removed. Now reader, mark; we pledge ourselves to the truth of it; Mr. Mathers the Serjeant [*sic*] at Arms, approached Judge Chase and told him, that he was instructed to inform him, that if he wished a seat he must apply to the Senate for the permission of one, and that upon such application it would be granted to him. Judge Chase did apply accordingly, and had the promised permission.

After listing other ways in which Chase had been treated demeaningly by the Senate at the beginning of the trial, the *Federalist* launched into an attack on Samuel H. Smith and the accuracy of the accounts that the *National Intelligencer* was giving of the proceedings. Calling him "*Sammy Harrison Smith*" and that "*puling* pimping Smith," it said he and his paper could not be trusted. After all, it reminded its readers, Smith was to be a witness in the Senate trial because his "false and malicious account" of Chase's speech to the Baltimore grand jury in 1803 had served as the basis for one of the articles of impeachment. The *Federalist* also published the text of Chase's speech to the Senate at the opening of his trial, interspersing the text with editorial comments criticizing aspects of the impeachment, including the claim that judges could be removed simply for political reasons.

On January 9, the *Federalist* published another scathing note about the chair incident, again attacking Smith for having tried to make it seem, in his report, that the Senate had simply been solicitous of Chase's comfort in providing a chair. What the episode really showed, the *Federalist* said, was a pathetic attempt, either by Senate Republicans or by Aaron Burr on his own, to insult Justice Chase. Common courtesy, the paper said, would be to offer a chair to anyone, young or old, healthy or infirm. So making Chase "*beg* for a chair" had been nothing more than a "low attempt to insult those years and infirmities [and] degrade and humble" a great man who, while he may have declined physically, still had a mind "as unconquerable as his integrity is uncorruptible." The *Federalist* that day also published an intriguing note that would prove prescient. The "more moderate Republicans" in the Senate, it said, were becoming concerned that the Chase impeachment may "have lighted up a flame by which they may be themselves consumed." These "more reasonable" senators considered the impeachment charges "frivolous in some instances, and malicious in others."

On January 7, the *Intelligencer* printed its version of the speech Chase had delivered to the Senate on January 2. Chase made some brief, polite remarks on the charges and explained his request for more time to respond to them. He did slip in a dig at his accusers, by noting that when they were just babies "in their nurse's arms," he had been "contributing my utmost aid to lay the ground work of American liberty." At that point, the paper reported, Aaron Burr, who was presiding over the trial, interrupted Chase and told him he should stick to the matter at hand, which was his request for a delay in the proceedings. On January 9, the *Intelligencer* printed more of the Senate's procedural rules for the trial. On January 11, it printed the affidavit Chase had filed in the Senate to support his request for more time to prepare for the trial.

The actual trial began on February 4. The *Intelligencer* began reporting the proceedings two days later, noting that the reading of Chase's response to the charges, which was done by Chase himself and his lawyers, had taken three and a half hours. Somewhat ironically, the paper followed this report with a note that the Supreme Court had opened its session the previous day. The note listed the names of the justices, including, of course, Chase's.

The next issue of the *Intelligencer* on February 8 carried an account of the debate in the House of Representatives that had produced the House's stinging reply to the answer Chase had filed in the Senate about the impeachment proceedings against him. Among other things, the House asserted that Chase's answer had "endeavored to cover the crimes and misdemeanors laid to his charge, by evasive insinuations, and misrepresentations of facts," resulting in "a gloss and coloring utterly false and untrue to the various criminal matters" alleged in the articles. It urged the Senate to bring Chase to a "speedy and exemplary punishment."

The *Intelligencer* then filled the first two pages of its February 11 issue with the partial text of Chase's reply to the charges against him. That issue also noted that the House representatives had begun presenting their case two days earlier and that it would soon "lay before the public in this paper a detailed statement of the proceedings in this important trial as soon as it can be given with accuracy." The next two issues were similarly devoted exclusively, except for advertisements, to publishing the rest of Chase's reply.

That reply was markedly different from his newspaper screed ten months earlier. He had in the meantime put together a team of first-rate trial lawyers, and their influence showed. The first seven of the eight articles of impeachment had accused Chase of various legal missteps— all allegedly betraying an anti-Republican or anti-defendant bias—while presiding in 1800 over two trials (that of John Fries for treason and that of James Callender for sedition) and a grand jury. As to each of those articles, Chase's response was firm and legalistic, citing precedent or common judicial practice to defend everything he had done. He added that even if he might have made some honest errors in those cases, none of them rose to the level of an impeachable offense. Finally, he argued that to make vague, debatable criticisms of his judicial conduct a basis for impeachment would introduce into the impeachment process arbitrariness and, thus, the seeds of "despotism."

Only in his response to the eighth article, which had charged him with making an "intemperate and inflammatory political harangue" to the grand jury in Baltimore in 1803, did Chase take a more confrontational approach. Even then, though, he avoided any personal attacks on either Jefferson or those in the House of Representatives who had voted for his impeachment. He first denied that anything he had said to the grand jury had been intemperate, inflammatory, or indecent. He declared that he still believed everything he had said in the charge and that, in expressing those opinions, he had followed the long-established practice in the United States of judges presenting to grand juries "such political opinions as they thought correct and useful." He then argued that even if a judge expressed "incorrect" political opinions, that could hardly be a basis for impeachment and removal. If it were, "error in political opinion . . . might be a crime," and "a party in power might, under this pretext, destroy any judge, who might happen in a charge to a grand jury, to say something capable of being construed by them, into a political opinion adverse to their own system." Such conduct "would be utterly subversive of the fundamental principles on which free government rests."

Rather than impugning anyone's motives or saying anything negative about their character, Chase stuck to the merits of the case. Framing the eighth article as a threat to political liberty in America was a powerful way to appeal to the moderate Republicans whose support Chase needed (and would get) in the trial.[21] All astute Republicans would have realized that as the number of Republican judges grew, making partisan behavior in judges an impeachable offense could be turned against their side too.[22]

A few issues later, on February 25, the *Intelligencer* reported that each of Chase's several lawyers had made long closing arguments. It also reported Chase's last brief remarks to the Senate. He said he was too ill to remain at the Senate proceedings any longer and regretted having to depart before hearing the Senate's verdict. He thanked the Senate for "its patience and indulgence in the long and tedious examination of the witnesses."

The March 1 paper reported the close of the trial proceedings that day. Saying that the Senate would be voting on the articles later in the day, the report characterized the proceedings as a "full, patient, and deliberate hearing" of the charges against Chase, conducted with "impartiality," "dignified deportment," and "order and decorum." It said the proceeding reflected "high honor on the Senate of the United States and the individual who presides over their deliberations," Vice President Aaron Burr.

There was a strong irony in the appearance of the next issue of the *Intelligencer*. It was published on March 4, 1805, the date of Jefferson's inauguration to a second term. Remarkably, in the newspaper that day, the decision in the Chase impeachment case received more space than Jefferson's inauguration. The Chase story was headlined, in all capitals and an unusually large font, "JUDGEMENT PRONOUNCED ON THE IMPEACHMENT AGAINST SAMUEL CHASE." In pitifully stark contrast, in the paper's regular small print was just this mention of Jefferson's inauguration: "*This day*, at 12 o'clock, the PRESIDENT takes the oath of office, when it is expected he will deliver an INAUGURAL SPEECH." On the glorious day of Jefferson's second inauguration, his own presidential newspaper devoted its entire first page and more than half of its second page to the speech that John Randolph had given at the opening of Chase's impeachment trial in the Senate. Centered on the third page was a full account of the final verdict, with a chart showing how each senator had voted on each article of impeachment. (That detailed information may well have come from Jefferson himself, who had been keeping a running tally of the voting.)[23]

It is hard not to ascribe some meaning to this hugely disproportionate coverage in Jefferson's newspaper. Why did the newspaper not publish the text of Jefferson's second inaugural address on the day it was given, as it had his first?[24] Was there, as it surely seems, an editorial decision that the importance of the Chase verdict required it to be published as soon as possible, at the expense of pushing coverage of Jefferson's inauguration to the next issue? Or could the editor just not bear to put both the news of Chase's acquittal and coverage of Jefferson's splendid triumph into the same issue? In any event, the paper's treatment of the news of Chase's acquittal certainly conveys the appearance that rather than having lost interest in the trial or thinking it inconsequential, Republicans still thought the trial had been hugely significant.

The entire first page of the *Intelligencer*'s next issue, published on March 6, printed Jefferson's inaugural speech. It also published a brief commentary on the speech and reported that, following the speech, Jefferson had been "waited upon by a large assemblage of members of the legislature, citizens, and strangers of distinction" and that "a procession was formed at the Navy Yard, composed of the several mechanics engaged, which marched to military music, displaying, with considerable taste, the various insignia of their professions." Even in this issue, though, the specter of Chase appeared, in the form of an advertisement headlined (in large print) "TRIAL OF JUDGE CHASE," promoting Smith's plan to "publish in a volume the proceedings on this interesting trial at full length, with as little delay as circumstances will admit." The ad solicited orders for the work and requested the editors of other newspapers to "confer a favor by inserting this advertisement a few times."

On the Federalist side, the *Washington Federalist* had been regularly publishing excerpts from Chase's defense brief since mid-February. It also published reports of the ongoing Senate trial proceedings. The newspaper celebrated Chase's acquittal in its March 2 issue: "It gives us pleasure to announce the triumph of reason and justice, over the spirit of party, in the acquittal of Judge Chase. We sincerely hope it will have a tendency to allay the spirit of intolerance, prejudice and party animosity, which has so long disgraced our country."[25]

The next issue of the *Intelligencer* that mentioned either Jefferson or Chase once again devoted more space to Chase. On March 13, 1805, the paper reported that Jefferson's reelection had been "celebrated with much distinction at New York, Philadelphia, Richmond, and Petersburg." While the paper said it had no space to give any "detail of these festivities," it did have space to print the resolution of the Senate commending Vice President Burr for his "impartiality, dignity, and ability" in presiding over Chase's trial, as well as Burr's response in which he expressed his appreciation to the Senate for "this flattering mark of their esteem."

On March 18, the *Intelligencer* began publishing parts of the transcript of the proceedings in Chase's trial in almost every issue for the next five months (until August 23, 1805). The March 18 issue, for example, carried the testimony of the two Republican attorneys who had sought to represent John Fries in his trial for treason. Both attorneys had testified that Chase had conducted the trial in an extremely biased manner. The April 3 and 5 issues of the paper notably carried the account of Chief Justice John Marshall's testimony in the impeachment trial. Marshall had been present at the Callender sedition trial as an observer. Called as a witness for Chase, he had unexpectedly provided testimony critical of some of Chase's conduct in the trial.[26] In August, the paper concluded its coverage of the trial by publishing the closing arguments of Chase's lawyers.

This in-depth, months-long coverage of Chase's impeachment in the *National Intelligencer* again contradicts the notion that Jefferson and his Republican allies had lost interest in the proceedings. If that were so, it seems inconceivable that Jefferson's newspaper would for so long have continued publishing so much of the proceedings, virtually verbatim. All the space devoted to the trial signals that Republicans wanted to spread a full account of it across the country. In this way, they could ensure that all the allegations against Chase would be known nationally and in great detail. Readers would have seen for themselves what Chase was accused of and why, in the eyes of Republicans, he had deserved to be removed from office. Anyone reading or hearing of the proceedings as recounted in the *Intelligencer* would thus have received an extensive education in what Republicans did and did not expect from a federal judge, especially one sitting on the nation's highest court.

The inference that Republicans viewed the impeachment proceedings as having been extraordinarily significant, despite the failure to convict Chase in the Senate trial, was essentially confirmed by the editor of the *Intelligencer* in a brief two-paragraph commentary on March 20, 1805. The first paragraph reported that Jefferson's second inauguration, on March 4, had inspired numerous celebrations around the country, all suffused with "general and lively joy." Then, in the second paragraph, Smith moved abruptly away from that good news.

> We exercise no small degree of self-denial in excluding these details [about the celebrations] from our columns. But the mass of original and interesting matters, which we have in readiness for the press, is so great as to render unavoidable the omission of many articles of merit,

which appear in other prints. It is our purpose to give the whole trial of judge Chase in its full details, with the least possible delay, constantly with the insertion of other matter of the first importance. *We are the more solicitous to do this, that there may be laid before the public, a correct statement of this important trial, which, viewed in its various aspects, merits and will reward as great attention, as any event which has occurred in the United States.* Under a full impression of its interesting nature, unremitting exertions have been made to present it in the most correct form; and it will appear, not only in the National Intelligencer, but likewise in one or more volumes, for which a copy right is obtained. (emphasis added)

Even allowing for the possibility of some commercial hyping by Smith, his characterization of Chase's trial as having been as notable as any other event in the history of the United States is striking. Clearly, Jefferson and his allies must have thought the impeachment effort had been worthwhile despite the result.

What motivation might have been behind this kind of thinking? As Jeremy Bailey has shown, Jefferson had a long-held view that the executive branch should be involved in the impeachment process. Bailey writes that the energy of the executive in sometimes seeking impeachment and removal of judges or executive branch officials could, in Jefferson's eyes, make impeachment more likely "by pricking the attention of the people, who too rarely rise up against tyrants, and by emboldening legislators." A corollary of this presidential participation was that it would strengthen the impeachment process "by improving the public's ability to understand the kind of questions that would be brought up by impeachments."[27]

In light of Bailey's points, the reason for the extraordinary attention paid to Chase's impeachment and trial in Jefferson's presidential newspaper becomes clear. Jefferson would have wanted the *Intelligencer* to carry out the task he envisioned for executive participation in the impeachment process: "improving" the ability of the American people to understand the bases for impeaching and removing officials, thus enabling them to judge for themselves both whether impeachment was warranted and whether their representatives had acted properly when engaged in the process. As noted previously, this is precisely how the editor of the *Intelligencer* had responded to Chase's complaint that the House committee report recommending his impeachment should not have been published in the newspaper. Disagreeing with Chase, Smith said, "The representatives of the people are responsible to their constituents. If they err, the people ought not to be left in the dark. If they act right, the people, whose interests they guard, ought not to be ignorant of their motives of action."

Smith's explanation also suggests a popular or "political" basis for the impeachment and removal of officials that fits with Jeffersonian popular democratic theory. Under that standard, impeachment is justified whenever any official, particularly a judge, is somehow seriously harming the nation but has not committed any criminal offense. This broad standard contrasts with the "legal basis" standard, which holds that only criminal conduct can justify the process.[28] In a speech in the House during the impeachment effort, Republican William Branch Giles justified the functional, "political" view of impeachment bluntly: "You hold dangerous opinions, and if you suffer to carry them into effect you will work the destruction of the nation. We want your offices for the purpose of giving them to men who will fill them better."[29]

Building on such statements, Stephen Engel asserts that Republican hostility to the Marshall court—and, by implication, to politically "out-of-step" justices such as Chase—was based not so much on hostility to the idea of judicial review but on the expectation that judges should hold views that were consistent with those of the American people as a whole. If they did, then even the judicial branch would reflect the concept of "popular sovereignty." Engel also concludes that, unexpectedly for both sides, out of the Chase trial emerged a bipartisan consensus that judges should behave in a politically neutral manner. He quotes one of the House impeachment managers as saying that Chase's impeachment had been intended to "teach a lesson of future instruction to judges that when intoxicated by the spirit of party, they may recollect the scale of power may one day turn, and preserve the scales of justice equal."[30]

Chase's impeachment also had more particular effects. Suitably castigated publicly by the Jeffersonians, he would have realized the danger in crossing them again. This public flogging could well have deterred him and other Federalist judges from publicly expressing anti-Republican sentiments ever again, as has been suggested.[31] Indeed, the Chase impeachment proceedings appear to have chastened even John Marshall. On the eve of the Senate trial, he wrote Chase to recommend abandoning judicial review in favor of "appellate jurisdiction in the legislature."[32] Then, when called to testify at the trial, he had appeared frightened, tentative, and accommodating to the prosecution.[33]

In conclusion, the research presented here provides a better understanding of the attitudes and strategies of Thomas Jefferson and his Republican allies regarding the impeachment of Samuel Chase. In many ways, the findings lead to different scholarly understandings. Most significantly, they highlight that rather than saying nothing publicly during the House impeachment proceedings against him, as had been commonly thought, Chase went on a major public relations offensive. In a letter he sent to newspaper editors around the country, he attacked not only the House Republicans but Jefferson himself. Accusing the president of acting out of partisan and personal animosity, Chase argued that his impeachment was an obvious assault against the constitutional independence and integrity of the federal judiciary. The bluntness of Chase's attack on Jefferson is stunning and stands as the most strident public confrontation ever between a president and a member of the Supreme Court.

The extraordinary attention paid by Jefferson's presidential newspaper to Chase's impeachment also undermines major scholarly opinions on Jefferson's attitude toward the impeachment effort. Some scholars have concluded that Jefferson was uninvolved in the effort as it unfolded and that he soon lost interest in it.[34] Others have asserted that Jefferson backed off on the effort because he no longer viewed the Supreme Court as a serious threat, due to the "cautious and conservative approach" the Court had taken since *Marbury*.[35] To the contrary, all the attention paid to Chase's impeachment in Jefferson's presidential newspaper leads to the opposite inference that the president and his Republican allies cared deeply about the matter. That concern would have been apparent to the entire Washington political community at the time. Evidently, while the Court as a whole might have become nonthreatening, the antidemocratic and anti-Jefferson public statements by Samuel Chase (and the similarly held Federalist sentiments of the other Supreme Court Justices, especially John Marshall) were still considered a major threat to Jeffersonian Republicanism and to the president himself. Nothing else explains the constant attention the newspaper devoted to the controversy for months. Indeed, as several scholars have noted, the article condemning Chase's political speech to the Baltimore grand jury got the most votes in his impeachment trial.[36]

The inference that Jefferson actually wished for Chase's conviction suggests different interpretations for some of the other aspects of the impeachment effort. From the assumption that Jefferson opposed the prosecution of Chase, it has been inferred that John Randolph must have acted on his own in initiating the impeachment proceedings, to embarrass and pressure Jefferson and his allies. Similarly, Jefferson is said to have then begun courting Aaron Burr (who, as vice president, would preside over Chase's Senate trial) to get him to assist with the acquittal of Chase. If one assumes, as the coverage in the *National Intelligencer* seems to indicate, that Jefferson instead was trying to accomplish Chase's conviction and removal, then his use of Randolph makes much more political sense. Randolph may have been a political "wild card" (as he has been described), but Jefferson could well have found that crazy aggressiveness useful in the attack against Chase. Similarly, Jefferson's courting of Burr could have been with the design of encouraging Burr to do all he could to facilitate Chase's conviction. In this regard, it is noteworthy that when Chase first appeared before the Senate on January 2, 1805, to request a postponement of the proceedings, Burr used the occasion to "badger and embarrass the Judge."[37]

By the time of Chase's impeachment trial, the *Intelligencer* was firmly established, in the minds of both the public and political elites, as the mouthpiece of Jefferson's presidency. The paper's incredibly extensive coverage of Chase's impeachment would therefore have conveyed to its readers the clear impression that this was indeed a high stakes political battle between a president and the only threat to his power, the Federalist judges of the US Supreme Court. As shown in this chapter, that coverage adds even more drama and complexity to one of the great clashes in American political history.

CHAPTER 8

The New Orleans Port Closure and the Great Solution

The Louisiana Purchase

This chapter examines the most famous achievement of Jefferson's presidency, the Louisiana Purchase, as it was portrayed in the *National Intelligencer*. The impetus for the Louisiana Purchase actually began when the Spanish government's superintendent of the port of New Orleans unexpectedly ordered the port closed to American shipping in October 1802. The crisis was doubly challenging diplomatically, because at the time of the closure Spain was on the verge of ceding all of its Louisiana Territory to France. This meant, of course, that the United States would have to negotiate a short-term resolution with Spain and then a longer-term one with France.

The news of the port closure reached Washington, DC, by the last week of November in 1802.[1] The November 26 edition of the *Intelligencer* reported the news, along with the official administration reaction to it. Essentially, as soon as Jefferson received the news, he had it published in the newspaper. The November 26 issue not only reported the closure but also declared that the action violated the 1795 Treaty of San Lorenzo between Spain and the United States.

Just four issues later, on December 6, the paper carried calming news: "We understand that there is good reason to consider the late measures of the [Super]Intendent at New Orleans as having originated entirely with himself and as being, of consequence, unauthorized by the Spanish government." That statement reflected the discussions that Jefferson and Madison had held in Washington with the Spanish minister Marques de Casa Yrujo. The minister had told them that the action of the port superintendent must have been mistaken and was a violation of the treaty.[2] The commentary in the *Intelligencer* went on to say, "[F]rom the steps . . . taken by our government, rational expectation may be entertained that the decree will be revoked before it can have operated extensively to the injury of our trade on the Mississippi."

Perhaps out of a desire to minimize the issue, Jefferson did not even mention it in the Annual Message he sent to Congress on December 15. Two days later, however, the House of Representatives passed a unanimous resolution requesting all the documentary information the administration had on the matter. When he sent the papers on December 22, Jefferson said he had acted speedily upon hearing the news and included an official report from Madison concluding that the port superintendent had apparently acted on his own authority.[3] In a second response to Congress, on December 30, Jefferson included a letter from the Spanish governor of Louisiana to the governor of the Mississippi Territory; in that letter, the Spanish governor denied authorizing the action. The next day, the *Intelligencer* announced, "We understand that the Executive have received authentic information, that the late suspension of the right of deposit at NEW ORLEANS was undertaken without orders from the Spanish Government. . . . Under these circumstances and the interpositions of our own Government, it may be reasonably hoped that the matter will be peaceably and early adjusted."

The news of the closing of the port caused great concern in Washington and throughout the country. Feelings ran especially high in the Western states and territories with commerce that depended on the Mississippi and the New Orleans port. Federalists in Congress began accusing the administration of having mishandled the matter and not doing enough to resolve it. According to Dumas Malone, Jefferson "was well aware of the extreme agitation of the public mind" among residents in the West and "of the necessity of doing something to quiet it." Jefferson himself described the agitation as a "fever" and a "ferment."[4]

A piece published in the *Intelligencer* on December 27, 1802, reflected those sentiments. It was a letter from a resident of New Orleans reporting, among other things, that a shipment of clothing to American soldiers had been detained in New Orleans and that the "minds of the Americans as well as the Spanish subjects were much agitated, fully expecting a war." On December 31, the newspaper published the documents Jefferson had sent Congress regarding the controversy. One was a letter in which the governor of Kentucky reported to Jefferson about the shutting of the port. The governor said that the citizens of his state were "very much alarmed and agitated" and that the action, unless rescinded, would "at one blow cut up the present and future prosperity of their best interests by the roots."

Malone identifies two steps Jefferson took publicly to respond to the agitation. The first was the appointment of James Monroe, a known advocate for Western interests, as a special envoy to negotiate with the French and Spanish about the issue. The other step was to have numerous Republicans give speeches in the House of Representatives affirming their party's support for free navigation of the Mississippi and of Western commercial interests in general.[5] The nomination of Monroe was reported in the *Intelligencer* on January 12, 1803, and the paper published many of the House speeches as part of its regular coverage of the proceedings in Congress.

There were, however, other ways, not mentioned by Malone, of responding to the problem. One was through anonymous or pseudonymous commentaries in the *Intelligencer* and other Republican newspapers. On February 23, the *Intelligencer* reprinted, from the *Philadelphia Aurora*, a long commentary by "Camillus." The commentary began by noting that "for some weeks past the federal papers have teemed with inflammatory publications, evidently intended to dispose the people of the United States to hostility against France and Spain, on account of the proclamation of the Spanish intendant of New Orleans, and the reported cession of Louisiana to Spain." The commentary argued that the apparently mistaken act of one Spanish agent should not be a cause for war. Dismissing the "war whoop" heard from "various quarters," "Camillus" disparaged it as the language of "patricides" and "champions of murder." The commentary concluded, "No man but the callous hearted speculator in human affliction, he who calculates upon the plunder without partaking of the dangers or the miseries of war—those who have in view the accumulation of fortune at the expense of the best blood of their fellow citizens and the ruin of the national prosperity, could advocate such doctrines."

On February 28, 1803, in a commentary in its regular "Washington City" column, the *Intelligencer* commended the US Senate for, "with becoming firmness," having voted down a pro-war resolution offered by Federalists. The commentary called Federalists the "war party" and accused them of engaging in the kind of "party violence . . . that in its rage patriotism perishes." Of the defeat of the resolution, the commentary said, "[T]hus have measures calculated to inflame the passions of the nation, to sow discord among them, and to destroy that harmony between the executive and legislative departments of the government, so preeminently necessary at this crisis, been nipped in the bud."

The April 1 and 6 issues of the *Intelligencer* carried a similarly themed two-part essay, signed "Penn" and entitled "An Estimate of the Motives of Those Who Are Clamorous for War." The part of the essay published on April 6 argued against the demands from Federalists in Congress that Jefferson disclose the basis for his announcement, in his Annual Message, that Spain had ceded its Louisiana Territory to France. "Penn" argued that the disclosure would have undercut the president's efforts to avoid war through diplomatic efforts, saying, "It belongs to the Executive to preserve peace and to conduct the foreign relations; and to the legislature exclusively to declare war." He said that if the material had been turned over to Congress, France would have concluded that the United States had resolved on war, because Congress possessed the war power and was not interested in a negotiated resolution of the crisis.

In another commentary in the "Washington City" column, published on March 16, the *Intelligencer* mixed the threat of war with the urge for restraint and patience. The commentary followed the newspaper's publication of two letters to the Spanish governor of Louisiana, one each from the Spanish and French ministers to the United States, in which both foreign ministers disavowed any desire of their governments to close New Orleans to American commerce. Noting that James Monroe had sailed for Europe a week earlier, the commentary praised him as the best emissary possible for such a mission. Citing the Spanish and French letters, the commentary said it would "take a degree of skepticism bordering on lunacy" not to conclude that the port closure had been the mistaken act of one individual rather than the dictate of either government.

The commentary concluded on an ominous note, however, regarding the threatened loss of the use of the New Orleans port: "There is, and can be but one opinion in America, and there is but one sentiment. The spirit that exists on the Atlantic is as indignant as that beyond the mountains; and if negotiation should fail, if moderate means should not avail; there is an appeal which the undissenting suffrage of America would call for, and which her united strength would render successful." Such a commentary, carried in the newspaper known to be speaking for Jefferson, must have been intended not only to assuage concerns among

Americans but also to publicly signal to the Spanish and French governments that the United States would use force if necessary to resolve the situation.[6] As noted previously, it was common practice for European ambassadors in the United States to send their governments copies of the *National Intelligencer* so that their leaders could gauge the positions of Jefferson's administration. Therefore, when the French were negotiating with Monroe over Louisiana, they could well have had in hand the March 16 commentary and other, similar material from the paper.

Another, more direct way the *Intelligencer* could indicate Jefferson's position on the New Orleans affair was to publish statements attributed to him. On March 18, the paper carried an excerpt from a March 3 article in the *Palladium*, a newspaper based in Frankfort, Kentucky. That article reported what the state's congressman, John Brown, had told the newspaper's editor about Jefferson's intentions after Brown recently returned from Washington. The "authenticity" of the information, the editor said, could not be doubted, as "Mr. Brown received it from the President himself, and has authorized us to make it public." The article said, first, that the congressman had been told by Jefferson that the United States had received assurances from France that the New Orleans port would be kept open to its shipping. Significantly, the article further reported that Jefferson had told Brown that his ultimate goal was the acquisition of at least part of the Louisiana Territory from France: "Mr. Jefferson further observed that although the re-establishment of things on their former footing was all we had a right to demand—experience had shown it would not be sufficient to ensure the protection of the western commerce, or to restore confidence to the minds of our citizens— the government would therefore make every exertion in its power to obtain one entire side of the Mississippi."

Similarly, on April 13, 1803, the *Intelligencer* reprinted a letter regarding the New Orleans situation from US Senator Joseph Anderson to his constituents in Nashville, Tennessee. Anderson reported that he had spoken personally with Jefferson and received the president's assurance that he had "taken immediate steps to have the injury redressed." Anderson said Jefferson had told him that the Spanish minister in Washington had shown "very great anxiety" over the situation and had immediately, by "express," sent his superiors a communication regarding it. The senator then wrote,

Our fellow citizens may rest assured, that nothing within the power of the Executive will be left undone, to restore to them (as speedily as possible) *all* the benefits which they have heretofore enjoyed, conformable to the Spanish treaty. If, however, the powers and exertions of the President, should not be able to effect this, to us, *all important,* and very desirable object, I feel authorized to say, that *we the people* (in conjunction with the Executive) will use our *best* endeavors to effect it.

With his letter, Anderson included the resolution the House had passed the previous day in support of Jefferson's handling of the matter.

The congressional members' accounts of their recent meetings with Jefferson show how the *Intelligencer* could be used to communicate Jefferson's positions on policy issues without anything coming directly from the president himself. Jefferson used respected leaders in the affected areas as his surrogates, to report to their constituents (and the public) what he was doing about the crisis. Through them, he could assure concerned Americans that he was actively trying to resolve the problem, that there was reason to believe it would be resolved peacefully through diplomatic means (even perhaps by purchasing some of the territory), and that if it were not resolved peacefully, then the nation's "best endeavors" would be employed to resolve it by other means—clearly a euphemism for the use of force.

Scholars have not previously noted these public communications by Jefferson through the *Intelligencer.* Dumas Malone, for example, describes the "noiseless course" that Jefferson pursued during the crisis.[7] Forrest McDonald similarly asserts that Jefferson avoided any public mention of acquiring territory from France, so that he could operate "without political interference."[8]

Obviously, the short-term solution to the crisis was to have the Spanish government confirm that the closure of the New Orleans port to American shipping had been a mistake by the superintendent of the port. Jefferson and his Secretary of State, James Madison, pursued that course of action, and on April 20, the *Intelligencer* announced they had succeeded. Under the heading "OFFICIAL" (printed in much larger type than usual), the paper carried the text of a letter to Madison from the Spanish minister in Washington. Dated the previous day, the letter informed Madison that the minister had received instructions from his government that the port should be reopened to American commerce. The minister said the news had been "brought by a Brig of war of the King my master, dispatched for this purpose alone," and that the dispatch had confirmed "all the assurances" the minister had previously given to the US government that the closure of the port had not been ordered by the Spanish government.[9]

In a May 13 commentary, the *Intelligencer* announced that in the cession of the Louisiana Territory by Spain to France, "*all our rights under the Spanish treaty were secured to us.*" This meant that even when possession of New Orleans passed to France, the American right to use the port, granted under the treaty between the United States and Spain, would continue. The essay was signed "Curtius," and the writer said the information was "from an authentic and undoubted source," which was clearly a way of saying that the information came from the administration itself.

"Curtius" marveled how well the crisis had been resolved. "Who can doubt," he asserted, "the policy, the wisdom and the justice of the present administration, or who doubt the madness, if not the iniquity of the leaders of the opposition, in their attempts to drive us into a war with France and Spain! For such would have been the consequence of our seizing upon New Orleans." Jefferson's wise conduct needed to be recognized, he said: "The time has now arrived in which the citizens of this country must appreciate the foresight and the conciliatory disposition of our executive."

The May 18 *Intelligencer* reprinted an essay originally published in the *Philadelphia Aurora* by Thomas Paine, entitled "To the Citizens of the United States." Paine argued that the Jefferson administration had wisely chosen diplomatic over military means to resolve the crisis. He contrasted the administration's calm, peace-loving approach with that of the "career of the former administration." The Adams presidency, Paine observed, had been marked by "uproar and extravagance" and had kept the country in "continual agitation and alarm" at the possibility of being drawn into the "troubles and tumults of the European world."

Jefferson's diplomatic efforts ultimately succeeded far more spectacularly when Napoleon offered to sell the United States all of the Louisiana Territory. On July 4, 1803, the *Intelligencer* reported, again in larger print and with the caption "OFFICIAL," that "the Executive ha[d] received official information" that the Louisiana Purchase Treaty had been signed in Paris on April 30. The timing of the one-paragraph announcement was remarkably fortuitous, making it possible to couple the news with a long commentary—perhaps authored by Jefferson himself, judging from its language—celebrating the American Revolution and the many blessings that had resulted from it. Inserted after the commentary was the text of the Declaration of Independence.

Over the course of several months, the *Intelligencer* carried a number of glowing articles extolling the benefits of the Louisiana Purchase. On July 25, it reprinted an *Aurora* article describing New Orleans as a "modern Alexandria, at the mouth of our American Nile," and predicting that "hence our ship-owners, mariners, manufacturers and mechanics will derive great and constant advantages from this new acquisition of territory." Many similar articles followed.[10] Two articles reported on celebrations in Kentucky (September 5) and Natchez (September 9); a resolution passed by the Pennsylvania legislature to celebrate the purchase was published in the *Intelligencer* on December 30.

The paper frequently carried responses to Federalist objections to the purchase. A number of articles responded to Federalist complaints that the purchase price was too high (August 29; September 12, 14, 30; October 10, 14). Others attacked Federalists for not having been fully supportive of the purchase. The September 2 issue carried a commentary, signed "Columbus," chastising Federalist newspapers for having tried to undermine the negotiations, so that the United States would instead have to go to war to get the territory. From reading those newspapers, the commentary charged, the French government might have concluded that the United States was not sincere in negotiating a settlement.

On September 26, the *Intelligencer* carried a satirical commentary signed "Watty Watersnake, Possum Town." "Watty" railed against the purchase, calling New Orleans a "paltry little island . . . [in] nothing but a downright swamp." He wished, as "all my brother *feds* most sincerely hope it will," that Jefferson and the "democrats" would get no credit for the purchase and all the blame if it led to anything bad.

On January 16, in print three times as large as normal, the *Intelligencer* published a lavish commentary marking the day Louisiana officially became part of the United States. The first paragraph of the commentary follows:

> AMERICANS! The event, for which we have all looked with so much solicitude, is at length realized. LOUISIANA is a part of the union— The acquisition is great and glorious in itself; but still greater and more glorious are the means by which it is obtained. In them are developed the energy and justice of a republican government, and its perfect competency; with the least practicable injury to others, to redress the wrongs and to secure the rights of the nation it protects. Never have mankind contemplated so vast and important an accession of empire by means so pacific and just. . . . May the example go forth to the world, and teach rulers the superiority of right to violence!

Then, the newspaper began publishing reports of celebrations. The January 23 issue described one in Alexandria and reprinted the texts of eighteen toasts given on that occasion, "accompanied," it said, "with martial music, and the utmost hilarity." The first toast, addressed to "citizens on both sides of the Mississippi," entreated that "one interest rivet the union." The second toast, to Jefferson, observed that "his enemies fear and admire him, his friends glory in their chief, and the world venerate[s] his wisdom." The tenth toast was bluntly partisan: "Federalist, tories, and royalists—may their principles never be disseminated in our newly acquired country." The January 25 issue featured the words of a song celebrating the peaceful acquisition of a territory described as bigger than France and England combined.

On January 30, the paper described a "most superb dinner" given by members of Congress to celebrate the purchase, with the president, vice president, and other officials of the executive department as guests. The members had escorted Jefferson from "his own house" to the celebration on Capitol Hill. His approach was "announced by a discharge of artillery," and he was "welcomed by a full band of music playing 'Jefferson's march.'" There were about a hundred attendees, and of them, the report declared, "An assemblage so numerous, to celebrate an event, at once so glorious and so happy, may not occur for centuries to come." Following seventeen toasts, Jefferson was serenaded by an "Ode, translated from the Latin, by one of the company, and adapted to the occasion." It ended with this stanza:

> To Jefferson, belov'd of Heav'n,
> May golden Peace be ever given,
> And when Death at last, shall come,
> To lay him in the silent tomb,
> May weeping Angels gather near,
> And Laurel strew around his bier,
> And waft him, on the wings of Love,
> To everlasting Peace above.

The February 3 issue described an even more lavish ball, held in Georgetown by a number of members of Congress to celebrate the acquisition. The assemblage of personages, "about 200 Ladies and near 300 Gentlemen," was described as "the most numerous and brilliant which has ever met in this district." The walls of the room were "decorated with festoons of Laurel," and at one end of the room, in the center, "was placed a transparent portrait of the President of the United States" that could be seen outside, reflected in the snow, for a "considerable distance." The report observed that the "most perfect good order, and the highest flow of hilarity were kept up," with "every difference of opinion or contrariety of intention being melted into one single and unanimous sentiment of social and patriotic joy." For months thereafter, the paper would publish many more such reports, including accounts of speeches, toasts, and poems glorifying the purchase.[11]

In its commentary on the following Fourth of July, in 1804, the *Intelligencer* noted that news of the signing of the Louisiana Purchase Treaty had reached the capital exactly one year earlier. Reflecting on the "happy completion of this great event," the commentary crowed that "the fears and awful forebodings, then so loudly run through the land, have been hushed and that vast territory has become ours without the effusion of one drop of blood."

As this chapter shows, readers of the *Intelligencer* would have received the complete Republican education about the Louisiana Purchase, the crisis that had led up to it, and Jefferson's perfect presidential leadership. First, those readers were assured that Jefferson was handling the crisis prudently, keeping the nation out of war for the time being but reserving that option if necessary. Then, with the news of the purchase, the president was portrayed as having acquired a spectacular jewel for the country, with no bloodshed, at a reasonable cost, and with the enthusiastic approval of the vast majority of Americans. As the story was portrayed in the *Intelligencer*, the country's trust in Jefferson had indeed been well placed.

CHAPTER 9

Getting Reelected

The young American Republic faced a critical time in 1804. It was a presidential election year, with Republicans aiming for Jefferson's reelection and increased Republican representation in Congress, governorships, and state legislatures across the country. Federalists, in turn, wanted just the opposite. On a deeper level, both parties were fighting to impose their visions of the public interest on the new nation and its governmental institutions. The *National Intelligencer* naturally played a key role for Republicans in these battles. As will be seen in this chapter, the paper took a number of approaches in advocating for Jefferson and Republicanism.

One approach is reflected in the "official" material the *Intelligencer*'s editor chose to publish. For example, in the early months of 1804, in issue after issue, the paper carried reports of the debates in the House and Senate over the proposed amendment to the US Constitution that would require presidential electors to cast separate votes for a president and a vice president. This amendment, ratified later in 1804 as the Twelfth Amendment, was strongly supported by Republicans, who wanted to avoid a repeat of the 1800 election, and was vehemently opposed by most Federalists. (Not surprisingly, the *Intelligencer* mostly published excerpts of congressional speeches favoring the amendment.) As discussed previously, the paper also carried long accounts of the debates and congressional reports regarding Republican efforts to impeach Supreme Court Justices John Pickering and Samuel Chase.

Throughout 1804, the paper frequently found a place for reports of favorable state official proceedings. On January 4, for instance, it published a resolution passed by the South Carolina legislature praising Thomas Jefferson for his conduct as president in acquiring the Louisiana Territory. That action, the resolution said, was proof that Jefferson would do everything possible to secure peace and honor for the country.

Similarly, on July 2, the paper published a resolution that was passed by a majority of the New Hampshire legislature and was full of pro-Republican rhetoric. The resolution first lamented that "the presses of the United States are daily teeming with abuse and invective" spread "through the medium of free press . . . to alienate the affections of the people from the general government, and to abuse and vilify the President and principal officers of the United States." The legislators then affirmed their "fullest confidence in the justice, benevolence and wisdom of the President of the United States" and cited the Louisiana Purchase as having "secured to us those rights which were lately invaded without an appeal to arms." Probably as a reflection of the fierce electoral battles going on between Republicans and Federalists in Eastern states like New Hampshire, the *Intelligencer* also somewhat surprisingly printed the protest Federalist state legislators made to the resolution. In the dissenters' view, such resolutions could only "increase the flame of party contentions which already threaten the destruction of our happy country." As for the Louisiana Purchase, they said its accomplishment "without the expense of blood" was irrelevant. The price had been far too high, they contended, and the acquisition had brought in an "unwieldly and undefined territory" that could result in the "total dissolution of th[e] confederation."

In another unusual example, the *Intelligencer* of October 26 reprinted, from the New Orleans *Moniteur,* the texts of a letter Jefferson had received from the Ursuline nuns in New Orleans and his reply. In their letter, the nuns asked Jefferson, as president, to assure them that their title to their convent and home and school for the young was secure after New Orleans had come under the jurisdiction of the United States via the Louisiana Purchase. They said they were pleading for this assurance not on their own behalf but for the "cause of the orphan, of the helpless child, of want, of the many who may be snatched from the paths of vice and infamy under their guidance, and be trained up in the habits of virtue and religion to be happy and useful." Jefferson replied in kind. He assured the nuns that their property would be preserved "sacred and inviolate" and that they would be permitted to "govern themselves by their own voluntary rules without interference from the civil authority." He praised the nuns for their work in furthering the "wholesome purposes of society, by training up its younger members in the way they should go." Obviously, Jefferson had seen the communication from the nuns as an opportunity to publicly reinforce his commitment to religious freedom, his appreciation for the role of religion in society, and the separation of church and state.[1] (Interestingly, Jefferson's more stridently worded letter of January 1, 1802, to the Danbury Baptists, in which he famously asserted that there should be a "wall of separation" between church and state and that religious beliefs were solely a matter of individual conscience, was not published in the *Intelligencer*. As Peter Onuf has noted, the sentiments in the letter to the Baptists may not have been shared by a majority of Americans at the time.[2] That realization might have been the reason for not publishing the letter.)

Although such reports of official proceedings or actions were obviously printed in the *National Intelligencer* for political purposes, they were published there without commentary and were relatively few in number. Much more frequently, the paper was publishing a variety of more explicitly electoral material. This included reports on events and topics of particular importance or advantage to Republicans—candidate promotion and overt political commentary.

In the February 29 issue, the paper reported on the recent Republican congressional caucus that had chosen the party's nominees for president and vice president. It noted the unanimous nomination of Jefferson for president and the nomination, "by a very large majority," of New York governor George Clinton for vice president. No mention was made of Aaron Burr.

The next issue, published on March 2, fawned, "It would be a work of supererogation to attempt any eulogium upon the political deportment of THOMAS JEFFERSON. . . . [H]e was emphatically denominated the *man of the people*, and . . . in the discharge of the high duties of his station, he has demonstrated that the honorable epithet was not misapplied." The nominations were sure to be welcomed, the *Intelligencer* proclaimed, by "the friends of liberty throughout the union." Dozens more such glowing commentaries would appear in the newspaper throughout 1804.

Some other commentaries, though, reflected the partisan rancor of the time. For example, on July 11, an essay signed "Franklin" began by praising the "superior talents and patriotism which distinguish the *present* from the *former administration*." He said the national government was now headed by "a *band of patriots*," whose wisdom and prudence had produced an "unparalleled state of prosperity." Still, "Franklin" complained, Federalists were attacking Jefferson with "the most glaring *misrepresentations*" and "*scurrilous attacks* upon the private character of the chief magistrate of our country." The essay described the Federalists' daily diminishing "faction" as "implacable in their enmity to the President." Fortunately, "Franklin" said, "their *arrows* though *dipped* in *wormwood* and *gall*, and *stained* with *malice* and *aimed* with *fury* and *vengeance* are *ineffective*."

Federalist Attempts at "Disunion"

In his July 11 *Intelligencer* essay, "Franklin" also complained that Federalists were trying to "prejudice the eastern people, against their fellow-citizens of the south, particularly against the Virginians." Themes of North-South conflict and anti-Virginia prejudice would be raised repeatedly in the paper. On May 25, another "Franklin" essay railed against the "*self-stiled federalists*," those "enemies of the government," who "actually contemplate a dissolution of the union." Acknowledging the political power of newspapers, "Franklin" said that while such outrageous reports would once "have been hardly credited," they now had to be taken seriously because "many of the opposition papers have of late avowed [such] sentiments," thus manifesting "the real views and designs of this party, at least of its leaders." Saying that "the cry of what is called *Virginia influence* is now the *order of the day*" among the Federalists, "Franklin" argued that, to the contrary, James Madison was "almost the only Virginian who holds an office of importance under the administration."

Similarly, the July 13 issue pronounced that Federalists were "anxious to bring about a northern and a southern party." This charge was in a commentary the paper reprinted from the *Richmond Enquirer*, entitled "The Vindication of Virginia" and signed "A Virginian." The commentary was to be part of a series showing "that the principal complaints . . . made against Virginia, have sprung rather from the invidious policy of party spirit, than from an enlightened view of our political history." "Virginian" identified the attacks as dangerous because they were not "confined to a small number of northern federalists" but had "crept into the high-toned prints of Boston, New York, Philadelphia, and other northern towns." The commentary asserted that, like the election of 1800, the 1804 election would be another national referendum in which Americans would be asked to choose between two opposing views of government. Federalists, he said, "wished to strengthen the federal government by lessening the power of the states and liberties of the people," whereas

Republicans "viewed with suspicious vigilance the gradual encroachments of the general government upon the rights of the states or of individuals."[3]

On September 26, the *Intelligencer* reprinted a commentary from the *National Aegis* addressed to the "Men of Massachusetts." It warned that the ultimate effect of Federalist anti-union arguments would be "*Civil War!*" Reinforcing this argument, the October 17 *Intelligencer* reprinted an editorial from the *Republican Advocate* that asserted, "It is better to go to the election ground than to the field of battle. Voting is easier than fighting. Federalism breeds war; republicanism bears peace. You who have wives and children, think upon it."

On October 31, the paper printed a long commentary, signed "Concordia," in which the writer spoke of being finally forced to take the talk of disunion seriously after having read it in the Federalist newspapers. He claimed that the "dismemberment of the federal union" was now being portrayed in those papers as a "measure *devoutly to be wished for*" and charged, "[t]his, then, is federalism with a vengeance." The commentary belittled the Federalists as "a few vain-glorious individuals" who, thanks to the luck of speculation or inheritance, operate under the "conceit that they are a superior order of beings." It concluded by condemning the talk of "dissolution" as an attempt to "counteract one of the great dispensations of Providence, which God in his goodness has intended for the human race."

Sarcasm and Satire

Then, as now, sarcasm and satire were weapons in political battles. In its first issue in 1804, on January 2, the *Intelligencer* carried an example. Entitled "Ruins" and signed "One of the ruined citizens of the United States," it responded to an anti-Republican commentary in the previous day's *Washington Federalist*.[4] According to the *Intelligencer*, the commentary was "a lamentable tale of the 'Jefferson' system of ruins brought upon the United States." Those "ruins" were said to have included the US "army, navy, judiciary, bankrupt[cy] system, internal taxes, and the mint." Observing facetiously that the *Federalist* had "strangely forgotten to enumerate other equally important ruins produced by the same 'Jefferson' system of administration," the writer asked the *Intelligencer*'s editor for "leave to supply [them] for the benefit of the Washington Federalist and its supporters, through the medium of your useful Gazette." The writer then listed other "ruins": the "marine corps, sedition law, alien law, federalism, and monarchy." "Last of all," the writer said, had been the ruin of the American people, who now found themselves in a most "*unfortunate* and *distressing* state of public affairs." The list of those affairs was long: under Jefferson, a "long and bloody war" had been avoided, the country was at peace and respected abroad, and its people were "happy at home . . . in the full enjoyment of liberty and independence with a national credit and reputation unknown and unequalled by any other people in any other nation or empire."

The *Intelligencer* of August 3 published an imagined report of Federalists caucusing in the Capitol to discuss how to win the upcoming election. In this fictionalized account, Federalists conceded they could not contest the measures of the administration, which had the "confidence of the people." Instead, they agreed, their only chance was to undermine the "public esteem" for the administration through "gradual and insidious means." So they would arrange to demean the public and private character of Republicans through their own Federalist newspapers, sure that the administration would be "too magnanimous to appeal to law for redress." The exchange concluded with their claimed political strategy: "Above all things, never abandon one ground. Endeavor to convince the people that they are miserable; and that the national character is the scorn of the world." In a similar vein, the *Intelligencer* of October 8 satirized the view of America that Federalists were promoting. According to them, "America is one of the greatest curiosities the world ever produced," burdened by

> a president "drenching his country in blood" by averting war, and cultivating peace—evincing "infidelity," by steady attendance upon public worship and liberal donations for the support of Christianity. . . . A people oppressed with light taxes; ruined and involved in bankruptcy by an annual saving of millions, a full treasury, and a rapid decrease of national debt—establishing a military despotism for want of [a] Standing Army!

Another "Franklin" campaign piece appeared in the October 10 issue. The essay begins aggressively, charging that Federalist newspapers were full of "falsehood, misrepresentation, scurrility, and personal abuse." The writer then argued that the best way to judge the Federalist opposition is to take a "retrospective view" of the measures they enacted when they were in power in the beginning of the new national government. He attributed the advent of "party spirit" to the vote by the Federalist majority in Congress, over the objections of James Madison and other Republicans, to assume all the state debts incurred during the Revolutionary War, even though most of it had been bought cheap by speculators who would reap all the profits in place of the original lenders. "Franklin" explained how that "obnoxious act," coupled with a complicated system of public finances, "created a powerful opposition to the then Secretary of the Treasury and his friends in Congress." During the Adams administration, the essay continued, Americans then saw

> an army raised in time of peace, who in all probability were ready to support any of the despotic and ruinous measures of government. They saw almost daily, numbers of their fellow citizens thrown into dungeons for having virtue and patriotism enough to denounce these arbitrary measures, and for asserting those rights and privileges which were secured to them by the constitution. In a word our citizens saw the *"reign of terror,"* completely established in this country, and were convinced that nothing short of an entire change in the administration could preserve their liberties.

Under Jefferson, "Franklin" observed, things were vastly better. The army had been reduced, internal taxes repealed, a "vast number of useless offices" abolished, the public debt reduced every year, and the Louisiana Territory acquired for an "inconsiderable sum when compared with the advantages which will result to the American Republic."

The essay ends by warning that Federalists, even though they "despair of preventing the re-election of our *illustrious President*," will nevertheless make every effort to "*excite divisions* of the friends of the administration." In particular, therefore, care had to be exercised by Republicans in selecting their presidential electors. Republicans should appoint no one "unless they are fully convinced of his firmness, & attachments to *republicanism*. The *intrigues* of some *pretended patriots* have already been discovered, and they have justly lost the confidence of the public."

Another satirical piece appeared in the October 19 issue, addressed to the editor of the *Intelligencer* and signed "A Friend." It portrayed a dialogue "between two staunch Tories," as the writer archly described them, adding, "for I will not term them Federalists." The writer explained he was passing the dialogue on to readers of the *Intelligencer* so that, when they heard similar arguments, "the latent motive may be understood." In the imagined dialogue, the two Federalists wrestled with the difficulty of coming up with a good political campaign strategy to counter the successes of the Jefferson administration over the past four years.

The "Tories," labeled "A" and "B," began by considering, "How shall we conduct the ensuing campaign?" They agreed that if a war with Spain broke out, they could argue it should have been fought earlier, when Spain was unprepared and before the United States had paid out $15 million to France for Louisiana. They acknowledged, though, that peace was likely to continue. If so, "B" said, "we may dwell upon the President's pusillanimity, and expatiate upon national dignity, honor, glory, etc.— these are fine topics for eloquence." Agreeing that those were "certainly noble themes for declamation," Tory "A" then pointed out other problems for Federalists: the "damned democrats produce their treaties for compensation to our merchants by the Belligerent powers [France and England]"; and that "cursed calculator, [Treasury Secretary] Gallatin, is constantly giving statements of increased imports and exports, and of increasing revenue." "B" acknowledged that all seemed good in the country, but suggested they could always "complain of partiality in appointments, and by urging this with vehemence inflame the people, who always wish for a change, and look to men more than measures." "A" was not convinced this tactic would work, because "the people . . . are become free-thinkers and free agents," and will now "not risk their comforts, fortunes or lives without some real grievance, or great exciting cause." Unfortunately, he added, "We erred in predicting anarchy before, and alarm is now not so easily disseminated." Recognizing the problem presented by all this good news, "B" urged his partner to not give up hope; there are always circumstances, he said, "which ably handled can annoy the government, and keep up the hopes of our party." The dialogue ended with the two hoping for some misfortune to change their dismal electoral outlook:

A. We have made every exertion for four years to very little effect, and I see no prospects of a change.

B. I must candidly acknowledge, that Jefferson has been more prudent than I expected: but let us rely on the chapter of accidents; it is impossible for him always to run an uninterrupted career of prosperity—So keep up your spirits; retrospection is fruitless, look forward with hope.

The Fourth of July

At least as portrayed in the *National Intelligencer*, the Fourth of July had, by 1804, become the major holiday in America.[5] It obviously presented promotional opportunities for Jefferson and Republicanism. Jefferson was linked to the day as the author of the Declaration of Independence, and the natural inclination to celebrate the continuing glory of the American Revolution could be translated easily into proof that Jefferson's presidency and the principles of Republicanism deserved most of the credit for those good times.

The *Intelligencer* began its "coverage" of the holiday in its July 4 issue, with a patriotic, elegantly written essay entitled "The Day." In two full columns of the paper and in language that suggests the possibility Jefferson himself wrote it, the essay presents an inspiring history of a divinely favored and popularly governed America. It begins by stating that there is "no country more deeply indebted for the happiness she enjoys, to the Supreme disposer of events, than the United States." From the "vigorous germ" of the Jamestown and Pilgrim settlers, America was now the largest empire in the world. It was also a bold new model of governance to the world. With the American Revolution, a "new day" had dawned and made "the PEOPLE the basis of all power." To them "it assigned the power of raising up and of putting down their rulers; not with the fury of a mob, but with the calm decision of an enlightened judgment." On "this MIGHTY FOUNDATION our governments, our laws, our liberty rest." So "successful has this experiment been in rendering us happy," the commentary exclaimed, "that we fearlessly predict its adoption, at some future period, by every nation of the civilized world. A century hence, and our population will exceed fifty millions. The example of such a nation enjoying peace and prosperity will be irresistible. The world will know and imitate it."

In eight other issues, the first published on July 6 and the last on October 19, the *Intelligencer* carried reports of Fourth of July celebrations around the country.[6] After describing the celebrations, the reports usually printed the toasts that had been given. In the rank of toasts, Thomas Jefferson, as president, always preceded any other living person and any reference to current events or institutions. Among the toasts printed in the July 9 issue were, first, one to "the day we celebrate"; second, one to "The President—whose virtues afford an ample shield to repel the bolts of his enemies, without the aid of a Sedition Act"; third, one to

"The government of the United States—the world's last and best hope"; fourth, one to "The Congress of the United States"; and, fourteenth out of seventeen, one to "The Tree of Liberty—May it never produce Burrs."

The July 16 issue reported on a celebration in "Powhatan County," which included toasts to the American patriots of '76, the Constitution, Louisiana, Thomas Jefferson, the memory of Washington, a free press, the Republicans of Connecticut and Massachusetts, and the youth of America. There was an intriguing toast to "The Fair Sex," who were likened to "the women who saved Rome when Cariolanus thundered at her gates. May they be virtuous, generous, and patriotic." Cariolanus was a Roman general and politician whose story was told by Plutarch and turned into a political play of the same name by William Shakespeare. Portrayed by Shakespeare as a "proud and conceited Roman aristocrat" who had "nothing but contempt for the people," Cariolanus achieved his fame chiefly by having been dissuaded by the pleas of his wife and mother from burning Rome down as an act of political revenge.[7] Thus, the toast would have been taken as yet another dig at Federalists, as well as an entreaty that the women of America use their persuasive resources to resist the modern-day threat Federalism posed to the survival of the American republic.

The *Intelligencer*'s accounts of the festivities sometimes had an aggressive political cast, as illustrated in its July 13 description of a "GLORIOUS CELEBRATION" in Boston on July 4. It began, "Yesterday, there was a republican Triumph at Faneuil Hall, where upwards of two hundred Citizens assembled to celebrate our political emancipation." The account then turned into an attack on Federalists, charging that "an insidious and baneful party" had sought, for the past ten years, "to introduce the elements of an aristocracy under various, specious disguises." All along, they had worked to "seditiously interweave one word for the prosperity of America, amid twenty for the prosperity of Great Britain."

After toasts to "The Day," "The People," and "The American States United and Indivisible," the next toast at the Boston celebration was to "Our beloved President THOMAS JEFFERSON, whose eulogy is proclaimed in the prosperity of his country and the despair of her enemies"; it was followed by a salute of nine guns. There were twenty-four toasts in all, including one to "our sister state Virginia" and another against "Ely's Amendment," a proposed amendment to the Constitution to remove the three-fifths rule and only count freemen for representation in the House of Representatives. Two other toasts concerned the politics of Massachusetts: one favored the Republicans' preferred selection method for presidential electors, and the other referred to the "Federal plot lately contrived to blow up the republicans, on the 5th of November [the general election day in the state]; may it prove as disastrous to them as the powder plot did to the Roman Catholics." Another toast honored "The federal Judiciary—May the sanctuary of justice never be outraged by the oppressor's wrong, or the madman's profanity."[8]

Aaron Burr

In 1804, there would only be a few mentions in the *Intelligencer* of the political status of Aaron Burr and of why he had been denied renomination as vice president.[9] On April 20, the paper carried an "Address to the Republican Voters of New York," written by a committee of the New York State Republican Party to explain why they had not chosen Burr as their nominee for governor. The committee noted, "Mr. Burr has long been publicly accused of intriguing with federalists at the last presidential election." Whether the accusations were "with or without foundation," they said, was not "for us to pronounce." They did, however, point out that Burr had not received "a single vote" for renomination as vice president at the party's recent congressional nominating caucus, which was "high evidence that suspicions exist to Mr. Burr's prejudice on the ground of republicanism."[10] The committee urged all Republicans in New York to avoid any support for Burr, warning that most of Burr's supporters were Federalists and that his candidacy for governor was part of a Federalist plan to "*divide and conquer*" the Republicans.

On its front page on April 23, probably to reinforce the New York committee's warning about supporting Burr, the *Intelligencer* reprinted a humorous fable that had appeared in the *Hampshire Gazette*. It told the story of a man who had been asked for his written opinion on two matters, one involving quarreling church members, and the other on directions to the manager of his farm. Somehow, the messages were misdirected, and the one to the farm manager was given to the church members. When they opened the message, they at first did not understand what it meant: "You will see to the repair of the fences, that they be built high and strong, and you will take special care of the *old Black Bull.*" After some thought, however, they decided it was just the advice they needed. They realized they must "keep out strange cattle from the fold" and "in a very particular manner set a watchful guard over the Devil, the *old Black Bull,* who has done us so much hurt of late." Because the church members followed this advice, the story explained, "peace and harmony were restored to the long afflicted church."

The only direct political discussion of Burr by the *Intelligencer* itself would come on May 16, after Burr had lost his attempt to win the governorship of New York. The *Intelligencer* reported that Burr had received no support for renomination as the Republican vice presidential candidate because "he had by his conduct forfeited the national confidence." The paper asserted that when Burr had then failed to obtain the Republican nomination for the governorship of New York, he should have withdrawn from the race. Instead, Burr had run and had received the votes of "the *federalists*, and the *federalists alone*." The result, Burr's loss and the election of the Republican nominee, was "glorious to the cause of republicanism." The election had demonstrated the "prevalence of principle among the republicans of the United States" and had averted a "serious division" among Republicans that could have extended beyond New York and reached the "friends of the general government."

The paper concluded its treatment of Burr on May 25, in the "Franklin" essay previously discussed. Thwarted in their attempts to "destroy the popularity of our chief patriotic Magistrate," "Franklin" charged, Federalists had "by art and intrigue" tried to "effect a division among the friends of the administration." During the previous session of Congress, he said, Federalists had tried to "form a party under the banners of a man (who had long been denounced as an apostate to the principles he once professed)." "Fortunately for the cause of republicanism," he said, "those intrigues were discovered and measure[s] taken to counteract them."

State Elections

The *Intelligencer* regularly reported and commented on matters of electoral interest to Republicans at the state level. On February 5, April 6, and September 14, for example, it published the lists of the Republican presidential elector nominees for Maryland, Pennsylvania, and Massachusetts, respectively. The paper also regularly printed election results, especially in the New England "battleground" states where Republicans were trying to make inroads on the previous Federalist dominance. Massachusetts was particularly a prize Republicans hoped to wrest from the Federalists.

On April 13, the *Intelligencer* carried a message by the Republican

Party of Massachusetts to the voters of that state. The message included a lengthy indictment of Federalism and the measures of the Adams administration, as well as an equally long defense of the Jefferson administration. It argued to Massachusetts voters that their votes in the upcoming state election would be determining the "momentous question for the whole human race," which was "whether the anglo-federal system shall be restored, with all its attendants and consequences, or that of the republican administration be continued in its present prosperous state." On May 2, the paper reprinted, from the *Boston Chronicle,* another address "To the People of Massachusetts," arguing that the state legislature election in Massachusetts would be "of infinite consequence to the whole nation." It warned, "Unless this state shall have a republican house of representatives this year, there will be much done towards sowing those seeds of discord among the states, which will tend strongly to a dissolution of the federal government and to a subversion of our nation."[11] On April 20, after the results were known for various elections in New Hampshire, Massachusetts, Connecticut, Vermont, and Rhode Island, the *Intelligencer* surveyed with joy the "rapid growth of Republicanism" in those states. The commentary found Rhode Island and Vermont "now completely reformed," New Hampshire now almost equally divided between Republicans and Federalists, and Massachusetts making huge electoral strides toward Republican majorities.

As these electoral commentaries illustrate, a major thrust of all the paper's reporting and commentary was to "nationalize" state and local elections in New England by turning them into referendums on Republicanism versus Federalism. This evidence from the *Intelligencer* supports the conclusion of Noble Cunningham Jr. that, to a significant degree, the Republican Party was a "new growth that sprang from the divisions in Congress and the national government; it was a product of national rather than state politics."[12] It also undermines the more recent judgments of other scholars, such as John Gerring and Daniel Klinghard, that true political parties, as measured by having a nationalized political ideology and organization, only appeared decades later in America.

Gerring asserted that in the early 1800s, "Subpresidential elections tended to be based on personal ties rather than abstract ideologies. This was an age of 'deferential' politics, . . . an age in which it was not necessary to form cohesive ties either within legislatures or within the general electorate."[13] Similarly, Klinghard asserted that party leaders began working in the late 1800s to "craft a truly national party-in-the-electorate" that required "national party politics" to be "defined and defended." The result was a political "transformation," he said, because "the parties had been originally organized to resist just this kind of nationalization."[14] Gerring's and Klinghard's assessments simply do not match up with the *Intelligencer*'s nationalized, rabidly partisan approach toward the 1804 state elections.[15]

Another problem that must be noted is with Klinghard's assertion that a "definitive feature" of the new approach toward political parties at the turn of the nineteenth century was a "new means of mobilizing national politics called the educational campaign, the premise of which was that local prejudices had to be enlarged and replaced by 'educated' views on questions of public policy."[16] To the contrary, as this book shows, "educating" the public in this way was actually a central component of Jefferson's (and Madison's) political philosophy, and one of the main functions of the *National Intelligencer*.

On May 16, the paper featured the words of a "New Song, taken from the Boston Chronicle," that it said represented "a becoming temper in the republicans of that town." The song, sung to the tune of "Yankee Doodle," began:

> We'er all asleep, the federalists say,
>   And never will awaken,
> But on the next election day
>   We'll shew them they're mistaken.
>   *Chorus*
> Republicans in freedom's cause,
>   Will make a glorious stand sir,
> And guard their government and laws
> From faction's furious band sir.

The June 20 issue celebrated Republican success in New Hampshire by reprinting a report from the *New Hampshire Gazette* headlined "New Hampshire politically regenerated." Another headline in the report spoke of the "old republican spirit of New Hampshire revived" and of "the delusion of false federalism dissipated by the light of truth." On the same page, the paper reprinted a commentary, entitled "Serious Questions, and True Answers," from the *True American*. The commentary asked why Federalists impugned the "private characters of public officials" and used "misrepresentation and falsehood" when attacking "public measures." The answer was that Federalism could not stand up to genuine "facts and arguments." How was it, the commentary asked sarcastically, that Federalism had been "defeated in almost every quarter of the Union by the *illiterate* and *half witted* democrats (as they contemptuously style the republicans)?" The answer was simple: "Because the cause of Federalism IS A BAD ONE . . . while the cause of republicanism IS A GOOD ONE." The commentary concluded by asserting that "*truth*, even without talents or learning," would cause Republicanism to grow and prosper.

Responding to Federalist pamphleteering, an October 15 *Intelligencer* commentary said, "The best Pamphlet that can be read on public men and measures, is the Pamphlet of Experience." It urged that when citizens "see another federal pamphlet or take up a federal newspaper to read," they should "compare it with the volume of experience—a volume which is widespread before you, and is near you, even in your mouth and in your hearts, in your barns, in your houses and in your coffers, the volume of Mr. Jefferson's administration." The commentary concluded by warning voters not to exchange their current happiness for "visionary dreams and unsubstantial pretenses."

When the November election in Massachusetts for presidential electors and state representatives produced Republican majorities for the first time, the *Intelligencer* rejoiced. The November 23 issue reprinted an essay from the Worcester *National Aegis* that, after hailing the "dawn of FREEDOM'S day" over the "hills of Massachusetts," boasted,

> With cordial congratulations on the glorious result of the late important election, we salute our republican friends in every part of the union: The return of Massachusetts to the principles of republicanism, forms an era in her history, on which patriotism will delight to dwell. . . . The issue of the late election will be quoted as the most illustrious triumph of Republican energy over "*powers and principalities*," wealth, influence and hypocrisy. . . . The defeat was total—the victory complete. . . . They [Federalists] have been defeated on their own ground.

On November 30, the *Intelligencer* printed its own gloating commentary on the Massachusetts elections.

> This colossus of federalism, which has so long and so vigorously resisted the tide of popular opinion, has at length, . . . asserted her claim to republican character, [and] she has proclaimed to the union the origin of a new political era in the East [that] . . . proves the

people of the United States to be one people. . . . The measures of the administration of the general government were made the criterion; measures emphatically those of peace, economy, and moderation.— These were loudly and vehemently denounced. . . . The republicans, the sleeping Sampsons of New England, awoke from their slumbers. . . . They fought and triumphed.

The *Intelligencer* commentary's comparison of Republicans to the biblical character Sampson evokes several classic Republican themes. One was that except for a small group of irredeemable Federalists, the great mass of Americans shared the same Republican principles. Another was that the great "will of the people" was irresistible, just like Sampson's strength. Finally, the reference to the awakening of a sleeping Sampson echoes the same theme found in the "Liberty" play (discussed in chapter 4) that celebrated Jefferson's election. The theme (also alluded to in the *Yankee Doodle* song discussed above) was that many Americans had been lulled into a virtual slumber during the era of Federalism but, fortunately, had reawakened in time to take their country back to its proper, founding (Republican) principles.

Defending and Praising Jefferson

There was, of course, a constant stream of Federalist newspaper campaign claims to which the *Intelligencer* could respond. One way the paper approached the task was to print rebuttals in a series headlined "Federal Misrepresentations." Every time the paper responded to a particular statement in a Federalist newspaper, the *Intelligencer* response was numbered as the latest in the series.[17]

Typically, an *Intelligencer* reply first quoted a claim (sometimes even reprinting the whole article) that had been published in a Federalist newspaper. The *Intelligencer* would then provide the Republican response. For instance, on April 11, 1804, the *Intelligencer* reprinted, in full, the Federalist *New York Evening Post*'s scathing description of an event involving Jefferson and a "Mammoth Loaf" of bread, about twelve feet by two feet, which Washington bakers had carried, with great ceremony, into a Senate committee room next to the Senate chamber. According to the *Post* account, the bakers also brought along a "huge cold roasted sirloin and two quarter casks, one containing wine and the other the more republican liquor cyder." In the *Post*'s telling, Jefferson had behaved boorishly,

and the crowd gathered for the free food and drink had become so boisterous that the Senate had been forced to adjourn. The *Post* said it had
no doubt Jefferson had schemed to create the "mob procession" to demonstrate, before leaving town, that he was, "in reality and practically, the
Man of the people."

The *Intelligencer* essentially labeled the story fake news, saying that
there had not been the "least disorder" and that the Senate proceedings had not been interrupted. It provided a point-by-point refutation of
some of the most "mischievous" charges. A few days later, on April 25,
the bread story appeared again in the *Intelligencer*. The paper reprinted a
claim, from the Federalist *Boston Repertory*, that when Jefferson had seen
the giant loaf and beverages, he had "sneeringly compared the unhal-
lowed bread and wine . . . to the sacred symbols of our Redeemer's sacrifice." The *Intelligencer* said only, "We shall offer no comment on the above
falsehood; we are confident that no man in America believes it."

An item on May 2 dealt with another attack on Jefferson that had
been published in the *Boston Repertory*. That attack, which the *Intelligencer*
published in full on its first page, alleged that Jefferson was heading the
effort by Southern states to dominate the Union at the expense of the
Northern states. Even the Louisiana Purchase was cited as part of the
conspiracy. The *Repertory* commentary is quoted at length here to convey
a sense of the raw political discourse of the time.

But by his [Jefferson's] *pretensions* he has achieved every object which
Virginia and her Southern allies wished for. He has brought to cooperate with him, in the Northern states, all the enthusiasts of a good
cause, and all the leveling, blood thirsty ruffians of a bad one. The
herd of foreign renegadoes [*sic*] echo his success, and his triumphal
car drawn by a million of enslaved Negroes, drives over the necks
of those who have not bent the neck to Baal. And are WE to submit
to the guidance & the tyranny of the South? Are the states from the
Chesapeake to the River St. Croix to be only the satellites of Virginia?
That fact is, that our Representatives yield with feeble resistance to
the current that carries them away. . . . There was not found one
man in Congress . . . who had the spirit to bring forward an amendment [to the Constitution] by which the aristocratical influence of
the Southern states should be checked—by which their millions of
Negro slaves should cease to be represented in Congress. Is there anything more scandalous in the abuse of the British Constitution, than
this mockery of representation? Are the rotten boroughs of England

more infamous than our Negro boroughs? Why should *their* slaves be represented if denied the right of suffrage, in preference to *our* horses and oxen? There is this principle adopted in all republics. The representatives are always taken from the people represented. Let us then have at least, their Members in black—real Negroes. Will Mr. Jefferson who certainly has no scruples, when he wishes to debauch the wife of a friend, or defraud his creditors, or recompense a flattery, or get rid of an enemy, will he make any delicate objections? Or are we to believe the account of the French traveler in the southern states, who mentions that though a Planter would have no objection to sleep with a slave, he would disdain to see her sitting at the same table.[18]

Also on its first page, the *Intelligencer* carried a point-by-point refutation of the *Repertory* piece's charges about Jefferson's official conduct. Regarding the innuendos, the response said it would not "descend to take any notice of the vulgar and pitiful calumnies so impotently leveled against the private character of Mr. Jefferson," and predicted that "the lot of his traducers will be that infamy which they unblushingly attempt to fix upon him."[19]

In May, news arrived of Stephen Decatur's successful recapture and destruction of an American ship that had been seized by pirates in Tripoli. On May 28, after having devoted several issues to the news, the *Intelligencer* complained that Federalists were denigrating even that success. The commentary said the Federalists' rule was simple: "Everything is to be condemned."

On September 12, the *Intelligencer* took a similar approach to criticism from another newspaper, the *Charleston Courier*, about Jefferson's dress and behavior in public. The *Courier* had said his actions were "greatly reprehensible," beneath "the dignity of that office," and "cheapen the authority of the magistrate in vulgar estimation."[20] Specifically, the *Courier* had charged, Jefferson was known to "dress with shabby frugality, whether real or affected, to ride to Congress without an attendant, and hitching his horse's bridle on a peg, leave it to stand there while he himself is employed in the public discharge of his great trust." Introducing its reprint of the *Courier*'s commentary, the *Intelligencer* said only, "The following extract is from the *Charlotte Courier*. Need we inform our readers that the print is *federal*. We offer it as an evidence of the ignorance and folly of many of those who attempt to lead the public opinion."

In addition to many such replies to specific Federal attacks, the *Intelligencer* also printed occasional general responses to what it characterized as the basic rhetorical strategies of its Federalist newspaper opponents. One example of that technique is found in the June 20 paper, which reprinted from the *True American* an essay, signed "Plain Truth," that critiqued Federalist newspapers in general. The critique took the form of what the essay called "Serious Questions, and True Answers" about how the Federalist newspapers did their work.

> Why do the Federal papers, in treating of public measures, resort to *misrepresentation* and *falsehood?*
> Because if those measures were *fairly* and *truly* represented by them, every honest reader they have, would become a supporter of the administration.
> Why do the Federal papers substitute *assertions* and *abuse*, for *facts* and *arguments?*
> Because *facts* and *arguments* all make against them, and would, if used, effect their own destruction.

Sometimes, the *Intelligencer* would preface its reprint of a specific Federalist newspaper attack with a broad attack on all Federalist newspapers. An example is the *Intelligencer's* response, on July 25, to the *Boston Repertory's* claim that recent Republican electoral successes in Massachusetts were just proof that in democratic governments, "demagogues who are instinctively skillful in all base arts will inevitably come to govern the 'multitude.'" The *Intelligencer* said derisively,

> The following extract from the *Boston Repertory* is a specimen of the matter with which that and many other federal New England prints are constantly filled. They breathe the utmost violence of denunciation against Virginia, and democratic governments. As power is passing from their hands, their political passions rise, until they have really swelled to a tempest, in which all coolness and reason are drowned.

On November 9, in three columns of extra-large type that filled one page of the paper, the *Intelligencer* published the Annual Message Jefferson had delivered to Congress the previous day at noon. The paper then devoted its next three issues (November 12, 16, and 19) to a detailed, effusive commentary on the message. The overall tone is exemplified by its description of life in the United States under Jefferson: "If all is not sunshine, we may truly affirm that no portion of the world has ever enjoyed a more cloudless sky."

In a separate commentary on November 19, the *Intelligencer* responded to another attack in a Federalist newspaper, from a "Major Jackson." The charge was that the failure of Jefferson in his Annual Message to mention some American sailors who were being held captive by the Tripoli government meant that he had not made an effort to secure their release. Denying the charge as "an unfounded insinuation, a deduction not warranted," the *Intelligencer* asserted that the administration was employing both threats of force and negotiations (including the possibility of ransom) to secure the captives' release. Nevertheless, it concluded, there was no way the administration could win in the eyes of its opponents.

> The truth is simply this, if the next advices from our squadron announce the release of our seamen by *ransom*, the major will talk of the expense; he will exclaim, is this economy? If the captives are released by the employment of *force*, the major will refuse the administration any share of the credit. Such is the inconsistency of men governed by vindictive, unworthy passions, and not by a respect for truth or principle.

Jefferson as a Constitutionally Proper President

Even at this early time in American political history, the appropriate place of the presidency in the American constitutional system of government had become the source of deep contention.[21] Disagreements on that subject swelled in the election of 1800, as Republicans complained bitterly about the constitutional transgressions of the Adams administration, while Federalists warned about the collapse of American government into debilitating "democracy." In effect, that election became a great national argument over which of the presidential candidates and which of their parties best conformed to the American constitutional plan.

It is not surprising, then, that the subject of how well Jefferson had behaved constitutionally during his first term was addressed in the *Intelligencer* as part of the effort to reelect him in 1804. This was done at great length, in twenty essays published from September 7 to November 19, entitled "For the Defense" and signed "Curtius."[22] The actual author was John Taylor of Virginia, a close ally of Jefferson and a respected Republican constitutional theorist.[23] Unwaveringly supporting everything Jefferson had done, the commentaries would have served as a semiofficial assurance to readers that Jefferson had always behaved correctly from a constitutional perspective and was therefore above reproach on that ground.[24]

Jefferson's Opponent: Charles Cotesworth Pinckney

Remarkably, from reading the *National Intelligencer* in 1804, one would never know that Thomas Jefferson had an opponent in that year's presidential election. Charles Cotesworth Pinckney was only mentioned three times in the newspaper that year, never once as Jefferson's opponent. The first mention was on February 27, when the paper reprinted a *Washington Federalist* account of how Federalists had celebrated Washington's birthday. In that account, Pinckney was simply identified as one of the people who had been toasted. The second mention came on August 31, when an *Intelligencer* commentary complimented Pinckney on his public opposition to dueling. The third came on October 10, when the paper published the text of a South Carolina legislative resolution condemning dueling and signed by Pinckney among others.

The Celebration of Victory

Around mid-November, the *Intelligencer* began publishing reports of state presidential election results. The first, published on November 12, reported that Jefferson had won all the electoral votes in Virginia and Pennsylvania. The news about Pennsylvania would have been enormously gratifying to Republicans; in the 1800 election, Jefferson had defeated Adams there by only one vote (eight to seven). On November 14, the paper reported incomplete results showing that Republicans had made huge gains in Massachusetts, a former Federalist stronghold. While Jefferson might not win the state, the *Intelligencer* said, those gains alone were grounds for rejoicing.

In December, the pace quickened as the newspaper regularly reported results from one or two states. On December 14, the *Intelligencer* reported, surprisingly without comment, that Jefferson currently had 99 Electoral College votes while his Federalist opponent had just 11. Jefferson was thus assured of reelection, because he had already won a majority of the total 176 votes at stake.

One week later, the paper dropped its editorial silence on the electoral battle with a commentary entitled "PRESIDENTIAL ELECTION."

It did so, though, in an understated tone that reprised the cool, collected behavioral guidance it had promoted so heavily to Republicans back in 1801–2. The commentary began not with any celebratory language but by observing, "There frequently occur events of great importance, which from peculiar circumstances, do not command the attention to which their intrinsic merit entitles them."

Then came the surprise: Jefferson's reelection was *not* one of those "great" events. Rather, the reelection was but an event of a "subordinate character" that had nevertheless "animated the nation." The truly "great event," the *Intelligencer* proclaimed, had been the "tremulous and . . . strenuous contest of 1800." In that election, "two great parties claimed an ascendancy with pretensions nearly equal" and turned the presidential contest into one "fought for with avidity." Then, just four years later, Jefferson had been reelected "without awakening either the rapturous exultation of his friends, or the angry passions of his enemies."

Continuing in this cool mode, the commentary said it would avoid "indulging in expressions of triumph, which the occasion would well warrant." Instead, it would "proceed to extract" from Jefferson's reelection the "sound and rational inferences of which it is susceptible." One lesson was that the American system of government had demonstrated to the world a solution to the "extreme and paramount difficulty" that "all writers on government" had identified regarding the "executive power of the government." The difficulty was how to "organize" that power "efficaciously to promote the general welfare without endangering the liberty or peace of the nation."

Out of this concern and based on the lessons of history, many writers had recommended a "hereditary chief," for two reasons. They had argued, first, that the "body of the people are incapable of making a judicious decision" and, second, that a popular election would "inevitably, by awakening the fiercest passions of the human breast, . . . produce disorder, and an eventual resort to violence." Yet even though the Founders had chosen an elected chief executive, America had now had five "legal, regular, and rational" elections, without any "bloodshed, or violence." The *Intelligencer* argued that the reason for that American success story was the "*representative* principle of our government."

> This is the gravitating principle of our government. Its mighty influence, like that kindred power which holds the universe in concord, adjusts and harmonizes the complicated machinery that composes the various systems of government that unite the respective portions

of the nation. . . . Its vortex embraces the whole physical force of the nation, and gives it a moral direction. At one instant of time, the representatives of six millions vote that Thomas Jefferson shall be their President. To the force of such a vote, what is an army of one hundred thousand veterans, or the combined artillery of stratagem, fraud, or seduction? Let us then, fellow-citizens, hallow in our hearts this sacred feature as new to the world, as propitious to us.

Another lesson the *Intelligencer* found in Jefferson's reelection concerned the conclusive triumph of Republicanism over Federalism. Republicanism had stood for a government of "*limited powers*, derived at short periods from and at all periods *responsible* to the people." Federalists, in contrast, "strove to extend the powers of the government, so as to increase its influence over the people" and had demonstrated "an indifference to take public opinion as their guide."

Federalists had captured control of the federal government in 1796, and the *Intelligencer* commentary condemned their reign as a "dark and gloomy" time for the country. The experience had, though, "roused the revolutionary feelings of whiggism into action; and as they had once, so again they triumphed." But the Republican victory in 1800 had been "long doubtful, and the triumph, though great, far from decisive." Refusing to concede defeat, Federalists instead had fought incessantly to recover their power in all possible venues: "the floor of Congress, in the state legislatures, and in the public prints." As the commentary put it, "On these great theatres of investigation they were met. Enquiry was challenged. Both sides were heard. The nation was enlightened; and what is the result?—Thomas Jefferson, who in 1800, was elected by a majority of but eight votes, out of 138 is in 1804 elected by a majority of 148 out of 176." According to the commentary, Jefferson's reelection proved that the "more faithfully and completely" Republican principles are "transfused into the measures of government," the more will the government and its representatives "consolidate the affections of a free people."

The commentary declared that the whole American experience was a profound demonstration to the "visionary statesmen of Europe." Rather than popular rule containing the "elements of anarchy and dissolution," as those statesmen had taught, there was a new, contrary lesson to be drawn from the American system of government. It was evident, the commentary proclaimed, that, "under a wise direction," democratic rule could be turned into "the very elements of union, harmony, and stability."

Conclusion

In many ways, reading the *National Intelligencer* of 1804 is like sampling the partisan media of today. One's own candidate, party, and their associates are presented as largely above reproach. The obnoxious opposition is derided as wrong and, depending on the line of attack chosen, also stupid, scheming, ridiculous, illogical, and/or out of touch with most Americans. Then as now, these attacks were often made by first quoting a statement from the opposition and then critiquing or ridiculing the statement.

The *Intelligencer* also frequently used the technique of reprinting favorable commentaries drawn from other Republican newspapers. That rhetorical strategy magnified the circulation of those commentaries and created the impression that the Republican sentiments of the *Intelligencer* were being reflected in the states as well. The *Intelligencer* and its newspaper allies were serving as mutual media "echo chambers" for the Republicans, enabling pro-Republican messages to bounce around the country as quickly as possible given the technological constraints of the time. The technique of quoting favorable commentary from other politically aligned media sources is common today as well, especially on web-based media sites where such links can be made so easily.[25]

Another technique employed by the *Intelligencer* and frequently used today is labeling material printed in opposition newspapers as biased, slanted, unreliable, or just plain false. The cumulative effect is to create the impression that nothing in them should be believed or, at least, that everything in them should be doubted strongly. Many politicians create the same impression today by railing against "fake news."

The *Intelligencer* also served the same functions that partisan-based media outlets do today. As noted in chapter 2, the *Intelligencer* is a classic illustration of how the political newspapers in the nineteenth century worked, providing readers with "a common rhetoric, a common set of political ideas, and a common interpretation of current affairs."[26] Similarly, in their case study of modern conservative media outlets, Kathleen Hall Jamieson and Joseph N. Cappella found that major outlets such as Fox News and Rush Limbaugh perform a variety of functions "once associated with party leaders." The first is to "reinforce a set of coherent rhetorical frames that empower their audiences to act as conservative opinion leaders." A second function is to "insulate their audiences from persuasion by Democrats by offering opinion and evidence that make Democratic views seem alien and unpalatable."[27] The conservative outlets work to convince their listeners to discount information from other, non-conservative media sources as biased and untrustworthy.[28] These findings by Jamieson and Cappella also serve as good descriptions of the rhetorical efforts made by the *National Intelligencer* in 1804 on behalf of Thomas Jefferson and Republicanism and against their Federalist opponents.

Another modern aspect of the political content of the *Intelligencer* in 1804 is its treatment of the fortunes of President Thomas Jefferson and Republicanism as being intertwined. Commentaries that begin on the topic of Jefferson and his presidency often morph into discussions of Republican principles or threats to Republicanism, and vice versa. Similarly, commentaries on upcoming state and local elections frame support for those Republican candidates as a way of ensuring that the policies and principles of the Jefferson administration will also be continued at the national level.

Despite all these similarities, the campaign efforts of the *Intelligencer* were different in 1804 in significant ways. Jefferson speaks rarely in the paper's issues, never directly addressing the American people or anything related to the campaign. His voice comes through only briefly in the texts of a few official proclamations and letters on matters of state that the *Intelligencer* published in the months preceding the election. He is heard extensively in the text of his Annual Message to Congress, but that message was not delivered and published in the newspaper until the second week of November, when many pledged presidential electors would have already been chosen. Instead, anonymous or pseudonymous commentaries did almost all the talking and campaigning on Jefferson's behalf.

CHAPTER 10

The Newspaper Presidency
of Thomas Jefferson

Imagine the presidency of Thomas Jefferson without the *National Intelligencer*. Jefferson is known as a "man of the people," who believed in the primacy of "public opinion" and turned the presidency into a plebiscitary office. Yet he hardly communicated with the people directly. His formal public communications were two inaugural speeches, his annual messages to Congress, and some special messages. He also wrote some short public responses to letters and addresses sent to him by citizen groups. As Robert Johnstone Jr. puts it, "most people never saw" Jefferson, "never heard his voice, never had an opportunity to receive firsthand impressions of him." Yet, as Johnstone also observes, Jefferson "possessed a formidable power over the public imagination," even "without direct appeals to the people, with in fact little direct contact with the masses."[1]

So where does Jefferson's public persona come from? It must come more from what was said about or for him than from what he said publicly himself. When Jefferson's presidency is viewed from this perspective, the *National Intelligencer* becomes an important part of both his presidency and the promotion of the principles of Jeffersonian democracy. The *Intelligencer* (and the rest of the Republican newspaper chain) was promoting the popular image of Jefferson. To millions of Americans, he became a symbol, "unchecked," as Johnstone puts it, "by any direct awareness" of the man.[2] The *Intelligencer* was fleshing out for Americans just what Jeffersonian Republicanism meant and what it required of them.

Under the supervision of Jefferson and his allies, the pages of the *Intelligencer* were constructing not only images of Jefferson and his presidency but also approved articulations of government principles, citizen behavior, and America as a nation. Those constructs then circulated throughout the country, helping turn the American people into the kind of citizens Jefferson believed were best suited for democratic self-government: those who had been informed and educated "correctly." On October 19, 1803, an *Intelligencer* commentary proclaimed that "the greatest practical happiness is to be acquired by consulting and respecting the sentiments of the people." Yet this did not mean "that a government is to yield implicit obedience to every prejudice that takes possession of the public mind." When public sentiment was mistaken, the commentary said, it was the duty of the *government* "to dissipate it, and to inspire the people with more correct sentiments."

Viewing the *Intelligencer* as the tool to do this informing on behalf of the government suggests an explanation for an important observation made by Stephen Skowronek regarding Jefferson's success in reworking fundamental aspects of the American political system.

> Jefferson pursued the reconstruction of American government and politics relentlessly, and the regime he created in the end was profoundly different from the one he displaced. Yet, the most remarkable aspect of his transformation is how little resistance he encountered in the process from the institutions and interests previously attached to the old order. Jefferson's authority to reconstruct proved singularly disarming and all-encompassing.[3]

Skowronek attributes that success to two factors. First, with the recent death of George Washington, Jefferson, as the recognized author of the Declaration of Independence, could "stamp patently political actions with a unique claim to insight into original intent." Second, after the controversies during the Adams administration and the ensuing electoral "rout of 1800," Jefferson found himself in a "uniquely liberating" position politically. With "Federalist heresies fully exposed," Jefferson possessed a strong popular "warrant" for change, in Skowronek's terminology.[4]

The *Intelligencer*, along with the entire Republican newspaper network, must have played a key role in creating such openings for change.

After all, how else could most of the voting public have found out about the "Federalist heresies" that prompted the demand for change? As has been shown, the *Intelligencer* did a lot of that "informing"—all under the implicit imprimatur of the man who, as Skowronek observed, had a unique claim to understand the Founders' true intentions regarding the system of government they created.

Of course, as the bitter battles between Federalists and Republicans demonstrated, one party's "heresy" can often be another's "truth." In a government that ultimately depends on the consent and electoral support of voters, there have to be ways for each side to promote its version of the truth and show the public why the other side is wrong. The winner of that battle, even if by a narrow margin, can then claim to be representing the democratically expressed "national will." Under classic Jeffersonian democratic theory, this was the role of political newspapers: to prepare "the people" to express their considered electoral judgments after having been fully educated and informed.

As a May 2, 1803, commentary in the paper observed, "In the contentions of party the national good is often lost sight of." Because of partisanship, opponents of the administration in power are sure to condemn, "with indiscriminate vengeance," everything the government has done. Here is where newspapers come in: to create a public space in which all political arguments, pro and con, are displayed to all Americans. As the commentary put it, "On this *partial* ground the opponents and friends of the administration meet. They are gladiators before the assembled people." After all citizens have been duly "enlightened," they vote in their "comprehensive wisdom" and render "the decision of a nation." Said the commentary proudly, "a virtuous government will ever be ready to appear before a tribunal thus constituted." This essay is a remarkable real-world expression of the ideal "sphere of public discourse" conceptualized by Jurgen Habermas.[5] It also negates James Sterling Young's assertion that national government affairs at the turn of the nineteenth century were conducted "at a distance and out of sight."[6] To the contrary, through newspapers, interested Americans could be quite well informed about those affairs, as the preceding chapters demonstrate.

Obviously, Jefferson and his allies wanted the national "tribunal" to be stocked with good Republicans. So Americans had to be educated on the "proper" (i.e., "Republican") principles of American government and provided with the necessary factual information (again, from a Republican perspective) to do the judging. In the early 1800s, the only feasible way to accomplish that goal nationally, in a consistent, organized fashion, was through newspapers that could circulate throughout the country spreading the Republican message—slowly but surely.[7]

That is the role played by the *National Intelligencer*. Through it, Jefferson's actions could be announced, explained, and defended. That function corresponds to part of David Zarefsky's formulation of presidential rhetoric: defining "political reality" by "shap[ing] the context in which events or proposals are viewed by the public."[8] Especially in an era when presidents were not supposed to be publicly involved in partisan affairs, the *Intelligencer* was the perfect tool for Jefferson. It could publicly promote everything connected with his presidency and party without Jefferson ever being publicly connected to it. Viewed in that light, a close reading of Jefferson's presidential newspaper can be expected to add new understandings and perspectives on the study of his presidency, as the research presented here demonstrates that it does.

When Federalists threatened to hijack the presidential election in 1800, the *Intelligencer* played a key role in the Republican resistance. It declared publicly that the only acceptable outcome was for the House of Representatives to choose between Jefferson and Burr. In sophisticated commentaries, it explained why no other option was possible under the Constitution and rebutted Federalist claims to the contrary. It then raised the dispute to the ultimate level, by asserting that a continued deadlock would mean a collapse of the federal government and a return, constitutionally and even perhaps socially, to a virtual state of nature. Federalists could have had no doubts about how strongly Republicans viewed the crisis.

Once they had emerged victorious, Jefferson and his allies set about consolidating their victory. The main features of that effort in the *Intelligencer* were invocations of the need for national unity, promotion of Jefferson himself, defenses of his actions (e.g., his appointments and removals of federal officials), and guidance on how good Republicans should behave and think so as to attract more political converts. The paper's repeated entreaties for moderation, as well as its discouragement of citizen addresses to government leaders, would also have helped temper the wave of democratic populism that Jefferson rode to victory but that many elites, Republican and Federalist alike, had come to view as a potential threat to the stability of the country.

When the public and Congress clamored for strong action by Jefferson after the New Orleans port was closed to American commerce in 1803, the *Intelligencer* was a vital communications tool for Jefferson. The paper was used to explain Jefferson's approach and assure Americans that, should it not work, he was prepared to use force to resolve the problem. On the other hand, there probably was not any nationwide demand for the impeachment of a Supreme Court justice. But that was something many Republicans thought was warranted. So when they decided to try to remove Samuel Chase from the Court for his blatantly anti-Republican actions and statements, they needed to explain publicly why that effort was necessary. Once again, the *Intelligencer* was the obvious tool for the job, as its dedicated, months-long coverage of the effort demonstrates. Finally, reading how the *Intelligencer* advocated for Jefferson's reelection lets us see the arguments and strategies that Republicans were using in 1804. Besides the obvious promotions of Jefferson the man and of Republicanism as the correct party philosophy, there was even the promotion of Jefferson as a constitutionally proper president.

Thus, the *Intelligencer* was always serving two functions for Jefferson and his fellow Republicans. On one level, it was promoting and defending Jefferson and his policies. But on another, deeper level, it was educating regular readers of the *Intelligencer* on the correct precepts of Jeffersonian Republicanism, presented in the context of real-life political disputes in the young American Republic. And this was not just a fleeting educational experience for the nation. After all, some concepts promoted in the newspaper, such as those concerned with the "will of the people" and "public opinion," are still bedrock principles of American political theory. Equally, some critiques that were frequent themes in the paper, such as those regarding judicial review and extreme political partisanship, continue to be heard today. Issue by issue, the *Intelligencer* was constructing for its readers a communal understanding of what being a Jeffersonian Republican meant. Reading it today lets us see what Jefferson and his allies wanted everyone to know.

Notes

Chapter 1

1. *Founders Online*, National Archives, https://founders.archives.gov/docu ments/Jefferson/01-11-02-0047; original source: *The Papers of Thomas Jefferson*, vol. 11, *1 January–6 August 1787*, ed. Julian P. Boyd (Princeton: Princeton University Press, 1955), 48–50.

2. *Founders Online*, National Archives, https://founders.archives.gov/docu ments/Jefferson/01-14-02-0196; original source: *The Papers of Thomas Jefferson*, vol. 14, *8 October 1788–26 March 1789*, ed. Julian P. Boyd (Princeton: Princeton University Press, 1958), 420–24.

3. *Founders Online*, National Archives, https://founders.archives.gov/docu ments/Jefferson/01-33-02-0116-0004; original source: *The Papers of Thomas Jefferson*, vol. 33, *17 February–30 April 1801*, ed. Barbara B. Oberg (Princeton: Princeton University Press, 2006), 148–52.

4. For example, Dumas Malone cites items from the *Intelligencer* in some of the accounts in his two-volume history of Jefferson's presidency, entitled *Jefferson the President* (Boston: Little, Brown, 1970–74). Material from the *Intelligencer* is also cited extensively in Jerry W. Knudson, *Jefferson and the Press: Crucible of Liberty* (Columbia: University of South Carolina Press, 2006). Knudson focuses on presenting an overall view of how various issues during Jefferson's presidency were "reported" (in the modern sense of the word) and commented on by the newspapers of the day. The present study has different purposes: first, to show how the *Intelligencer*, as the official "spokesperson" for Jefferson and his administration, addressed key controversies during his first term; second, to analyze what that messaging revealed about the likely thinking and goals of Jefferson and his allies.

5. Throughout this book, the terms *Republican* and *Republicanism* are almost always capitalized, to distinguish the Republican political party and its principles from the concept of republicanism, which references a government based on popular consent and some degree of popular participation. Federalists and Republicans both saw themselves as "republican" but understood that identity very differently. The difference has been nicely described by Stephen John Hartnett and Jennifer

Rose Mercieca in "'Has Your Courage Rusted?': National Security and the Contested Rhetorical Norms of Republicanism in Post-Revolutionary America, 1798–1801," *Rhetoric and Public Affairs* 9, no. 1 (2006): 79–112, at 82–83. They explain that the Federalists had a "tragic view," convinced that average citizens were not capable of enlightened, uncorrupted participation in government, whereas Republicans had a "romantic view," convinced that average Americans were essentially virtuous and, if well-informed, were the best directors of the government. See also Gordon S. Wood, *The Radicalism of the American Revolution* (New York: Alfred A. Knopf, 1992), chap. 19.

On the development of the partisan split that began early in George Washington's first presidential term and led to the formation of early versions of the Federalist and Republican parties by 1792 and rabidly partisan ones by the mid-1790s, see Noble E. Cunningham Jr., *The Jeffersonian Republicans: The Formation of Party Organization, 1789–1801* (Chapel Hill: University of North Carolina Press, 1957); James Roger Sharp, *American Politics in the Early Republic: The New Nation in Crisis* (New Haven: Yale University Press, 1993); Sean Wilentz, *The Rise of American Democracy* (New York: W. W. Norton, 2005), chap. 2. As Wilentz shows, the Republican Party of Jefferson and Madison came about as an alliance between them and the so-called Democratic-Republican societies that sprang up in the mid-1790s. The opposition interest Jefferson and Madison represented was known as the "Republican interest," and the appellation *Republican* was used initially for the amalgamated early party. As the quotation from Appleby suggests, Federalists essentially sneered at the idea of ordinary Americans having a continuing role in political affairs and sought to insult Republicans—and scare responsible Americans—by calling them "Jacobins" (after the radicals who led the French Revolution) or, worse, "democrats." For a vivid description of the Federalists' attacks in the 1800 election, see Charles O. Lerche Jr., "Jefferson and the Election of 1800: A Case Study in the Political Smear," *William and Mary Quarterly*, 3rd ser., 5, no. 4 (1948): 467–91. In apparent acknowledgment that the appellation really did describe what they stood for, many Republicans began calling themselves "Democrats" or "Democratic-Republicans." See Robert M. S. McDonald, *Confounding Father: Thomas Jefferson's Image in His Own Time* (Charlottesville: University of Virginia Press, 2016), 125. Finally, the party settled on the name *Democratic*, leaving *Republican* for the taking in the 1850s by deserters from the American Whig Party, including, most notably, Abraham Lincoln. See John Aldrich, *Why Parties? The Origin and Transformation of Political Parties in America* (Chicago: University of Chicago Press, 1995), chap. 5. I use the term *party* to describe the deep partisan division between Republicans and Federalists at the time, because those affiliated with each side spoke and acted just as do those affiliated with modern political parties. See Robert M. Johnstone, Jr., *Jefferson and the Presidency: Leadership in the Young Republic* (Ithaca: Cornell University Press, 1978), 119–25. For a discussion of how the "first parties" differed from the "true modern political party," see Aldrich, *Why Parties?*, chap. 3.

6. Benedict Anderson, *Imagined Communities: Reflections on the Origin and Spread of Nationalism*, rev. ed. (London: Verso, 1991), 62.

7. Jurgen Habermas, *The Structural Transformation of the Public Sphere*, trans. Thomas Berger (Cambridge, MA: MIT Press, 1989). Habermas dismisses the nineteenth-century political newspapers as a "party-bound press" with content controlled by political elites for their narrow purposes (186). But Michael Warner has argued that there was a functioning public sphere of public policy discourse in the print culture of the American colonies as early as the mid-eighteenth century. Warner, *Letters of the Republic: Publication and the Public Sphere in Eighteenth Century America* (Cambridge, MA:

Harvard University Press, 1992). Richard R. John has similarly argued that by the first quarter of the nineteenth century, newspapers circulating through the postal system had "created an imagined community that incorporated a far-flung citizenry into the political process." John, *Spreading the News: The American Postal System from Franklin to Morse* (Cambridge, MA: Harvard University Press, 1995), 167–68. The existence of such a sphere is taken for granted in Saul Cornell, *The Other Founders: Anti-Federalism and the Dissenting Tradition in America, 1778–1828* (Chapel Hill: University of North Carolina Press, 1999). On the limited extent of the "public sphere," see Brian Steele, *Thomas Jefferson and American Nationhood* (Cambridge: Cambridge University Press, 2012), 166.

8. Jeffrey Tulis, *The Rhetorical Presidency* (Princeton: Princeton University Press, 1987).

9. Mel Laracey, *Presidents and the People: The Partisan Story of Going Public* (College Station: Texas A&M University Press, 2002), introd., chap. 6. For subsequent exchanges on the point, see Laracey, "Presidents' Party Affiliations and Their Communication Strategies," and Jeffrey Tulis, "*The Rhetorical Presidency* in Retrospect," *Critical Review: A Journal of Politics and Society* 19, nos. 2–3 (2008): 359–65, 481–500; Laracey, "The Rhetorical Presidency Today: How Does It Stand Up?," and David A. Crockett, "'The Rhetorical Presidency': Still Standing Tall," *Presidential Studies Quarterly* 39, no. 4 (2009): 909–32, 932–40. Richard J. Ellis, with Alexis Walker, found that "nineteenth century presidents were continually forced to navigate between conflicting expectations about how they should behave and speak in public" and that those conflicting expectations, "not settled norms or an agreed-upon doctrine," were "the hallmarks of the mid-nineteenth-century rhetorical presidency." Ellis and Walker, "Policy Speech in the Nineteenth Century Rhetorical Presidency: The Case of Zachary Taylor's 1849 Tour," *Presidential Studies Quarterly* 37, no. 2 (2007): 248–70, at 268. Ellis provides extensive additional historical evidence for that conclusion and elaborates on it perceptively in *Presidential Travel: The Journey from George Washington to George W. Bush* (Lawrence: University Press of Kansas, 2008).

For other works in the broader "rhetorical presidency" field, see Richard J. Ellis, *The Development of the American Presidency*, 3rd ed. (New York: Routledge, 2018); Ellis, ed., *Speaking to the People: The Rhetorical Presidency in Historical Perspective* (Amherst: University of Massachusetts Press, 1998); Karen S. Hoffman, *Popular Leadership in the Presidency: Origins and Practice* (Lanham, MD: Lexington Books, 2010); Martin J. Medhurst, ed., *Beyond the Rhetorical Presidency* (College Station: Texas A&M University Press, 1996); David K. Nichols, *The Myth of the Modern Presidency* (University Park: Pennsylvania State University Press, 1994); Anne C. Pluta, "Re-assessing the Assumptions behind the Evolution of Popular Presidential Communication," *Presidential Studies Quarterly* 45, no. 1 (2015): 70–90; Ryan Lee Teten, *The Evolutionary Rhetorical Presidency: Tracing the Changes in Presidential Address and Power* (New York: Peter Lang, 2011); Teten, "The Evolution of the Rhetorical Presidency and Getting Past the Traditional/Modern Divide," *Presidential Studies Quarterly* 38, no. 2 (2008): 308–14; special issue, *Critical Review: A Journal of Politics and Society* 19, nos. 2–3 (2008).

10. Jeffrey L. Pasley, "1800 as a Revolution in Political Culture," in *The Revolution of 1800: Democracy, Race, and the New Republic*, ed. James Horn, Jan Ellen Lewis, and Peter S. Onuf (Charlottesville: University of Virginia Press, 2002), 121–52; see also Carol Sue Humphrey, *The Press of the Young Republic, 1783–1833* (Westport, CT: Greenwood, 1996).

11. Joanne B. Freeman, *Affairs of Honor: National Politics in the New Republic* (New

Haven: Yale University Press, 2001), 147; Richard L. Rubin, *Press, Party, and Presidency* (New York: W. W. Norton, 1981), 23.

12. Philip E. Converse, "The Nature of Belief Systems in Mass Publics," in *Ideology and Discontent*, ed. David E. Apter (New York: Free Press, 1964).

13. Culver H. Smith, *Press, Politics, and Patronage: The American Government's Use of Newspapers, 1789–1875* (Athens: University of Georgia Press, 1977); Richard L. Rubin, *Press, Party, and the Presidency* (New York: W. W. Norton, 1981), 21–22.

14. Paul Starr, *The Creation of the Media: Political Origins of Modern Communications* (New York: Basic Books, 2004), 87–91; Pasley, "1800 as a Revolution in Political Culture," 8–9, 77, 196–97. Postal delivery rates for newspaper subscriptions were also heavily subsidized under federal law. A letter cost one dollar to mail, while the rate for a newspaper was one and a half cents. See Smith, *Press, Politics, and Patronage*, 6–9. An account of how Samuel Harrison Smith established a Republican Party newspaper in Philadelphia in 1797 noted that the paper was "published weekly, so as to fit it for diffusive circulation through the country by the mails, which, at that day, were, with few exceptions, transmitted but once a week." Joseph Gales and William Seaton, "The Late Samuel H. Smith," *National Intelligencer*, December 2, 1845. For a detailed description of how partisan themes and essays flowed between the partisan newspapers, see Pasley, "1800 as a Revolution in Political Culture," 140–43.

15. Quoted in Donald H. Stewart, *The Opposition Press of the Federalist Period* (Albany: State University of New York Press, 1969), 637. (Unless otherwise indicated, throughout this book all emphases in quotations are original.) As another observer explained in 1800, the reason for the perceived power of the media was that while "a large part of the nation reads the Bible, all of it assiduously peruse the newspapers. The fathers read them aloud to their children while the mothers are preparing the breakfast" (Pierre Dupont de Nemours, quoted in Stewart, 630). As noted in the text, even those who could not read or could not afford a newspaper subscription themselves could still be exposed to the contents of the papers. Newspapers were shared and passed around and could be found at public gathering places such as post offices, inns, and taverns, where they were often read aloud. One newspaper found that 506 people in 107 families were sharing the issues that had been sent to one post office. See Thomas C. Leonard, *News for All: America's Coming-of-Age with the Press* (New York: Oxford University Press, 1995), 15. Of course, the contents of the newspapers would have been spread by word of mouth also.

16. On Alexander Hamilton's pioneering use of the *Gazette of the United States*, a newspaper linked to the administration during Washington's presidency, see Laracey, *Presidents and the People*, 49–53; Richard L. Rubin, *Press, Party, Presidency* (New York: W. W. Norton, 1981), 11–13. Hamilton wrote many of the commentaries in the *Gazette*. According to James Madison, John Adams was also a frequent contributor as vice president. See McDonald, *Confounding Father*, 29.

17. Thomas Jefferson to John Garland Jefferson, January 25, 1810, *Founders Online*, National Archives, https://founders.archives.gov/documents/Jefferson/03-02-02-0145; original source: *The Papers of Thomas Jefferson*, Retirement Series, vol. 2, *16 November 1809 to 11 August 1810*, ed. J. Jefferson Looney (Princeton: Princeton University Press, 2005), 183–84; quoted and discussed in Ralph Ketcham, *Presidents above Party: The First American Presidency, 1789–1829* (Chapel Hill: University of North Carolina Press, 1984), 105–6.

18. Dumas Malone explains that "by the end of the summer if not earlier," Jefferson would have been confident of a Republican majority in the new Congress and

would have had "good reason" to expect his own election to the presidency. Malone, *Jefferson and the Ordeal of Liberty* (Boston: Little, Brown, 1962), 486.

19. The two significant Federalist newspapers serving the capital were the Georgetown *Washington Federalist* and the *Alexandria Advertiser and Commercial Intelligencer.* Both papers were supported by Federalist politicians and merchants and promoted Federalist Party positions. See Stewart, *Opposition Press of the Federalist Period*, app., 871, 891; David Hackett Fischer, *The Revolution of American Conservatism: The Federalist Party in the Era of Jeffersonian Democracy* (New York: Harper and Row, 1965), 138.

20. In 1795, around 150 newspapers were published in the United States. Federalists had a major newspaper advantage. Three-fourths of the newspapers in America were either Federalist supporters of the administration or nonpolitical; there were only eighteen or so Republican newspapers, mostly concentrated in large cities. Just five years later, Republicans had essentially achieved newspaper parity with Federalists. In 1800, there were 85 Republican-oriented newspapers out of a total newspaper population of about 260; by the time Thomas Jefferson took office in early 1801, "the Republican cause had a dedicated promoter of its views in every major city and in most of the principal smaller towns of every state." Pasley, "1800 as a Revolution in Political Culture," 106, 126, chap. 7, chart 2 in app. 1.

21. *Founders Online*, National Archives, https://founders.archives.gov/docu ments/Jefferson/01-31-02-0005; original source: *The Papers of Thomas Jefferson*, vol. 31, *1 February 1799–31 May 1800*, ed. Barbara B. Oberg (Princeton: Princeton University Press, 2004), 9–11; quoted and discussed in Cunningham, *Jeffersonian Republicans: The Formation of Party Organization*, 129.

22. *Founders Online*, National Archives, https://founders.archives.gov/docu ments/Jefferson/01-34-02-0506; original source: *The Papers of Thomas Jefferson*, vol. 34, *1 May–31 July 1801*, ed. Barbara B. Oberg (Princeton: Princeton University Press, 2007), 657–69; quoted and discussed in Noble E. Cunningham Jr., *Jeffersonian Republicans in Power: Party Operations, 1801–1809* (Chapel Hill: University of North Carolina Press, 1963), 240.

23. Ralph Ketcham, "The Education of Those Who Govern," in *Thomas Jefferson and the Education of a Citizen*, ed. James Gilreath (Washington, DC: Library of Congress), 281.

24. Benjamin R. Barber, "Education and Democracy: Summary and Comment," in Gilreath, *Thomas Jefferson and the Education of a Citizen*, 135.

25. Richard D. Brown, *The Strength of a People: The Idea of an Informed Citizenry in America, 1650–1870* (Chapel Hill: University of North Carolina Press, 1996), 52, 53.

26. Jefferson to Joseph Priestley, June 19, 1802, *Founders Online*, National Archives, https://founders.archives.gov/documents/Jefferson/01-37-02-0515; original source: *The Papers of Thomas Jefferson*, vol. 37, *4 March–30 June 1802*, ed. Barbara B. Oberg (Princeton: Princeton University Press, 2010), 625–27. See also Jefferson's letter to James Madison on March 15, 1789, in which Jefferson argues for a Bill of Rights to give state governments (which are "only agents" of the people) the "principles . . . whereon to found their opposition" to any future excesses of the federal government. *Founders Online*, National Archives, https://founders.archives.gov/documents/Madi son/01-12-02-0015; original source: *The Papers of James Madison*, Congressional Series, vol. 12, *2 March 1789–20 January 1790*, and supplement, *24 October 1775–24 January 1789*, ed. Charles F. Hobson and Robert A. Rutland (Charlottesville: University of Virginia Press, 1979), 13–17.

27. In his letter to Carrington (cited in n. 1), Jefferson even asserts that informa-

tion is more important than government in a society: "[W]ere it left to me to decide whether we should have a government without newspapers, or newspapers without a government, I should not hesitate a moment to prefer the latter."

28. On Jefferson's plans, see Gilreath, *Thomas Jefferson and the Education of a Citizen*; Jean M. Yarbrough, *American Virtues: Thomas Jefferson on the Character of a Free People* (Lawrence: University Press of Kansas, 1998); Michael P. Zuckert, *The Natural Rights Republic: Studies in the Foundation of the American Political Tradition* (Notre Dame: University of Notre Dame Press, 1996), 224–26. On the state of education in America at the time, see Lorraine Smith Pangle and Thomas L. Pangle, *The Learning of Liberty: The Educational Ideas of the American Founders* (Lawrence: University Press of Kansas, 1993).

29. Yarbrough, *American Virtues*, 145–46.

30. See also the opening section of Jefferson's 1779 Virginia Bill for the More General Diffusion of Knowledge, which stated that the "most effectual means" of preventing democratic political degeneracy was to "illuminate, as far as is practicable, the minds of the people." Yarbrough, 125.

31. One good example of how the informative and educational role of newspapers has been ignored by many Jeffersonian scholars is found in Robert M. S. McDonald, ed., *Light and Liberty: Thomas Jefferson and the Power of Knowledge* (Charlottesville: University of Virginia Press, 2012). As described by its author, that book's aim was to present different scholarly views on "Thomas Jefferson's multitudinous efforts to enlighten America's citizens and encourage them, in innumerable capacities, to embrace and advance his expansive vision for a free society" (xv). Yet there is no mention of the role that newspapers might have played in those efforts. Similarly, in *Thomas Jefferson and American Nationhood*, Steele describes Jefferson's view of popular governmental control as a "kind of cycle in which an enlightened public opinion would shape the character of electoral politics, leading to the election of wise statesmen . . . cultivating enlightened public opinion" (152), but Steele does not mention newspapers as a possible agent in the process.

32. Colleen A. Sheehan, *James Madison and the Spirit of Republican Government* (Cambridge: Cambridge University Press, 2009), 20–21.

33. Sheehan, 94, 103.

34. Sheehan, 94, 103–4. Jefferson's and Madison's great nemesis Alexander Hamilton said much the same in 1799: "[T]he first thing in all great operations of such a government as ours is to secure the opinion of the people" (quoted in Laracey, *Presidents and the People*, 50). See also Hamilton's statement in his Federalist Paper No. 84: "[P]ublic papers will be expeditious messengers of intelligence" about government actions, informing even the "most remote inhabitants of the union." David Wootton, ed., *The Essential Federalist and Anti-Federalist Papers* (Indianapolis: Hackett, 2003), 307.

In light of what Jefferson said in 1787 about the role of newspapers in republican self-government, whether Madison deserves full credit for coming up with the idea is debatable. It seems more likely to have been a mutual enterprise, as was so often the case. Of particular relevance would be the long and frequent contacts that Madison and Jefferson had in 1791 after Jefferson's return from France, during which Madison was writing his "Notes on Government" and then his newspaper essays. See Sheehan, *James Madison and the Spirit of Republican Self-Government*, 15–16. As Yarbrough puts it, Madison and Jefferson "shared a fifty year relationship that was fundamentally political: what bound these two together was their lifelong devotion to the republican cause" (*American Virtues*, 168).

That role for newspapers had been promoted by at least two other people: Jefferson's and Madison's good friend Benjamin Rush and Benjamin Franklin Bache, the son of postmaster general Richard Bache and the grandson of Benjamin Franklin. In an "Address to the American People" published in 1787, Rush declared that a key duty of the new central government was to circulate "knowledge of every kind . . . through every part of the United States" to shape the "principles, morals, and manners of our citizens to our republican forms of government." The "only means" of doing this, he wrote, was through newspapers circulated free of charge throughout the country. In a series of newspaper commentaries in 1791, Bache echoed this argument. The federal government had a fundamental obligation to provide all citizens with information about its conduct, he said, because republican governments depend upon the "enlightened approbation" of their citizens. Newspapers, he said, were the only channels through which this information could flow effectively to "every part of the empire." John, *Spreading the News*, 30, 36.

35. Johnstone, *Jefferson and the Presidency*, 250.

36. Another measure of the regard Jefferson had for newspapers is that he subscribed to dozens of them during his presidency (Cunningham, *Jeffersonian Republicans in Power*, 253–54).

37. Well-documented strong divisions within the Republican Party were managed and kept in check by Jefferson during his time in office. They are not addressed in the present study, because the *Intelligencer* obviously, with very few exceptions, was presenting Jefferson's version of Republicanism and his favored policy positions. For a good overview of the divisions, see Cunningham, *Jeffersonian Republicans in Power*, chap. 9. Cunningham concludes, "Party unity was a constant problem throughout Jefferson's administration, but Republican loyalty to Jefferson was not seriously endangered. The party never was so united while in power as it had been in opposition, but aided by the massive popular support which the President commanded and his policy of forbearance toward intra-party disputes, factionalism was kept in check as long as Jefferson remained in office" (235). See also Lance Banning, *The Jeffersonian Persuasion: Evolution of a Party Ideology* (Ithaca: Cornell University Press, 1978), 281–85.

38. Adrienne Koch, *Jefferson and Madison: The Great Collaboration* (Lanham, MD: University Press of America, 1950), 275.

39. Yarbrough, *American Virtues*, 142.

40. Quoted in Cunningham, *Jeffersonian Republicans in Power*, 259.

41. Quoted in Cunningham, 259.

42. On the "shattering rise of the plebiscitary presidency to constitutional prominence," see Bruce Ackerman, *The Failure of the Founding Fathers* (Cambridge, MA: Harvard University Press, 2005), with quote on 113; Terri Bimes, "The Practical Origins of the Rhetorical Presidency," *Critical Review: A Journal of Politics and Society* 19, nos. 2–3 (2008): 241–56.

43. Sheehan, *James Madison and the Spirit of Republican Government*, 105, 179.

44. Yarbrough says, "[A]lthough Jefferson *thought* more about the virtues Americans would need to cultivate than perhaps any other Founder, he did not . . . place his table of virtues before the public. . . . Much of what we know about Jefferson's understanding of virtue and character comes from his private correspondence, or indirectly through his efforts to shape public policy, rather than from his public statements" (*American Virtues*, xx).

45. Some other major events in his first term have been omitted from this study for one or more of the following reasons: they are not that interesting to most modern

readers, the topic has been well covered by historians, little or nothing new of note could be found in the *Intelligencer*'s coverage, or the coverage of the topic in the *Intelligencer* was essentially reflective of the public debate in Congress. The omitted topics include the fight in Congress over the Republicans' 1802 repeal of the Federalists' 1801 Judiciary Act, the public furor over Thomas Paine's return (at the invitation of Jefferson) to America in 1802, and the proposal and ratification of the Twelfth Amendment. For an account that references the *National Intelligencer*'s handling of the Paine affair, see Dumas Malone, *Jefferson the President: First Term, 1801–1805* (Boston: Little, Brown, 1970), 192–200.

46. August 3 and 10, 1801 (Rousseau); August 7 and 12, 1801 (Abolition Society Convention).

47. October 28, 1803 (Louisiana); February 29 and March 2, 5, and 16, 1804 (import tax).

48. Peter S. Onuf, *The Mind of Thomas Jefferson* (Charlottesville: University of Virginia Press, 2007), 152, 153–55, 229.

49. One reason Jefferson offered for his public silence on the issue was that for him to speak publicly against slavery would be counterproductive politically. Declining to endorse an antislavery pamphlet sent to him by a friend in 1805, he wrote, "I have most carefully avoided every public act or manifestation on that subject. Should an occasion ever occur in which I can interpose with decisive effect, I shall certainly know & do my duty with promptitude and zeal, but in the mean time it would only be disarming myself of influence to be taking small means. The subscription to a book on this subject is one of those little irritating measures which, without advancing its end at all, would, by lessening the confidence and good will of a description of friends comprising a large body, only lessen my powers of doing them good in other great relations in which I stand to the publick." Jefferson to George Logan, May 11, 1805, *Founders Online*, National Archives, https://founders.archives.gov/documents/Jefferson/99-01-02-1709

50. See the brief discussions of this topic in chapters 5 and 9. For an overview of Callender's attacks, see the editors' note to a letter from John Barnes to Jefferson, August 31, 1802, *Founders Online*, National Archives, https://founders.archives.gov/documents/Jefferson/01-38-02-0286; original source: *The Papers of Thomas Jefferson*, vol. 38, *1 July–12 November 1802*, ed. Barbara B. Oberg (Princeton: Princeton University Press, 2011), 323–25. See also Dumas Malone, *Jefferson the President: First Term*, 209–20. On Sally Hemings, see Annette Gordon-Reed, *Thomas Jefferson and Sally Hemings: An American Controversy* (Charlottesville: University of Virginia Press, 1997); Gordon-Reed, *The Hemingses of Monticello: An American Family* (New York: W. W. Norton, 2008).

51. Quoted in the previously cited editors' note to the letter from Barnes to Jefferson, August 31, 1802, *Papers of Thomas Jefferson*, 38:324.

52. On these points, see Fred I. Greenstein, *Inventing the Job of President: Leadership Style from George Washington to Andrew Jackson* (Princeton: Princeton University Press, 2009); Stephen Skowronek, *The Politics Presidents Make: Leadership from John Adams to Bill Clinton* (Cambridge, MA: Harvard University Press, 1997); Keith Whittington, *Constitutional Construction: Divided Powers and Constitutional Meaning* (Cambridge, MA: Harvard University Press, 1999).

53. Skowronek, *Politics Presidents Make*, 28.

54. See Skowronek, *Politics Presidents Make*; Ackerman, *Failure of the Founding Fathers*; Whittington, *Constitutional Construction*.

Chapter 2

1. Alexis de Tocqueville, *Democracy in America*, trans. Henry Reeve, 2 vols. (New York: Alfred A. Knopf, 1945), 2:119–20; quoted and discussed in Rubin, *Press, Party, and Presidency*, 9–11.

2. *Founders Online*, National Archives, https://founders.archives.gov/documents/Madison/03-03-02-0427; original source: *The Papers of James Madison*, Presidential Series, vol. 3, *3 November 1810–4 November 1811*, ed. J. C. A. Stagg, Jeanne Kerr Cross, and Susan Holbrook Perdue (Charlottesville: University of Virginia Press, 1996), 366–67.

3. Cunningham, *Jeffersonian Republicans: The Formation of Party Organization*, 259. For a vivid treatment of how politicians of the time used every form of communication available, see Freeman, *Affairs of Honor*.

4. *Founders Online*, National Archives, https://founders.archives.gov/documents/Jefferson/01-34-02-0018; original source: *Papers of Thomas Jefferson*, 34:21–24.

5. Granger to Jefferson, September 5, 1802, *Founders Online*, National Archives, https://founders.archives.gov/documents/Jefferson/01-38-02-0309; original source: *Papers of Thomas Jefferson*, 38:356–57; quoted in Cunningham, *Jeffersonian Republicans in Power*, 239.

6. Quoted in Jeffrey L. Pasley, *"The Tyranny of Printers": Newspaper Politics in the Early American Republic* (Charlottesville: University of Virginia Press, 2001), 230. Ames still articulated an elitist view of the role of the press. The papers he envisioned would appeal to the "passions of the citizens" by educating the people under the direction of "able men," rather than "uneducated printers, shop boys, and raw schoolmasters being, as at present, the chief instructors in politics" (quoted in Fischer, *Revolution of American Conservatism*, 135).

7. Joyce Appleby, *Thomas Jefferson* (New York: Times Books, Henry Holt, 2003), 23.

8. Pasley, *Tyranny of Printers*, 106, chart 2 in app. 1.

9. Pasley, 126.

10. John, *Spreading the News*, 4, 38. The population (free white) is taken from https://www.census.gov/history/www/through_the_decades/fast_facts/1800_fast_facts

11. John, *Spreading the News*, 154–55.

12. Starr, *Creation of the Media*, chap. 3; Pasley, *Tyranny of Printers*, chap. 9; Rubin, *Press, Party, and Presidency*, chap. 2; Freeman, *Affairs of Honor*, chap. 3. Freeman's description of the common understanding of the role of the political press in American political culture at this time seems to focus more on the Federalist than the Republican view of such newspapers; for comparison, see Fischer, *Revolution of American Conservatism*, 133.

13. See Laracey, *Presidents and the People*, 49–53. In *Press, Party, and Presidency*, Rubin characterizes Jefferson's denials to George Washington of his connection to Freneau as "evasive and disingenuous" (13). For the story of the newspaper and its editor and on Jefferson's and Madison's involvement in the enterprise, see Marcus Leonard Daniel, *Scandal and Civility: Journalism and the Birth of American Democracy* (London: Oxford University Press, 2010), chap. 2.

14. Dumas Malone, *Jefferson and the Rights of Man* (Boston: Little, Brown, 1951), 462. Freneau later recanted his denial and claimed that Jefferson had authored some of the paper's fiercest commentaries. Laracey, *Presidents and the People*, 212n17. See also note 69, this chapter.

15. Paul L. Ford, ed., *The Works of Thomas Jefferson*, 12 vols. (New York: G. P. Put-

nam's Sons, 1904–5), 12:176. For an informative discussion of how this newspaper war influenced Jefferson's thinking about the role of newspapers in the new partisan era in American politics, see Michael Lienesch, "Thomas Jefferson and the American Democratic Experience," in *Jeffersonian Legacies*, ed. Peter S. Onuf (Charlottesville: University of Virginia Press, 1993), 316–37.

16. Quoted in Pasley, *Tyranny of Printers*, 105. In 1801, shortly after retiring from the presidency, the defeated John Adams agreed, "If we had been blessed with common sense, we should not have been overthrown by Philip Freneau, Duane, Callender, Cooper, and Lyon, [all Republican newspaper editors] or their great patron and protector [Jefferson]." Quoted in Willard G. Bleyer, *Main Currents in the History of American Journalism* (Boston: Houghton Mifflin, 1927; repr., New York: Da Capo Press, 1973), 125.

17. Pasley, *Tyranny of Printers*, 174, 155. Pasley notes that during the Adams administration, Jefferson had tried to raise sponsorship for a "national newspaper" that would be printed in Philadelphia, then the capital, and circulated nationwide. James Sterling Young somehow missed the flagship status and national circulation of the *Intelligencer* in his study *The Washington Community, 1800–1828* (New York: Columbia University Press, 1966). The *Intelligencer* "had only local circulation," he wrote, which meant it should be "considered principally as [an] organ of internal propaganda, rather than a presidential device for reaching the larger public outside Washington, although items appearing in the *Intelligencer* were occasionally reproduced in the partisan press of other localities" (174).

18. Introductory note to a letter from Jefferson to Smith, March 6, 1809, *Founders Online*, National Archives, https://founders.archives.gov/documents/Jeffer son/03-01-02-0017-0001; original source: *The Papers of Thomas Jefferson*, Retirement Series, vol. 1, *4 March 1809 to 15 November 1809*, ed. J. Jefferson Looney (Princeton: Princeton University Press, 2004), 30.

19. Samuel Harrison Smith, "Education in a Republic: Remarks on Education," in Noble E. Cunningham Jr., ed., *The Early Republic, 1789–1828* (Columbia: University of South Carolina Press, 1968), 227–39, at 228, 237; also discussed in Robert A. Ferguson, *Reading the Early Republic* (Cambridge, MA: Harvard University Press, 2004), 33. Jefferson would use a similar phrase in his second inaugural address, on March 4, 1805, attributing all the good that had come to the country to the "reflecting character of our citizens at large, who, by the weight of public opinion, influence and strengthen the public measures." Merrill D. Peterson, ed., *Thomas Jefferson: Writings* (New York: Library of America, 1984), 521.

20. Margaret Bayard Smith, *The First Forty Years of Washington Society in the Family Letters of Mrs. Samuel Harrison Smith (Margaret Bayard) from the Collection of Her Grandson, J. Henley Smith*, ed. Gaillard Hunt (New York: Charles Scribner's Sons, 1906), 9.

21. For an informative sketch of Smith, see William E. Ames, *A History of the "National Intelligencer"* (Chapel Hill: University of North Carolina Press, 1972), chap. 1.

22. Pasley, *Tyranny of Printers*, 286–87. For a vivid sketch of Duane, his newspaper career, and Jefferson's treatment of him, see Daniel, *Scandal and Civility*, chap. 6.

23. Quoted in Pasley, *Tyranny of Printers*, 299.

24. Ames, *History of the "National Intelligencer*, "9. The entire Federalist attack against Duane, spurred by President Adams himself, is recounted vividly by George Henry Payne in *History of Journalism in the United States* (New York: D. Appleton, 1920; repr., Westport, CT: Greenwood Press, 1970), chap. 13. For an overview of Duane's tumultuous career, see Knudson, *Jefferson and the Press*, 14–19.

25. These details come from Smith, *Press, Politics, and Patronage*, 24–29.

26. Ames, *History of the "National Intelligencer,"* 11–12.

27. Ames, 11–12. In a commentary published on November 13, 1801, under the pseudonym "Portencius," the *Washington Federalist* first praised Smith's Philadelphia newspaper for its political "impartiality," then blasted the *National Intelligencer* for its blatant partisanship.

28. Pasley, *Tyranny of Printers,* 259.

29. Quoted in Luther Mott, *American Journalism: A History of Newspapers in the United States through 250 Years, 1690 to 1940* (New York: Macmillan, 1941), 177–78.

30. Jefferson to Madison, August 16, 1803, *Founders Online,* National Archives, https://founders.archives.gov/documents/Madison/02-05-02-0332; original source: *The Papers of James Madison,* Secretary of State Series, vol. 5, *16 May–31 October 1803,* ed. David B. Mattern, J. C. A. Stagg, Ellen J. Barber, Anne Mandeville Colony, and Bradley J. Daigle (Charlottesville: University of Virginia Press, 2000), 314–15.

31. Madison to Jefferson, August 13, 1803, *Founders Online,* National Archives, https://founders.archives.gov/documents/Madison/02-05-02-0321; original source: *Papers of James Madison,* Secretary of State Series, 5:301–3. In his letter, Madison referred to "Smith's paper" as performing that communication function for the administration.

32. This judgment differs from that of Cunningham, who wrote, "it was indeed true that Jefferson exercised no control over the *National Intelligencer,* and editor Smith was completely his own agent in determining the policies and publications of his paper." Cunningham provided no evidence for that assertion, made incongruously in the middle of a lengthy discussion of how Jefferson had obvious influence over Smith and his newspaper and how Jefferson was widely understood to be using that paper frequently to publicize his administration's views (Cunningham, *Jeffersonian Republicans in Power,* 259–60).

33. Ames, *History of the "National Intelligencer,"* 38.

34. Ames, 38. Through his paper in Philadelphia and an unsuccessful start-up of an offshoot in Washington, Duane stubbornly tried to maintain his leading role as a Republican apologist. His efforts were no match, however, for the benefits Jefferson's support conferred on the rival *Intelligencer.* See Pasley, *Tyranny of Printers,* chaps. 8, 12.

35. Smith, *Press, Politics, and Patronage,* 42–47, including a list of the newspapers at 46–47. Many other Republican newspapers around the country, though they did not get this benefit, received the *Intelligencer* postage free and took their cues from it. The example of the Boston-based *Republican Gazetteer* is discussed in chapter 4.

36. Quoted in Ames, *History of the "National Intelligencer,"* 30.

37. See Johnstone, *Jefferson and the Presidency,* 247; Ames, *History of the "National Intelligencer,"* 36.

38. Ames, 36, 41.

39. Mott, *American Journalism,* 177.

40. Ames, *History of the "National Intelligencer,"* 36.

41. William E. Smith, "Samuel Harrison Smith," in *Dictionary of American Biography,* vol. 17, ed. Dumas Malone (New York: Charles Scribner's Sons, 1932), 343–44; quoted in Knudson, *Jefferson and the Press,* 13. Margaret herself observed in a letter in 1804 that "[o]f an evening some one or more of the gentlemen of congress are always here [in their home in Washington]" (Smith, *First Forty Years of Washington,* 45).

42. Ames, *History of the "National Intelligencer,"* 29–33; Smith, *Press, Politics, and Patronage,* 27–29.

43. Smith, *First Forty Years of Washington,* 7.

44. In the March 4 issue of the *Intelligencer*, Smith, who wrote that Jefferson had given him an advance copy of the speech so that it could be published on the day of the president's inauguration, noted that the issue had been "published at an earlier hour than usual [to] communicate to our subscribers the earliest account of the interesting proceedings of this morning."

45. Smith's notes on the viewing, dated June 18, 1804, are on file in the archives of the Papers of Thomas Jefferson at Princeton University.

46. In a letter sent to James Madison on August 30, 1823, Jefferson said he still had the document, "with the corrections of Doctor Franklin and Mr. Adams interlined in their own hand writings. Their alterations were two or three in number, and merely verbal." *Founders Online*, National Archives, https://founders.archives.gov/documents/Madison/04-03-02-0113; original source: *The Papers of James Madison*, Retirement Series, vol. 3, *1 March 1823–24 February 1826*, ed. David B. Mattern, J. C. A. Stagg, Mary Parke Johnson, and Katherine E. Harbury (Charlottesville: University of Virginia Press, 2016), 114–16.

47. McDonald, *Confounding Father*, 19. Similarly, in *American Scripture: Making the Declaration of Independence* (New York: Alfred A. Knopf, 1997), Pauline Maier says, "Jefferson did not consciously seek to exaggerate his own role. Indeed, he tried to avoid focusing attention on himself" (184). To promote Jefferson politically in the 1790s, Republicans began proclaiming that he had been virtually the sole author of the Declaration. Jefferson's Federalist opponents, including John Adams, countered that the first draft of the Declaration had been a joint production of a committee composed of Jefferson as chair, Adams, Benjamin Franklin, Roger Sherman, and Robert R. Livingston. See Maier, *American Scripture*, 99–123, 170–75. In a letter to his and Jefferson's mutual friend Benjamin Rush in 1805, Adams quipped, "Was there ever a *coup de theatre* that had so great effect as Jefferson's penmanship of the Declaration of Independence?" (quoted in McDonald, *Confounding Father*, 13). That letter by Adams could well have been spurred by the 1804 claim in the *Intelligencer*.

48. Maier, *American Scripture*, 122, 102, 183–87.

49. Pasley, *Tyranny of Printers*, 203. On January 5 and 11, 1802, the *Washington Federalist* republished commentaries from the *Columbian Centinel* and the *Anti-Democrat*, respectively, that responded to a pro-Republican essay signed "A Farmer." The *Centinel* response said that the "Farmer" essay had been written by a "great Officer of State," and the *Anti-Democrat* response attributed the essay to "the Attorney General of the U. States." Under the title "Federal Misrepresentation, No. XI," the *Intelligencer* of May 26, 1802, reprinted an excerpt from the May 21 *Washington Federalist* asserting, among other things, that Levi Lincoln was the author of that whole series and the two-part review of the accomplishments of the last session of Congress that had been published in the *Intelligencer* on May 14 and 17. The *Intelligencer*'s denial was curiously limited: "Mr. Lincoln is charged with having written a piece entitled 'Federal misrepresentation, No. IV.' This is absolutely false." Twelve installments of the series were printed in the *Intelligencer* in May, the first on May 7 and the last on May 28.

50. Malone, *Jefferson the President: First Term*, 209 n. 9.

51. Laracey, *Presidents and the People*, 60; on Madison's *National Gazette* commentaries, see Sheehan, *James Madison and the Spirit of Republican Self-Government*, especially chaps. 4–5.

52. Smith, *First Forty Years of Washington*, vii.

53. Margaret Bayard Smith's possible involvement in some of the commentaries published in the *Intelligencer* complicates how the authors of them should be referred

to, because all of the commentaries, except the few attributed to Samuel Harrison Smith in his editorial capacity, were anonymous or pseudonymous. For simplicity and because many of the commentaries have been connected to men while none have (yet) been connected to women, the male set of pronouns is used when referring to the authors of the commentaries.

54. See the editors' note to the letter, *Founders Online*, National Archives, https:// founders.archives.gov/documents/Jefferson/01-34-02-0421; original source: *Papers of Thomas Jefferson*, 34:546–49. On June 19, 1801, the *Washington Federalist* had questioned the legality of the spending without a specific appropriation by Congress. Lincoln wrote back to Jefferson on July 28, providing quite a bit of detail about the *Berceau* and the lodging of some French sailors at government expense, which had also come under attack. Lincoln said that he would not put together anything for the newspapers (he would "omit a public statement") until Jefferson confirmed that "the above account meets your approbation, in point of policy, & correctness." *Founders Online*, National Archives, https://founders.archives.gov/documents/Jeffer son/01-34-02-0506; original source: *Papers of Thomas Jefferson*, 34:657–69. On September 18, 1801, the *Intelligencer* published a commentary from the *Massachusetts Spy*, entitled "To the People" and signed "A Farmer," that defended the administration's handling of the two matters. As discussed in n. 49 above, Federalist newspapers publicly connected Lincoln to the "Farmer" commentaries.

55. *Founders Online*, National Archives, https://founders.archives.gov/docu ments/Jefferson/01-38-02-0404; original source: *Papers of Thomas Jefferson*, 38:448–49.

56. Note for the *National Intelligencer*, [ca. December 8, 1801], *Founders Online*, National Archives, https://founders.archives.gov/documents/Jeffer son/01-36-02-0034-0004; original source: *The Papers of Thomas Jefferson*, vol. 36, *1 December 1801–3 March 1802*, ed. Barbara B. Oberg (Princeton: Princeton University Press, 2009), 67–68.

57. Quoted and discussed in Cunningham, *Jeffersonian Republicans in Power*, 256.

58. *Founders Online*, National Archives, https://founders.archives.gov/documents/ Jefferson/99-01-02-0105

59. *Founders Online*, National Archives, https://founders.archives.gov/docu ments/Jefferson/99-01-02-0160. Smith wrote Jefferson on August 8, 1804, to ask for clarification and more information on the matter, and Jefferson wrote him back on August 12. *Founders Online*, National Archives, https://founders.archives.gov/ documents/Jefferson/99-01-02-0214

60. Ames, *History of the "National Intelligencer,"* 39.

61. *Founders Online*, National Archives, https://founders.archives.gov/docu ments/Jefferson/01-38-02-0504; original source: *Papers of Thomas Jefferson*, 38:544.

62. Frederick B. Marbut, "Decline of the Official Press in Washington," *Journalism Quarterly* 33 (Summer 1956): 335–41; Ames, *History of the "National Intelligencer,"* 39. On this point, see also Cunningham, *Jeffersonian Republicans in Power*, 253–74, especially 261–63; Appleby, *Thomas Jefferson*, 47.

63. Jefferson to W. A. Burwell, September 17, 1806, quoted and discussed in Jeremy D. Bailey, *Thomas Jefferson and Executive Power* (New York: Cambridge University Press, 2010), 242.

64. Bailey describes apparently the same letter as having been written by Jefferson "under the signatory 'of a Massachusetts citizen'" (165).

65. Cunningham, *Jeffersonian Republicans in Power*, 255–57; quoted and discussed in Bailey, *Thomas Jefferson and Executive Power*, 251.

66. Cunningham, *Jeffersonian Republicans in Power*, 255–67. Those examples, Cunningham wrote, "are ample proof to explode the myth of Jefferson's disassociation from the press and to show that as President he wrote, on more than one occasion, important pieces for newspaper publication" (258).

67. Malone, *Jefferson the President: First Term*, 387, 499–500 (full text of Jefferson's draft); Joyce Appleby, "Thomas Jefferson and the Psychology of Democracy," in Horn, Lewis, and Onuf, *Revolution of 1800*, 155–72, at 158.

68. Ackerman, *Failure of the Founding Fathers*, 44. In 1801 to 1803, five Federalist senators subscribed to the *Washington Federalist*, while twenty-two, including four Federalists, subscribed to the *National Intelligencer*. See Noble E. Cunningham Jr., *The Process of Government under Jefferson* (Princeton: Princeton University Press, 1978), 259. Cunningham notes that at least one of the Federalists subscribed to the *Intelligencer* because it was the only source of information on debates in Congress. Another compilation of the newspaper subscriptions of the thirty-two senators found that in December 1801, thirteen subscribed to both the *National Intelligencer* and the *Washington Federalist*, ten subscribed only to the *Intelligencer*, and seven took only the *Federalist*. Donald A. Ritchie, *Press Gallery: Congress and the Washington Correspondents* (Cambridge, MA: Harvard University Press, 1991), 16.

69. Interestingly, the Federalist press also suggested that Jefferson might have written pieces for the *National Gazette* during Washington's presidency. On January 1, 1802, the *Federalist* reprinted, from the Baltimore-based *Republican, or Anti-Democrat*, an essay on the origins of political divisions in the United States. The essay began by observing, "We all know that the United States are divided into two different parties, whose views, principles, and political faith, are in direct opposition to each other." That "division of sentiment" had begun with the "commencement of the constitution," and the "organization" that grew out of it a few years later was "now termed democrats." Blaming Republican newspapers for having stimulated those party divisions, the essay implicated Jefferson in the effort.

> The first publications against government, that assumed any degree of consistency or uniformity of attack, were those in a newspaper edited at Philadelphia, by Mr. Freneau, who received a salary from Mr. Jefferson, then secretary of state, as a clerk, though it is acknowledged that the office was merely nominal. There is ample evidence that these attacks came from the pen, or were made at the instigation, of the secretary.

70. Quoted in Bailey, *Thomas Jefferson and Executive Power*, 253.

71. Bailey, 254. As is well known to scholars, Jefferson sometimes denied any involvement with newspapers, including that he had written anonymously for them. In light of the information presented here and elsewhere, those denials were obviously untrue. See Cunningham, *Jeffersonian Republicans in Power*, 255–67; Laracey, *Presidents and the People*, 62–64.

72. *Founders Online*, National Archives, https://founders.archives.gov/documents/Jefferson/01-34-02-0067; original source: *Papers of Thomas Jefferson*, 34:95–97.

73. Quoted in Cunningham, *Jeffersonian Republicans in Power*, 259; Laracey, *Presidents and the People*, 60. See, generally, Cunningham, chap. 10; Laracey, *Presidents and the People*, 58–63; Cunningham, *The Process of Government under Jefferson* (Princeton: Princeton University Press, 1978), 33–34. When Smith died in 1845, the men who had succeeded him as the publishers of the newspaper, Joseph Gales and William

Seaton, memorialized him in the *National Intelligencer* on December 2 and described the relationship of him and his newspaper with Jefferson.

[D]uring the whole of the Administration of Mr. JEFFERSON, the relations of confidence and friendship which had for several years existed between Mr. JEFFERSON and Mr. SMITH were extended to the paper under the charge of the latter, which was justly considered as generally representing the views of the Administration, whose measures it espoused with the same earnestness with which its proprietor approved them. From the beginning to the end of the Jefferson Administration there was no sign of variableness or change of countenance on the part of Mr. JEFFERSON towards Mr. SMITH; who, on the other hand, cherished to his last day of life among his most pleasant memories those of his hours of intercourse and converse with Mr. JEFFERSON, as well at his residence at Monticello, where he had been a welcome visitor, as at the Presidential Mansion in the Federal City, as it was then familiarly termed.

74. James was actually the foster brother of Margaret. He was much older, though, and they apparently were not close. See Ames, *History of the "National Intelligencer,"* 21–22, 13 n. 55.

75. Quoted in Ames, 38–39.

76. Smith, *First Forty Years of Washington*, 40. In its January 13, 1804, issue, the *Gazette of the United States*, a Philadelphia Federalist newspaper, in commenting on a disagreement that had erupted between the *Intelligencer* and the *Aurora* over which was most responsible for Republican successes, referred to the *Intelligencer* as the "mouthpiece of the hero of Carter's mountain." A portion of what is known as Carter Mountain is part of Jefferson's Monticello estate: see "History of Carter Mountain Orchard," https://chilesfamilyorchards.com/about/history-of-carter-mountain-orchard/

77. "Demographics of Washington, DC," http://en.wikipedia.org/wiki/Demographics_of_Washington,_D.C.; James Sterling Young, *The Washington Community 1800–1828* (New York: Columbia University Press, 1966), 31. Even then, the inhabitants of the capital were prompting some startling assessments. In 1804, Margaret Bayard Smith wrote, "But certainly there is no place in the United States where one hears and sees so many strange things, or where so many odd characters are to be met with" (*First Forty Years of Washington*, 46).

78. See Laracey, *Presidents and the People*, 49–53. In a commentary entitled "Federal Misrepresentations, No. XVIII," in the *National Intelligencer* on June 12, 1802, Smith described the *Federal Gazette* as having been "the official print" of those administrations. Curiously, Chase's Memorial was titled, "To the Editors of the Federal Gazette." There was no such publication by that title in the capital.

79. The language of "Portencius" paralleled that used by George Washington in a letter to Judge Addison dated March 4, 1798, excerpted by the *Washington Federalist* on August 14, 1801, after the somewhat cryptic note "The Diffusion of Information, and Arraignment of all Abuses at the Bar of the public Reason. President Jefferson's Speech."

I wish sincerely, that your good Example, in endeavoring to bring the People of these United States more acquainted with the Laws and Principles of their Government, was followed. They only require a proper Understanding of them to judge rightly on all great National Questions; but, unfortunately, infinite more Pains is [*sic*] taken to blind them, by one Description of Men, than there is to open their eyes by the other; which, in my opinion, is the Source of most of the Evils we labour under.

80. Federalists would complain regularly about the *Intelligencer's* slanted "reporting." For example, the writer of the commentary signed "One of the Gallery" in the *Washington Federalist* of March 16, 1802 charged that the *Intelligencer* editor's report of recent congressional proceedings omitted any mention of a speech by a Republican member of Congress, Mr. Bacon. In that speech, the writer said, Bacon had disagreed with the "rest of his party" and "candidly stated" his opinion that judges did have the power to rule on the constitutionality of laws. The writer charged that Smith had omitted mention of the speech to conceal from his readers that there was any such disagreement among Republicans.

These are truths which you wish to conceal from the public eye; you wish it to be believed that every thing is carried on with perfect confidence—that no one hesitates or doubts of the propriety of the rash means which [you?] are pursuing. But this will not do; your "efforts," however vigorous, are not yet sufficient, to "sustain the character of an impartial reporter."

81. Jeffrey K. Tulis, "Reflections on the Rhetorical Presidency in American Political Development," in *The Rhetorical Presidency in Historical Perspective*, ed. Richard J. Ellis (Amherst: University of Massachusetts Press, 1998), 211–22, at 215–16.

82. Stephen Skowronek, "The Paradigm of Development in Presidential History," in *The Oxford Handbook of the American Presidency*, ed. George C. Edwards III and William G. Howell (Oxford: Oxford University Press, 2009), 760.

83. Terri Bimes, "Understanding the Rhetorical Presidency," in *Oxford Handbook of the American Presidency*, 213.

84. Malone provides one outstanding example. After seeing Jefferson's ghostwritten commentary on the new social environment in the capital, published in the *Philadelphia Aurora* in 1804, the French ambassador Pinchon had it translated into French and sent to Talleyrand in Paris (Malone, *Jefferson the President: First Term*, 387).

85. Laracey, *Presidents and the People*, 47–48. For examples of this form of intergovernmental newspaper communications during Madison's presidency, see Mel Laracey, "James Madison: The (Unknown) Great Communicator," paper presented at the September 2011 Annual Meeting of the American Political Science Association in Seattle, Washington.

86. Everett Somerville Brown, ed., *William Plumer's Memorandum of Proceedings in the United States Senate, 1803–1807* (Ann Arbor: University of Michigan Press, 1923), 600–601.

87. By 1804, the editor of the *Intelligencer* seems to have dropped the pretense that his paper was not the communications organ for Jefferson. Responding to attacks in a Philadelphia paper, *Relf's Philadelphia Gazette*, that had cited pro-Napoleon statements in "Mr. Jefferson's paper," Smith denied taking sides in the attempts to depose Napoleon but never denied the pro-Jefferson label.

88. See Sheehan, *James Madison and the Spirit of Republican Self-Government*, chap. 4.

89. Richard D. Brown, "Bulwark of Revolutionary Liberty: Thomas Jefferson's and John Adams's Programs for an Informed Citizenry," in Gilreath, *Thomas Jefferson and the Education of a Citizen*, 101.

90. Ironically, a few years later, the *Washington Federalist* would make the same point. On January 12, 1805, the paper declared that Republican postmasters were delaying its delivery to subscribers for weeks or months, while subscribers to the *Intelligencer* were receiving it regularly.

91. Solon was a wise Athenian statesman, often credited with having paved the way for the growth of democracy in Athens; see http//en.wikipedia.org/wiki/Solon. Nos. I–XI in the *Intelligencer* "Solon" series appeared between August 3 and November 20, 1801. Topics were: the need to carefully circumscribe the powers of the national government (No. II); the proper interpretation of the powers of the national government (No. III); the unconstitutionality of the Sedition Act of 1798, as determined by the presidential election of 1801 (No. IV); the unconstitutionality of the Alien Act of 1798 (No. V); whether the criminal "common law" in the United States had been incorporated into the US Constitution (No. VI); the power of Congress to build and maintain "public roads" (No. VII); the need for a clarifying amendment on congressional "privilege," to prevent Congress from holding citizens in contempt, as had been done with Republican newspaper editor William Duane (No. VIII); the treaty-making powers of the president and Congress (Nos. IX–X); and the possible need for an amendment to clarify how Congress should proceed if there were ever a challenge to the integrity of the presidential election process, such as a claim that electors had been unlawfully appointed by a state (No. XI).

92. The first two quotations are from No. I in the "Solon" essay series, the third from No. II.

93. Yarbrough, *American Virtues*, 121–25.

94. On the fractured aspects of the party, see, e.g., Malone, *Jefferson the President: First Term*, chap. 24, discussing John Randolph and the Yazoo question; Pasley, *Tyranny of Printers*, chap. 12.

95. Pasley, "1800 as a Revolution in Political Culture," 121–52, at 135. For other means of popular transmission, see Simon P. Newman, *Parades and Politics of the Street: Festive Politics in the Early American Republic* (Philadelphia: University of Pennsylvania Press, 1999).

96. Stephen Howard Brown, "'The Circle of Our Felicities': Thomas Jefferson's First Inaugural Address and the Rhetoric of Nationhood," *Rhetoric and Public Affairs* 5, no. 3 (2002), 409–38, at 412.

Chapter 3

1. James Roger Sharp, *American Politics in the Early Republic: The New Nation in Crisis* (New Haven: Yale University Press, 1993), 228.

2. Some of the material in this chapter and chapter 4 originally appeared in Mel Laracey, "The Presidential Newspaper as an Engine of Early American Political Development: The Case of Thomas Jefferson and the Election of 1800," *Rhetoric and Public Affairs* 11, no. 1 (2008): 7–46.

3. James E. Lewis Jr., "'What Is to Become of Our Government?' The Revolutionary Potential of the Election of 1800," in Horn, Lewis, and Onuf, *The Revolution of 1800*, 13. In ten of the sixteen states, state legislatures chose presidential electors. In another five states, electors were chosen via the popular vote. One state, Tennessee, used a combination of the two methods. See Sharp, *American Politics in the Early Republic*, 243. The five states that used the popular vote were Rhode Island, Maryland, Virginia, North Carolina, and Kentucky. See Noble E. Cunningham Jr., *In Pursuit of*

Reason: The Life of Thomas Jefferson (Baton Rouge: Louisiana State University Press, 1987), 227. Two of the five used statewide elections, and three used district elections. See Stanley Elkins and Eric McKitrick, *The Age of Federalism: The Early American Republic, 1788–1800* (New York: Oxford University Press, 1993), 741 and n. 143.

4. Sharp, *American Politics in the Early Republic*, 247.

5. There are many accounts of the endgame. See, e.g., Sharp, *American Politics in the Early Republic*, chap. 12; John E. Ferling, *Adams vs. Jefferson: The Tumultuous Election of 1800* (New York: Oxford University Press, 2004), chap. 12.

6. The same attack argued that Congress had been cowed by the president: "Such has been the mighty power of Presidential favour, such the dread of Presidential enmity, that Congress after Congress have exhibited the mournful spectacle of Republican independence at the commencement of their sittings, and of servile submission at their close."

7. Clinton Rossiter, ed., *The Federalist Papers* (New York: New American Library, 1961), 81.

8. On the controversy generated by Hamilton's pamphlet, see Cunningham, *Jeffersonian Republicans: The Formation of Party Organization*, 229–30.

9. See Cunningham, *Pursuit of Reason*, 227; Elkins and McKitrick, *Age of Federalism*, 741 and n. 143.

10. "Lycurgus," britannica.com/biography/Lycurgus-Athenian-statesman

11. https://en.wikipedia.org/wiki/Lycurgus_of_Sparta

12. See Elkins and McKitrick, *Age of Federalism*, 228.

13. Bimes, "Practical Origins of the Rhetorical Presidency," 245.

14. See Sean Wilentz, *The Rise of American Democracy, Jefferson to Lincoln* (New York: W. W. Norton, 2005), xvii; Appleby, *Thomas Jefferson*, chap. 1; Ackerman, *Failure of the Founding Fathers*, 44. As Ackerman observed, legal scholars have "barely notic[ed] that the American people repudiated these [original understandings of the Framers] after a brief decade of democratic experience" (246).

15. In addition to the issue of October 31, 1800 (previously discussed), election results and commentary were also printed in the issues of November 21, 24, and 26 and December 1.

16. On December 3, 1800, the paper reported that the federal ticket of electors was expected to win in Rhode Island; that the electors of Maryland had split their votes, with five for Jefferson and five for Burr; and that the North and South Carolina legislatures now had Republican majorities. The December 8 issue used the results of the voting for the Speaker of the House in the South Carolina legislature to infer that the "appointment of electors" would favor Republicans. The same issue reported the results of Electoral College voting in Pennsylvania, Virginia, and Georgia.

17. The paper also excerpted a letter from a Republican supporter in South Carolina recounting their struggle: "The talk was arduous here; as we had heard two days ago of the deficient vote of Pennsylvania, and knew that the burthen lay now upon this state." Although the news from Pennsylvania had also "excited the spirits and efforts of the Federalists," the writer said, the Republicans had managed to carry the day.

18. See Stephen H. Browne, *Jefferson's Call for Nationhood: The First Inaugural Address* (College Station: Texas A&M University Press, 2003).

19. Quoted in Malone, *Jefferson the President: First Term*, 20.

20. Quotes from the Priestley letter are found in Appleby, *Thomas Jefferson*, 12. The full letter, dated March 21, 1801, is available at *Founders Online*, National Archives,

https://founders.archives.gov/documents/Jefferson/01-33-02-0336; original source: *Papers of Thomas Jefferson*, 33:393–95.

21. The "General Smith" mentioned as the letter's recipient was Maryland congressman Samuel Smith. On Burr's overall presidential machinations, see Cunningham, *Jeffersonian Republicans: The Formation of Party Organization*, 242–43; *Jeffersonian Republicans in Power*, 38–39, 208–9; *Pursuit of Reason*, 232–34. See also Ackerman, *Failure of the Founding Fathers*, 101–4. Ferling (*Adams vs. Jefferson*, 178) indicates that Burr sent several letters to Jefferson and others. Only the letter quoted in the text was published in the *Intelligencer* (and other papers across the nation; see Ackerman, *Failure of the Founding Fathers*, 102).

22. "Aristides" asserted that in the new Congress that would take office on March 4, "there will be nine states Republican, four federal, and three doubtful."

23. In an unnumbered one-paragraph note in the *National Intelligencer* of February 16, 1801, "Aristides" warned again of the dire consequences that would result from the "*possible* event of no choice by our Representatives in Congress" and then referred the reader to one of the *Federalist Papers* (now known as No. 7, by Hamilton) that was reprinted in the *Intelligencer* following the "Aristides" note.

24. Robert A. Ferguson, *Reading the Early Republic* (Cambridge, MA: Harvard University Press, 2004), 161–65.

25. britannica.com/biography/Aristides-the-Just

26. See Laracey, *Presidents and the People*, 51.

27. See Elkins and McKitrick, *Age of Federalism*, 129 (on Hamilton's "passion for order"); David Waldstreicher, *In the Midst of Perpetual Fetes: The Making of American Nationalism, 1776–1820* (Chapel Hill: University of North Carolina Press, 1997), chap. 2; Gordon S. Wood, *The Radicalism of the American Revolution* (New York: Vintage Books, 1991), chap. 1; Pasley, *Tyranny of Printers*, 73.

28. Ackerman, *Failure of the Founding Fathers*, chap. 2. Dumas Malone cites a claim in the *Philadelphia Aurora* of January 10, 1801, that Federalists had held a meeting in Baltimore, in Justice Samuel Chase's home, to consider legislation that would install John Marshall as the president in the event of the deadlock continuing beyond the end of the Adams term. Dumas Malone, *Jefferson and the Ordeal of Liberty* (Boston: Little, Brown, 1962), 495.

29. In contrast to this Federalist argument, "Horatius" had argued that the existing presidential succession statute could not be utilized, because the successors named in the law, the Senate president pro tempore and the Speaker of the House, were not actually "officials" who could constitutionally succeed to the presidency. See Ackerman, *Failure of the Founding Fathers*, 42.

30. britannica.com/topic/Marcus-Curtius

31. See Lewis, "What Is to Become of Our Government?," 20–21.

32. Bimes, "Practical Origins of the Rhetorical Presidency," 241–56, at 251–52.

33. Robert A. Rutland et al., eds., *Papers of James Madison* (Charlottesville: University of Virginia Press, 1962–91), 14:170; quoted in Richard D. Brown, *The Strength of a People: The Idea of an Informed Citizenry in America, 1650–1870* (Chapel Hill: University of North Carolina Press, 1996), 90.

34. Ferguson, *Reading the Early Republic*, 13 (also 7, 86, 177); see also William L. Hedges, "The Old World Yet: Writers and Writing in Post-Revolutionary America," *Early American Literature* 16 (1981): 3–18.

35. Ferguson, *Reading the Early Republic*, 86.

36. See Wood, *Radicalism of the American Revolution*, chap. 13.

37. Jefferson to James Monroe, February 15, 1801. On February 18, 1801, he informed James Madison that Federalists had been deterred by "the certainty that a legislative usurpation would be resisted by arms, and a recourse to a convention to re-organize and amend the government." Both letters are available in *Founders Online*, National Archives, https://founders.archives.gov/documents/Jefferson/01-32-02-0430 and https://founders.archives.gov/documents/Madison/01-17-02-0312. See Cunningham, *Pursuit of Reason*, 236–37.

38. See Wilentz, *Rise of American Democracy*, chap. 2; Laracey, *Presidents and the People*, 25–31.

39. See Young, *Washington Community*, chap. 2.

40. For Maryland, "J. C. Thomas" was listed as having voted for Burr.

41. Ackerman, *Failure of the Founding Fathers*, 80 n. 7.

42. See also the 1801 issues of January 6, 22, 23; February 2, 6, 16.

43. See Psalm 7:15.

44. See the 1800 *Federalist* issues of October 18, 25, 28, 30.

45. The second quote in this sentence was presented in the newspaper commentary as a quote, but the source of the quote (if there really was one) was not specified.

46. See, e.g., Michal A. Bellesiles, "The Soil Will Be Soaked with Blood, Taking the Revolution of 1800 Seriously," in Horn, Lewis, and Onuf, *Revolution of 1800*, 77.

47. For excellent recent historical treatments of the crisis, see Ferling, *Adams vs. Jefferson*, chap. 12; Lewis, "What Is to Become of Our Government?"; Ackerman, *Failure of the Founding Fathers*, chaps. 4–5; Cunningham, *Pursuit of Reason*, chap. 16.

48. Lewis, "What Is to Become of Our Government?," 21; Elkins and McKitrick, *Age of Federalism*, 750.

49. *National Intelligencer*, February 18, 1801; Cunningham, *Jeffersonian Republicans: The Formation of Party Organization*, 245.

50. Quoted in Lewis, "What Is to Become of Our Government?," 21.

51. Jack M. Rakove, "The Political Presidency, Discovery and Invention," in Horn, Lewis, and Onuf, *Revolution of 1800*, 30–58, at 42, 48.

52. Lewis, "What Is to Become of Our Government?," 19.

53. See, generally, Ackerman, *Failure of the Founding Fathers*, especially 44, 205, 246.

54. Bimes, "Practical Origins of the Rhetorical Presidency," 252. For the now-classic elaboration of this point, see Skowronek, *Politics Presidents Make*, chap. 4.

55. Lewis, "What Is to Become of Our Government?," 21.

56. Ackerman, *Failure of the Founding Fathers*, 325 n. 15. At the time of the crisis, eyewitness Margaret Bayard Smith wrote: "[Had] Mr. Burr been elected to the Presidency, what an awful conflict, what civil commotions would have ensued" (*First Forty Years*, 10).

57. Bellesiles, "The Soil Will Be Soaked with Blood," 78. This conclusion was supported only by a statement from one issue of the *Washington Federalist* that was quoted in another newspaper, the *General Advertiser*. For perhaps the most vivid description of the warlike atmosphere that pervaded the crisis, see Sharp, *American Politics in the Early Republic*, chap. 12.

58. *Founders Online*, National Archives, https://founders.archives.gov/documents/Jefferson/01-33-02-0166; original source: *Papers of Thomas Jefferson*, 33:208–9.

59. Skowronek, *Politics Presidents Make*, 63.

60. See Appleby, "Thomas Jefferson and the Psychology of Democracy"; Appleby, *Thomas Jefferson*, chap. 2.

61. Wilentz, *Rise of American Democracy*, 82–85, 90, 96, 107.

62. Waldstreicher, *In the Midst of Perpetual Fetes*, 203–4.

63. Jefferson quoted in Cunningham, *Pursuit of Reason*, 223.

64. britannica.com/biography/Timoleon-of-Corinth

65. Cunningham, *Jeffersonian Republicans in Power*, 256–57.

66. Hartnett and Mercieca, "Has Your Courage Rusted?," 104–5; Cunningham, *Pursuit of Reason*, 239–40; Browne, *Jefferson's Call for Nationhood.*

67. For brilliant explications of these points, see Sheehan, *James Madison and the Spirit of Republicanism*; Bailey, *Thomas Jefferson and Executive Power*; Jeremy Bailey, *James Madison and Constitutional Imperfection* (New York: Cambridge University Press, 2015).

68. Jefferson to Spencer Roane, September 6, 1819, *Founders Online*, National Archives, https://founders.archives.gov/documents/Jefferson/98-01-02-0734; also available in Andrew A. Lipscomb and Albert Ellery Bergh, eds., *The Writings of Thomas Jefferson*, 20 vols. (Washington, DC: Thomas Jefferson Memorial Association of the United States, 1903–4), 15:212.

Chapter 4

1. Waldstreicher, *In the Midst of Perpetual Fetes*, 3, 134–37. For a complementary treatment of earlier American political and social culture, see David S. Shields, *Civil Tongues and Polite Letters in British America* (Chapel Hill: University of North Carolina Press, 1997).

2. Waldstreicher, *In the Midst of Perpetual Fetes*, 207.

3. Newman, *Parades and the Politics of the Street*, 167–70.

4. Appleby, "Thomas Jefferson and the Psychology of Democracy," 169. On February 15, 1801, in this midst of the electoral deadlock in Congress, Jefferson wrote to his daughter Mary Jefferson Eppes, "I feel a sincere wish indeed to see our government brought back to its republican principles, to see that kind of government firmly fixed; to which my whole life has been devoted. I hope we shall now see it so established, as that when I retire, it may be under full security that we are to continue free & happy." *Founders Online*, National Archives, https://founders.archives.gov/documents/Jefferson/01-32-02-0429; original source: *The Papers of Thomas Jefferson*, vol. 32, *1 June 1800–16 February 1801*, ed. Barbara B. Oberg (Princeton: Princeton University Press, 2005), 593.

5. Ferguson, *Reading the Early Republic*, 32.

6. Ferguson, 179.

7. Quoted in Malone, *Jefferson the President: First Term*, 19.

8. Brown, *Strength of a People*, chap. 4 (quote from title). Education was the "key to republican harmony and progress" (Ferguson, *Reading the Early Republic*, 33).

9. Ferguson, 181.

10. On the atheism charges, see Dumas Malone, *Jefferson and the Ordeal of Liberty* (Boston: Little, Brown, 1962), 480–83.

11. Ferguson, *Reading the Early Republic*, 66; Brown, "'The Circle of Our Felicities': Thomas Jefferson's First Inaugural Address and the Rhetoric of Nationhood," *Rhetoric and Public Affairs* 5, no. 3 (2002), 409–38, at 412.

12. Anderson, *Imagined Communities.*

13. For example, a commentary published in the *Intelligencer* on October 17, 1803, as the new session of Congress was about to commence, recounted the history of how America had been saved in the election of 1800.

Washington retired from the head of our affairs; and notwithstanding the benignity and wisdom of his advice, a spirit of the most alarming aspect sprung up under his successor. . . . The name of liberty became reproachful, and republicanism was denounced; while the ordinary instruments for subverting both were resorted to with an intemperate avidity. Armies were raised and a sedition bill passed. We all know the train of evils that ensued.

At this interesting crisis, when in the opinion of some of its warmest friends, the republic was in danger, her guardian genius roused the nation from its slumber, who, with a giant's strength, humbled her enemies, and replaced them with her firmest friends. Thomas Jefferson was called to the first chair of magistracy; and a majority of republicans to the two branches of the legislature.

14. Of course, the *Intelligencer's* newspaper nemesis, the *Washington Federalist*, mocked the gesture. On August 31, 1801, after quoting from an "Eastern print" regarding some details about the cheese, including that it had been made from the milk of nine hundred cows at one milking, the *Federalist* proposed that a procession be arranged to escort the cheese to the capital, that such notables as Thomas Paine and Samuel H. Smith could head the procession, that the "Merchants of New Haven could send a light skiff" to transport the cheese, that throngs of citizens could "crowd the shores as the tall ship passes, and make the concave roar with hymns," and that Smith, "in his official paper, with his usual glow of imagination," could record the event for prosperity. On December 23, the *Federalist* carried and commented on a humorous note from the (*Baltimore?*) *American*, "The RATS which left the federal ship last year were rather premature, for had they kept of guard until the present voyage, they might have been allowed to nibble at the *Mammoth Cheese*." Noting the arrival of the cheese, drawn by five horses, in the capital on December 31, the *Federalist* said that the plan was to present it to Jefferson as a New Year's Day present. On January 2, the paper reported that the cheese had been presented to the president the previous day, accompanied by "two Clergymen, and many other persons," and that "[t]he President stood in his door to receive it." On January 11, 1802, the *Federalist* published a long spoof "Message" by Jefferson "Relative to the Mammoth Cheese," which paralleled the wording of Jefferson's recent first Annual Message to Congress. Among other things, the spoof had Jefferson questioning whether his receiving the cheese would violate the prohibition against presidents receiving any "emoluments."

On January 7, 1802, the Federalist *New York Evening Post* published a brief account of the delivery, which read, in part, "It is said that the President stood in his door to receive it, dressed in his *suit of customary black*, with shoes on that closed tight round his ankles, laced up with a neat leather string, and absolutely without buckles, considering them as superfluous and anti-republican, especially when a man has strings." A few days earlier, on December 29, 1801, the *Post* carried a teasing note titled "Communication. *More of the Mammoth!*" The paper reported hearing of plans to prepare other giant gifts to Jefferson, including a loaf of bread as big as the mammoth cheese, a huge bottle for the "best American porter," hundreds of cigars "at least three inches in diameter," and a huge pipe constructed by "some of the *good republicans*" at Savannah. The pipe was so big, said the note, "that, while two negroes are to stand at the President's mouth to hold up the end which he is to use, eleven more are to stand in single file to support the remainder of the tube and bowl.—*Vive Le Citoyen Jefferson*."

15. Andrew W. Robertson, *The Language of Democracy* (Charlottesville: University of Virginia Press, 1995), 36.

16. Jefferson to the Committee of Cheshire, Massachusetts, [January 1, 1802], *Founders Online*, National Archives, https://founders.archives.gov/documents/Jefferson/01-36-02-0151-0004; original source: *Papers of Thomas Jefferson*, 36:252.

17. See Appleby, "Thomas Jefferson and the Psychology of Democracy." The mammoth cheese made another appearance in the pages of the *Intelligencer* more than a year later, this time linked to the day that symbolized America. On July 8, 1803, the paper reported that Jefferson had furnished pieces of the cheese on July 4 to the attendants at a morning White House celebration and for an afternoon dinner at Stelle's Hotel that was attended by all of the high government officials except, apparently, Jefferson and Burr. The cheese was reported to be aging well: "Good judges are of opinion that it has greatly improved, and that it only requires time to be an excellent cheese. It is in a state of the best preservation." As discussed in chapter 9, during Jefferson's reelection campaign of 1804, another "mammoth" food item appeared to honor the president, a huge loaf of bread made by capital bakers and delivered to the US Senate.

18. In September 1802, when James Callender published his claim about Jefferson's involvement with Sally Hemings, he taunted, "Duane and Cheetham [two other Republican newspaper editors] are not worth asking whether this is a lie or not? But censor Smith is requested to declare whether the statement is a FEDERAL MISREPRESENTATION." In capitalizing the last words, Callender was mimicking their capitalization in the *Intelligencer* series.

19. Appleby, *Thomas Jefferson*, 32.

20. Fred I. Greenstein, "Presidential Difference in the Early Republic: The Highly Disparate Leadership Styles of Washington, Adams, and Jefferson," *Presidential Studies Quarterly* 36, no. 3 (2006): 373–91, at 381.

21. Appleby, "Thomas Jefferson and the Psychology of Democracy." As is well known, Jefferson was roundly criticized for his departures from established norms of behavior and dress. The research for the present study uncovered another criticism raised by Federalists early in Jefferson's presidency. On November 18, 1801, shortly after it began publishing, the *Washington Federalist* said, "Among the numerous instances of economy shown by the present administration, we are surprised the National Intelligencer has taken no notice of the Fence around the President's house. It is made of rough split rails and posts, and appears more fit for a cowyard than a king's palace." For a detailed study of how Jefferson "presented" himself, see G. S. Wilson, *Jefferson on Display: Attire, Etiquette, and the Art of Presentation* (Charlottesville: University of Virginia Press, 2018).

22. Waldstreicher (*In the Midst of Perpetual Fetes*, 190) incorrectly attributes the reported statements to Jefferson rather than to Burr. Certainly, there would have been logic in having them come from Jefferson, who was linked to Republican principles far more than the discredited Burr. Perhaps the Jeffersonians wanted to make the negative point about addresses without Jefferson being associated directly with such an impolite response. It is possible that the paper fabricated either the encounter or what Burr was reported to have said. For Jefferson's recommendation to Madison, in another instance, that an explanation to be published in the newspaper should be attributed to an invented figure, "some one apparently from the North," see the second quotation at the opening of chapter 2 in the present study.

23. Malone, *Jefferson the President: First Term*, 93.

24. Appleby, "Thomas Jefferson and the Psychology of Democracy," 168–70.

25. Hartnett and Mercieca, "Has Your Courage Rusted?"; Waldstreicher, *In the Midst of Perpetual Fetes*, 161.

26. Laracey, *Presidents and the People*, 57; "Rhetorical Presidency Today."

27. *Papers of Thomas Jefferson*, 32:196–202. See also Waldstreicher, *In the Midst of Perpetual Fetes*, 160–64; Elkins and McKitrick, *Age of Federalism*, 588–89.

28. Jonathan J. Edwards, "Countersymbols and the Constitution of Resistance in American Fundamentalism, 1919–1922," *Rhetoric and Public Affairs* 17, no. 3 (2014): 421–54.

29. For a vivid, detailed account of those times, see Douglas Bradburn, *The Citizenship Revolution: Politics and the Creation of the American Union, 1774–1804* (Charlottesville: University of Virginia Press), especially chaps. 4–5.

30. *Founders Online*, National Archives, https://founders.archives.gov/documents/Jefferson/01-41-02-0075; original source: *The Papers of Thomas Jefferson*, vol. 41, *11 July–15 November 1803*, ed. Barbara B. Oberg (Princeton: Princeton University Press, 2014), 107–10. See the discussion of this point in Brian Steele, *Thomas Jefferson and American Statehood* (Cambridge: Cambridge University Press, 2012), 162–63. George Washington actually made a similar (albeit more extreme) point in his Farewell Address. He declared that "all combinations and associations under whatever plausible characters, with the real design to direct, control, counteract, or awe the regular deliberation and action of the constituted authorities are destructive of this fundamental principle" of the duty to "obey the established government." James D. Richardson, ed., *A Compilation of the Messages and Papers of the Presidents, 1789–1902* (Washington, DC: Bureau of National Literature and Art, 1904), 217–18.

31. Jeffrey Selinger, *Embracing Dissent: Political Violence and Party Development in the United States* (Philadelphia: University of Pennsylvania Press, 2016), 81.

32. Quoted and discussed in Bailey, *Thomas Jefferson and Executive Power*, 240.

33. Quoted in Appleby, *Thomas Jefferson*, 51–52.

34. *Founders Online*, National Archives, https://founders.archives.gov/documents/Jefferson/01-33-02-0156; original source: *Papers of Thomas Jefferson*, 33:196–97; quoted and discussed in Pasley, *Tyranny of Printers*, 205.

35. The commentary said that Americans should encourage the free expression of thought, congratulate themselves on their "entire exemption from ecclesiastical tyranny," and realize how much better off they were under a republican system of government. "All Europe is crimsoned with blood," the commentary asserted, and the monarchical systems of the Old World were plunging their countries "deeper and deeper into follies and crimes." The commentary concluded that the sentiments it expressed were "calculated to enlarge the boundaries of intellect" and to "draw man closer to man, by shewing him that all virtue and all good are impartial and diffusive." On July 8, the *Washington Federalist* published a sneering critique of the essay. Saying that "[n]o bad writer ought to pass unexposed," it characterized the essay as the product of "a brain giddy with the contemplation of our independence, and laboring to be delivered of some sentimental and sublime maggots, worth the day."

36. Federalists were not buying the celebratory Republican rhetoric. On July 13, quoting the reference to a "mantle of oblivion" having been thrown over past partisan divisions, the rival *Washington Federalist* asked archly of Smith why that attitude had not been "thought of *twelve months ago*," before "nearly all" Federalists had been "turned out of office" and before Smith himself had "unexpectedly obtained a *major part* of the printing business in the gift of the present administration." On July 15, the *Federalist* again apparently invoked the July 6 *Intelligencer* account, referring to Smith's description of the "fraternal feast on the 4th of July" as having been one characterized by "compliment without adulation." The *Federalist* commentary then essentially

accused Republicans of having been against all public fawning to government leaders until their own "Idol" had come into power.

37. The song began with "Hail Columbia!" Its first stanza celebrated the American Revolution, its second urged devotion to "social harmony," and its third celebrated the nation's hero, George Washington. The song concluded with the exhortation that Americans "despise all party zeal" and feel "but one attachment," to "our country's love" and the voice of the nation in its laws. On the phenomena of "acting out" American democracy through celebrations and performances, including politically and patriotically themed toasts, see Waldstreicher, *In the Midst of Perpetual Fetes*; Freeman, *Affairs of Honor.*

38. Yarbrough, *American Virtues*, 48, 28, 49.

39. Jeremy Engels, "Disciplining Jefferson: The Man within the Beast and the Rhetorical Norms of Producing Order," *Rhetoric and Public Affairs* 9, no. 3 (2006), 411–31, at 416–17.

40. Malone, *Jefferson the President: First Term*, 28.

41. Of course, it is possible that the real author of this evocative commentary could have been anyone, even Jefferson himself.

42. Malone (*Jefferson the President: First Term*, 92) points out that when the capital had been in Philadelphia, members of Congress had delivered the response formally by traveling the few blocks to the president's residence en masse in carriages. He notes that this could have been a logistical nightmare in the new capital, where Congress and the White House were a mile apart and where there were not a lot of horses and carriages.

43. Malone, 91–93. Malone cites Jefferson's letter to Nathaniel Macon on May 14, 1801, in which Jefferson said he would abandon the presidential address.

44. Johnstone, *Jefferson and the Presidency*, 59.

45. Appleby, "Thomas Jefferson and the Psychology of Democracy," 157; see also Malone, *Jefferson the President: First Term*, 92–93.

46. Tulis, *Rhetorical Presidency.*

47. Stephen E. Lucas, "Present at the Founding: The Rhetorical Presidency in Historical Perspective," in *Before the Rhetorical Presidency*, ed. Martin J. Medhurst (College Station: Texas A&M University Press, 2008), 35–43.

48. *Founders Online*, National Archives, https://founders.archives.gov/docu ments/Jefferson/01-36-02-0098; original source: *Papers of Thomas Jefferson*, 36:177–78.

49. Johnstone, *Jefferson and the Presidency*, 59 n. 12. Jefferson made essentially the same point later, on December 20, 1801, in a letter (also cited by Johnstone) to Dr. Benjamin Rush.

50. Jefferson's first annual message to Congress, December 8, 1801, *Founders Online*, National Archives, https://founders.archives.gov/documents/Jefferson/01-36-02-0034-0003; original source: *Papers of Thomas Jefferson*, 36:58–67.

51. Johnstone (*Jefferson and the Presidency*, 59) cites a letter of April 20, 1801, in which Speaker of the House Nathaniel Macon told Jefferson that "the people expect . . . that the communication to the next Congress will be by letter, not a speech," as well as Jefferson's reply of May 14, 1801, assuring Macon that the message would be handled in such a way. In his reply, Jefferson also declared the end of "levees and other ceremonial foolishness." See Malone, *Jefferson the President: First Term*, 93.

52. http: britannica.com/biography/Lucius-Licinius-Crassus. The commentary was in at least five parts. Part 1 was published December 17 and republished "in consequence of the demand" for it on December 18; part 2 was published on December

21; part 3 on December 24; part 4 on December 26; and part 5 on December 29. There was no other reference in these to the mode of delivery of the message.

53. Roger Griswold to David Daggett, December 8, 1801, William Griswold Lane Collection, Yale University; quoted and discussed in Cunningham, *Jeffersonian Republicans in Power*, 10.

54. Acknowledging that a "majority of the ministerial members would vote to whitewash their chief," the writer suggested that "many of the majority [were] men of nice honor who would never sacrifice their reputation for propriety and magnanimity to flatter any one." Published in the same issue was an "Anticipation" of Jefferson's address. Dated December 7, 1801, it was a satirical critique of Jefferson, presented in the guise of his imagined address to Congress. At one point, Jefferson is there made to say, "I have deemed it conformable with democratic ideas to abolish the parade of levees, and the expensive ceremonial of public dinners, and leave it with your wisdom to decide, whether the salaries of the national functionaries, including that of the President, may not be abridged, that as little as possible be taken from the mouth of labor."

55. The *Federalist*'s assertion conflicts with Malone's assessment that there would have been serious logistical difficulties for members of Congress to travel the "long mile" over a creek and through a swamp to the President's house (*Jefferson the President: First Term*, 92).

56. The commentary was originally published in the *Gazette* on February 20, 1805.

57. For an earlier Federalist characterization of the election of 1800 having been a "revolution," see the *Washington Federalist* of December 8, 1801.

58. I have not seen any previous mention of that story. Most likely, it references either the 1801 or the 1802 session of Congress. Under the Constitution, regular sessions of Congress begin on the "first Monday in December." Malone says that by the end of the first week in December 1801, enough members had "straggled" in to allow Congress to form a quorum. That week does not seem close enough to the "near a fortnight" that the commentary says it took for the Senate to form a quorum. In 1802, the first Monday in December was the sixth, and Jefferson did not deliver his message to Congress until the fifteenth, which suggests there must have been some kind of delay along the lines mentioned in the commentary.

59. Noting that some Federalists regarded Jefferson's action as an "insidious reflection on the conduct of his predecessors," Malone judges that it made practical sense and was a manifestation of Jefferson's determination to stop "aping English procedure" (*Jefferson the President: First Term*, 92–93). On December 8, 1801, the *Washington Federalist* reported that Jefferson, when visited by members of a joint congressional committee to inform him that the new Congress was now ready "to attend to any communication from him," had informed the members that 'the President *would communicate by message* on the morrow." The italicization must have represented an acknowledgment of the departure from prior practice, but nothing else was said in the paper. On December 28, 1801, the *Washington Federalist* referred somewhat obliquely to a letter that "reviles Mr. Jefferson for attempting to deviate from Washington and Adams' practice." Even in that brief account published so soon after the delivery of the address, the distinction between Jefferson's written message and a speech was vanishing. The account read, "The President speaks in his speech very animatedly on the naturalization law and on the judiciary—and on the militia laws and juries."

Chapter 5

1. The term *midnight appointments* refers to all the appointments that Adams and the Federalists made after Jefferson had been elected president by the House of Representatives. They included the lifetime appointments for the sixteen new circuit court judge positions created by the Judiciary Act that Federalists passed on February 13, 1801. Also appointed were DC justices of the peace, surveyors, collectors, port officers, supervisors, commissioners of loans, and US marshals and attorneys. See Richard E. Ellis, *The Jeffersonian Crisis: Courts and Politics in the Young Republic* (New York: Oxford University Press, 1971), 32–33.

2. Skowronek, *Politics Presidents Make*, 71–73; Richard J. Ellis, *The Development of the American Presidency*, 3rd ed. (New York: Routledge, 2018), 385–87.

3. Malone, *Jefferson the President: First Term*, 75.

4. The appointments of district attorneys, marshals, and justices of the peace for Alexandria and the District of Columbia were announced in the *Intelligencer* on March 18, 1801.

5. In an essay titled "History of the Last Session of Congress," published in the *Intelligencer* on April 17, 1801, the judicial appointees were described as "men whose political opinions were undisguisedly hostile to the national will as expressed in the recent election of Mr. Jefferson."

6. Lawrence M. Friedman, *A History of American Law*, 2nd ed. (New York: Simon and Schuster, 1985), 129.

7. Friedman, 155.

8. See also Jefferson's description of his attorney and marshal removals from 1801 to 1803 as quoted by Malone (*Jefferson the President: First Term*, 74 n. 17): "Attorneys & marshals removed for high federalism, & republicans appointed as a protection to republican suitors in courts entirely federal & going all lengths in party spirit."

9. *Founders Online*, National Archives, https://founders.archives.gov/documents/Jefferson/01-33-02-0353; original source: *Papers of Thomas Jefferson*, 33:413–15.

10. *Founders Online*, National Archives, https://founders.archives.gov/documents/Jefferson/01-33-02-0424; original source: *Papers of Thomas Jefferson*, 33:490–92.

11. Cunningham, *Jeffersonian Republicans in Power*, 250.

12. On April 24, the *Intelligencer* published a second response to the *Philadelphia Gazette*'s criticism of Jefferson's actions regarding Marbury's commission. The second response ridiculed the contradictory Federalist approaches toward government appointments. When Federalists had controlled the national government, the commentary said, they had always maintained that only "friends" of the controlling party should occupy positions in the government; once they had lost their control in the last election, Federalists had suddenly abandoned that principle by creating a host of new offices and filling them hurriedly with their supporters instead of leaving the appointments to the new administration.

13. As Jeremy Bailey puts it, Jefferson could claim "that his election conferred on him the painful duty to be executioner on behalf of the public will" (*Thomas Jefferson and Executive Power*, 168).

14. See, e.g., Ellis, *Jeffersonian Crisis*, 33.

15. In 1802, the *Intelligencer* published three commentaries defending Jefferson's appointments, with statistics and explanations that likely came from Jefferson himself. On January 11, the paper published a summary of all eighty-nine appointments Jefferson had made. Since Congress had not been in session until the past December,

they had all been recess appointments that now needed Senate confirmation. The paper stressed the accuracy of the information: "A gentleman who has examined it accurately, gives us the following analysis, which may be relied on." At least forty-seven of the appointments were explained on obviously partisan grounds. Twenty-one were replacement appointments for, in the words of the commentary, "what have been called midnight appointments, to wit: made in the last hours or days of Mr. Adams's being in office." Twelve were "of removal for misconduct, or revolutionary toryism." Three marshals and one attorney had been "removed, and republicans substituted, as a protection for republican citizens against the federalism of the courts." Another five were "removals" made "to give to those, who have been systematically excluded, some share in the administration of the government." Two were "removals on grounds of special propriety." A May 31 commentary said that many Federalists had been terminated for one or more of the following reasons: they "had solemnly declared they would hold no office under the present executive"; held offices that by "common agreement . . . ought exclusively to be filled by those who enjoy the entire confidence of the executive"; and/or "had been the instruments of carrying into effect unconstitutional laws, prostrating the liberty of the press, and persecuting the innocent for an honest difference in political opinion." An analysis published on June 2, 1802, and headlined "Federal Misrepresentations, No. XIII" gave similar reasons for what it said were the 123 appointments Jefferson had made from the beginning of his presidency through May 3.

16. Bailey, *Thomas Jefferson and Executive Power*, 168. Bailey's list of Jefferson's "three grounds for removal" of officials seems inappropriate for the same reason: "an officer could be removed because of corruption or abuse of office, because his absence was needed in order to restore a proper proportion of Republicans, or in order to strengthen the administration by replacing executives in office with others who were better respected by the public" (160).

17. That view is reiterated in J. David Alvis, Jeremy D. Bailey, and F. Flagg Taylor IV, and *The Contested Removal Power, 1789–2010* (Lawrence: University Press of Kansas, 2013), 53, 211–12.

18. Adrienne Koch observes, "It should not be overlooked that Jefferson's philosophy of the 'earth belongs to the living' conceived the 'will of the majority' honored by democratic theory not as the *primordial* majority will, but as the current or continuing majority" (*Jefferson and Madison*, 228).

19. Alvis, Bailey, and Taylor, *Contested Removal Power, 1789–2010*, 52.

20. Alvis, Bailey, and Taylor, 211–12.

21. *Founders Online*, National Archives, https://founders.archives.gov/documents/Jefferson/01-33-02-0353; original source: *Papers of Thomas Jefferson*, 33:413–15; also quoted in Ellis, *Development of the American Presidency*, 385 n. 23.

22. *Founders Online*, National Archives, https://founders.archives.gov/documents/Jefferson/01-35-02-0451; original source: *The Papers of Thomas Jefferson*, vol. 35, *1 August–30 November 1801*, ed. Barbara B. Oberg (Princeton: Princeton University Press, 2008), 543–44. Interestingly, Jefferson wrote this letter to Livingston to ask him to respond on his behalf to two New York Republican newspaper editors who had written Jefferson asking him to provide them with an explanation of the dismissal. The editors said that the news of the dismissal had become fodder for Federalist attacks and had even unsettled some Republicans, so they wished to have information they could use in defending the action. See Denniston and Cheetham to Thomas Jefferson, October 22, 1801, *Founders Online*, National Archives, https://founders.

archives.gov/documents/Jefferson/01-35-02-0395; original source: *Papers of Thomas Jefferson*, 35:480–81.

23. 1 *Annals of Congress*, 1st sess. (1789): 518; quoted and discussed by Bailey in *James Madison and Constitutional Imperfection*, 67, and *Thomas Jefferson and Executive Power*, 78.

24. Madison to Edmund Pendleton, June 21, 1789, in *James Madison: Writings*, ed. Jack Rakove (New York: Library of American, 1999), 465–66; quoted and discussed in Bailey, *Madison and Constitutional Imperfection*, 65. For an excellent overview of the 1789 controversy in Congress over the presidential removal power and Madison's key role in it, see Ellis, *Development of the American Presidency*, 380–83.

25. Koch, *Jefferson and Madison*, 184; as previously noted, this goal was referenced in the *Intelligencer* on January 11 and June 2, 1802, in commentaries saying that some federal marshals and attorneys had been removed "as a protection for republican citizens against the federalism of the courts."

26. The Shakespeare quotation is from *Henry VIII*, act 3, scene 2.

27. Smith wrote that although he had considered the matter "too unimportant" to pay attention to, he had learned "from an Alexandria paper" that the contempt citation had been issued for his June 12 publication of the "Friend to Impartial Justice" essay. Smith must have been referring to a note published that same day (July 1) in the *Washington Federalist* (which was published in Alexandria), reporting Smith's indictment for publishing a "libel against the judiciary of the United States in a piece signed 'A friend to impartial Justice.'"

28. Ellis, *Jeffersonian Crisis*, 40. See also Malone, *Jefferson the President: First Term*, 115. On October 23, Smith published an account of the court proceedings against him. He said he was not republishing the June 12 commentary, because it "has had an extensive circulation through the Union." On October 26 and 28, under the title "Remarks on Libels," he published an extensive defense of his actions and of the necessity for a free press in a republican form of government. On November 9, 1801, the *Washington Federalist* commented sarcastically that after reading Smith's two-part defense, "we . . . have received as much information, and seen as much light thrown on the subject, as if we had not read them."

29. The October 23 report in the *Intelligencer* describes the vigorous efforts by two of the judges, one of whom was James Marshall, John Marshall's brother, to get Smith charged. It reported that both the Republican Chief Justice William Kilty and the district attorney had opposed the effort, as had the members of the grand jury for the district. Ultimately, the grand jury rejected the judges' request to indict Smith for the common-law crime of "libel against the judiciary of the United States."

30. All of the argumentation in the *Intelligencer* at first fell on deaf ears, at least as far as the *Washington Federalist* was concerned. On June 29, the *Federalist* addressed a supposed inquiry from a "Correspondent" who "wonders" why it had not taken "notice of the long and labored attempt, in the National Intelligencer, to justify the Executive conduct in the removal of officers." The answer was simple: "Tho much is there said, we really cannot discover any arguments that tend to justify that conduct." On July 8, though, the *Federalist* reconsidered its stance and promised, "We shall soon have something to say of Executive control, etc."

31. Regarding the charges against Duane, Malone says that Jefferson "stopped the proceedings against him later in the year" (*Jefferson the President: First Term*, 35).

32. *Founders Online*, National Archives, https://founders.archives.gov/documents/Jefferson/01-35-02-0451; original source: *Papers of Thomas Jefferson*, 35:543–44.

33. Friedman, *History of American Law*, 289–90; Larry D. Kramer, *The People Themselves: Popular Constitutionalism and Judicial Review* (London: Oxford University Press, 2004), 94–95, 117.

34. *Founders Online*, National Archives, https://founders.archives.gov/documents/Jefferson/01-31-02-0142; Original source: *Papers of Thomas Jefferson*, 31:168–71.

35. The claim that there could be federal common-law crimes was rejected in 1812 by the Supreme Court in *United States v. Hudson and Goodwin*. Interestingly, that case involved a charge against two newspaper publishers for having committed a "libel on the President and Congress of the United States, contained in the Connecticut Courant of the 7th of May, 1806," by claiming the government had bribed Bonaparte to make a treaty with Spain. See Friedman, *History of American Law*, 290.

36. Ellis, *Development of the American Presidency*, 420.

37. For an impressive overview of the issue in the context of the president's power to remove officials in law enforcement from the executive branch and thereby affect federal law enforcement itself, see Ellis, *Development of the American Presidency*, chap. 8.

38. The commentary, by "An Enquirer," was addressed "To Solon." "Solon" had been the pseudonymous author of several essays in 1801 on the meaning of the US Constitution. In the commentary, "Enquirer" asked why "Solon" had not examined the constitutionality of Jefferson's action when he had had so much to say on so many other constitutional matters.

39. The commentary began by archly asking, "We wish we knew on what principles the President of the United States forgives sins; and whether there be any crime of which any person in the United States may be guilty which will not be pardoned by the President, provided the Culprit be a Jacobin."

40. Malone, *Jefferson the President: First Term*, 35.

41. See Saikrishna Prakash, "The Chief Prosecutor," *George Washington Law Review* 73, no. 521 (2005), 1701–87; Steven G. Calabresi and Christopher S. Yoo, *The Unitary Executive: Presidential Power from Washington to Bush* (New Haven: Yale University Press, 2008); Rebecca Roiphe and Bruce A. Green, "Can the President Control the Department of Justice?," *Alabama Law Review* 70, no. 1 (2018): 1–75; Kate Andrias, "The President's Enforcement Power," *New York University Law Review* 88, no. 4 (2013), 1031–1125. For impressive historical research which finds that the "faithful execution command" of Article II imposes on presidents the obligation to exercise a "diligent, careful, good faith, and impartial execution of law or office," see Andrew Kent, Ethan J. Leib, and Jed Handelsman Shugerman, "Faithful Execution and Article II," *Harvard Law Review* 132, no. 8 (2019): 2111–92, 2178. As this chapter illustrates, whether the obligation is met in a particular case can be debatable.

42. *Founders Online*, National Archives, https://founders.archives.gov/documents/Jefferson/01-34-02-0425; original source: *Papers of Thomas Jefferson*, 34:554–58. For good overviews of the controversy, see Ellis, *Jeffersonian Crisis*, 36–39; Malone, *Jefferson the President: First Term*, 75–79. In a letter to Levi Lincoln on July 11, 1801, Jefferson commented, "Mr. Goodrich's removal has produced a bitter *remonstrance*, with much personality against the two Bishops. I am sincerely sorry to see such inflexibility of the federal spirit there, for I cannot believe they are *all monocrats*." *Founders Online*, National Archives, https://founders.archives.gov/documents/Jefferson/01-34-02-0421; original source: *Papers of Thomas Jefferson*, 34:546–49. In a July 24 letter to Thomas McKean, the Republican governor of Pennsylvania who had pursued a similarly accommodating approach in his own appointments, Jefferson said he hoped the "ardent republicans" would "embrace" his reply to the merchants. Jefferson acknowledged that his reply would "furnish new texts for the Monocrats, but

from them I wish nothing but their eternal hatred. If that evidence of my conduct were to cease, I should become suspicious to myself. But between the Monarchist & the Federalist I draw a clear line. The latter is a sect of republicanism, the former its implacable enemy." *Founders Online*, National Archives, https://founders.archives. gov/documents/Jefferson/01-34-02-0477; original source: *Papers of Thomas Jefferson*, 34:625–27.

43. The commentary began by noting that "it is said" that Madison authored the "Friend to Impartial Justice" essay. Expressing dismay at the "serious charges of corruption exhibited against our national judges," the commentary emphasized that it was "devoutly to be wished that the published may be punished, and the author detected."

44. The *Intelligencer* carried a similarly themed commentary by "Plain Sense" on November 4. The commentary argued that just as the people had voted Adams out of the presidency for engaging in what they "deemed anti-republican and unconstitutional measures," Jefferson was justified in removing some Federalist officials for the same reason. Since the president is "responsible to the majority," argued the commentary, it was his "duty" to appoint "such characters only, as are most friendly to his own political sentiments, and those of the majority of the citizens of the United States."

45. On Jackson, see, e.g., Ellis, *Development of the American Presidency*, 390–94.

46. For a vivid sketch of this fundamental Federalist belief, see Koch, *Jefferson and Madison*, 136–38.

47. Two such examples are found in the issue of June 2 and August 20, 1802. The former presented an account of all the executive branch appointments and removals made by Jefferson; the latter did the same for post office positions.

48. See Malone, *Jefferson the President: First Term*, 83; Ellis, *Development of the American Presidency*, 387.

49. Calabresi and Yoo (*Unitary Executive*, 67) cite a letter from Jefferson to Edward Livingston on November 1, 1801, which strongly asserted Jefferson's position that he had absolute control over the direction of prosecutions. Mentioning that Jefferson asked Livingston to publicize his position, Calabresi and Yoo do not provide any information on how or if that was done.

50. See citations in n. 41.

51. These commentaries also illustrate an early version of the "hybrid presidency" thesis advanced by Vanessa Beasley, which notes that modern presidents now have two models of executive governance available to them: the "rhetorical presidency" model and the "unitary executive" model. Vanessa Beasley, "The Rhetorical Presidency Meets the Unitary Executive: Implications for Presidential Rhetoric on Public Policy," *Rhetoric and Public Affairs* 13, no. 1 (2010): 7–35.

52. In their discussion of John Adams directing that Sedition Act prosecution be dropped, Calabresi and Yoo say that while "Democrats complained repeatedly that the Sedition Act was unconstitutional, no one complained about Adams's direction of the district attorneys" (*Unitary Executive*, 61).

Chapter 6

1. Malone, *Jefferson the President: First Term*, 133.

2. Stephen Engel, *American Politicians Confront the Court: Opposition Politics and Changing Responses to Judicial Power* (Cambridge: Cambridge University Press, 2011).

3. Whittington, *Constitutional Construction*; Ackerman, *Failure of the Founding Fathers*.

4. Ackerman, 191.

5. Ellis, *Jeffersonian Crisis*, 66.

6. For an impressive survey that incorporates many newspaper accounts as well as a wealth of other interesting information on the *Marbury* controversy, see Cliff Sloan and David McKean, *The Great Decision: Jefferson, Adams, Marshall, and the Battle for the Supreme Court* (New York: Public Affairs, 2009).

7. Ellis (*Jeffersonian Crisis*, 58) notes that this had been the uniform Republican position during the debate on the repeal of the 1801 act. This assertion seems questionable in light of a commentary, signed "One of the Gallery," published in the *Washington Federalist* on March 16, 1802. There, the writer accused the *Intelligencer*'s editor of omitting, from Smith's own report of a speech by a Republican member of Congress, that Mr. Bacon had "candidly stated" his disagreement from the "rest of his party" on the issue of judicial review. Bacon had affirmed, the writer said, that every judge did have the power to rule on the constitutionality of laws. The writer thought Smith had made such omission to conceal from his readers, many of whom seldom saw any other newspaper, that there was such disagreement among Republicans.

> These are truths which you wish to conceal from the public eye; you wish it to be believed that every thing is carried on with perfect confidence—that no one hesitates or doubts of the propriety of the rash means which [you?] are pursuing. But this will not do; your "efforts," however vigorous, are not yet sufficient, to "sustain the character of an impartial reporter."

8. As also discussed in note 1 of chapter 5, *midnight appointments* was Jefferson's term for all of the judicial appointments Adams made after Jefferson had won the presidency in the House of Representatives. He and his Federalist allies wanted to plant as many good Federalists as possible into the judiciary before Jefferson and the Republicans took over. Dewey highlights the partisan excessiveness by pointing out, "There were only 8,144 persons (nearly one-fourth slaves) in Washington County and 7,121 (more than one-sixth slaves) in Alexandria County, so President Adams was thoughtfully supplying these counties with a justice of the peace of every 363 ½ persons, irrespective of age, sex, color, or condition of servitude." Donald O. Dewey, *Marshall versus Jefferson: The Political Background of* Marbury v. Madison (New York: Alfred A. Knopf, 1970), 76. Left with a free hand because none of the commissions for justice of the peace had been delivered, Jefferson pared the number of appointments down to thirty, omitting, in the process, seventeen of the justices appointed by Adams (Dewey, 80–81). See also Richard A. Samuelson, "The Midnight Appointments," White House Historical Association, http:whitehousehistory.org/the-midnight-appointments

9. See Malone, *Jefferson the President: First Term*, 73, 144–45. Interestingly, Malone (144) notes that none of the forty-two commissions for justice of the peace that were issued by Adams on March 2 have ever been found.

10. Malone, 147. According to Ackerman, Republicans at the time had a 17-15 majority in the Senate. *Failure of the Founding Fathers*, 138.

11. Both Malone (*Jefferson the President: First Term*, 147) and Dewey (*Marshall versus Jefferson*, 98) portray the Senate action solely as a condemnation of a constitutionally illegitimate attempt by the Supreme Court to exercise authority over presidential affairs.

12. Ellis, *Jeffersonian Crisis*, 58; Malone, *Jefferson the President: First Term*, 131.

13. Malone, 147.

14. See Ellis, *Jefferson Crisis*, 66; Ackerman, *Failure of the Founding Fathers*, 149; Forrest McDonald, *The Presidency of Thomas Jefferson* (Lawrence: University Press of Kansas, 1976), 51; Dewey, *Marshall versus Jefferson*, 142.

15. The first time the Supreme Court actually held an act of Congress unconstitutional was not in the 1803 *Marbury* decision but in 1792, when the Court said that the Invalid Pensions Act was unconstitutional. See Charles Gardner Geyh and Emily Field Van Tassel, "The Independence of the Judicial Branch in the New Republic," *Chicago-Kent Law Review* 74, no. 1 (1998): 75–76. On the history of the idea of judicial review in general, see Philip Hamburger, *Law and Judicial Duty* (Cambridge, MA: Harvard University Press, 2008); Nelson Lund, "Judicial Review and Judicial Duty: The Original Understanding," *Constitutional Commentary* 26, no. 1 (2009): 169–82; Shlomo Slonim, "Federalist No. 78 and Brutus' Neglected Thesis on Judicial Supremacy," *Constitutional Commentary* 23, no. 1 (2006): 7–31 and sources cited at 7–8 n. 2.

16. See Ackerman, *Failure of the Founding Fathers*, 138, 177–78. For a vivid description of the entire affair, see Sloan and McKean, *Great Decision*, chap. 9.

17. See, e.g., Ellis, *Jeffersonian Crisis*, 21, 206.

18. The *Federalist* was "sometimes referred to as Marshall's paper," according to Ellis (*Jeffersonian Crisis*, 67). Interestingly, in its edition of October 28, 1801, the *Federalist* challenged William Duane to provide proof of the claim in his Republican newspaper, the *Aurora*, that "many" of the commentaries in the *Federalist* were written by "clerks in the *very departments* the heads of which" were being attacked in its commentaries.

19. Malone, *Jefferson the President: First Term*, 151 and n. 44; Ellis, *Jeffersonian Crisis*, 66. H. E. Dean observes, "Even the most bitterly partisan Jeffersonian newspapers did not attack Marshall's assessment of the power of judicial review." Dean, *Judicial Review and Democracy* (New York: Random House, 1966), 27. Meanwhile, the *Intelligencer* had room to publish articles on other weighty subjects, such as "Instances of Sagacity in Dogs," published on April 6, 1803.

20. See, e.g., Dean, *Judicial Review and Democracy*. There is also, as noted previously, the view that judicial review was acceptable to all concerned, even most Jeffersonians. See Engel, *American Politicians Confront the Court*; Stephen Engel, "Before the Countermajoritarian Difficulty: Regime Unity, Loyal Opposition, and Hostilities toward Judicial Authority in Early America," *Studies in American Political Development* 23, no. 2 (2009): 189–217, at 193.

21. Editors' note to letter from John Langdon to Jefferson, May 8, 1803, *Founders Online*, National Archives, https://founders.archives.gov/documents/Jefferson/01-40-02-0250; original source: *The Papers of Thomas Jefferson*, vol. 40, *4 March–10 July 1803*, ed. Barbara B. Oberg (Princeton: Princeton University Press, 2013), 335–36.

22. Dewey, *Marshall versus Jefferson*, 142.

23. Keith E. Whittington, *Political Foundations of Judicial Supremacy: The Presidency, the Supreme Court, and Constitutional Leadership in US History* (Princeton: Princeton University Press, 2007), e.g., 117; see also Marc A. Graber, "Federalist or Friends of Adams: The Marshall Court and Party Politics," *Studies in American Political Development* 12, no. 2 (October 1998): 229–66, at 234.

24. Ackerman, *Failure of the Founding Fathers*, 195.

25. See also Dewey, *Marshall versus Jefferson*, 141. "Littleton" praised Marshall strongly: that act had been "the one memorable act of yours in supporting the gov-

ernment in the question of the repeal of the judiciary law. The time is remembered when you could despise the petty larceny consideration of party spirit, and against the clamors and flatteries of an infuriated opposition, support the constitutional rights of the legislature. The weigh[t] of your authority then calmed the tumult of faction, and you stood, as you must continue to stand, a star of the first magnitude."

26. That abdication was precisely what some prominent Federalists, including at least one member of the Supreme Court, Samuel Chase, had argued the justices should do. See Ellis, *Jeffersonian Crisis*, 60–62; Ackerman, *Failure of the Founding Fathers*, 166–72.

27. Ackerman, 173–75.

28. Quoted and discussed in Ackerman, *Failure of the Founding Fathers*, 185–86.

29. Kramer, *People Themselves*; Mark Tushnet, "Abolishing Judicial Review," *Constitutional Commentary* 27, no. 3 (2011): 581–89, at 587.

30. James M. O'Fallon, "The Case of Benjamin More: A Lost Episode in the Struggle over the Repeal of the Judiciary Act of 1801," *Law and History Review* 11, no. 1 (1993): 43–57.

31. O'Fallon, 48.

32. Ackerman, *Failure of the Founding Fathers*, 172–73, 276.

33. As O'Fallon puts it, Marshall "ducked" in the *More* case. James M. O'Fallon, "Marbury," *Stanford Law Review* 44, no. 72 (1992): 219, 241. On the idea that Marshall was determined to avoid a real confrontation with the Jeffersonians, see Ackerman, *Failure of the Founding Fathers*, chap. 8.

34. More's victory in the lower court would have been limited, protecting his right to collect the fees only for the duration of his five-year appointment. A new appointee or a reappointment would not have been able to claim that the 1802 repeal of the fees provision had violated the appointee's right to undiminished judicial pay, because the abolition of the fee would have predated the appointee's taking office.

35. O'Fallon, "Marbury," 241 n. 72.

36. Jefferson to Thomas Ritchie, December 25, 1820, *Founders Online*, National Archives, https://founders.archives.gov/documents/Jefferson/98-01-02-1702; also available in *Writings of Thomas Jefferson*, ed. Paul Leicester Ford (New York: Putnam, 1892), 10:170. Ample support for the characterization can be found in Henry H. Simms, *Life of John Taylor: The Story of a Brilliant Leader in the Early Virginia State Rights School* (Richmond, VA: William Byrd Press, 1932).

37. Quoted in Benjamin F. Wright, "The Philosopher of American Democracy," *American Political Science Review* 22, no. 4 (1928): 870–92, 876.

38. Jeffersonians made the attack in the context of a discussion of the claimed unconstitutionality of the repeal in 1802 of the 1801 Federalist act that had established sixteen new federal judgeships. The argument of unconstitutionality was based on the clause in the Constitution that provides that "judges shall hold their offices during good behavior," which could be read as implying that once a judgeship was created, it could not be abolished by Congress. See Jerry W. Knudson, "The Jeffersonian Assault on the Federalist Judiciary, 1802–1805: Political Forces and Press Reaction," *American Journal of Legal History* 14, no. 1 (1970): 55–75.

39. In an intriguingly timed letter written just two weeks before Taylor's essay would be published in the *Intelligencer*, Jefferson made a similar argument against judicial review to Abigail Adams. He wrote, "But the opinion which gives to the judges the right to decide what laws are constitutional, and what not, not only for themselves in their own sphere of action, but for the legislature and executive also in their

spheres, would make the judiciary a despotic branch" (quoted in Malone, *Jefferson the President: First Term*, 155).

Chapter 7

1. Some of the material in this chapter originally appeared in Mel Laracey, "The Impeachment of Supreme Court Justice Samuel Chase: New Perspectives from Thomas Jefferson's Presidential Newspaper," *Journal of Supreme Court History* 40, no. 3 (2015): 231–48.

2. For an account that incorporates newspaper reports and commentaries, including some from the *Intelligencer*, see Knudson, "Jeffersonian Assault on the Federalist Judiciary."

3. Dewey, *Marshall versus Jefferson*, 94. One example of that attitude is found in an unusual signed attack against James Callender by Robert Lawson, republished in the *Intelligencer* on October 27, 1802, from the *Richmond Examiner*. Lawson derisively dismissed Callender's claim that he was responsible for Jefferson's victory: "No, Mr. Callender you are very much mistaken; the sedition law, and the improper and rigorous conduct of Judge Chase, did more injury to the Federalists, than the writings of a thousand Callenders." Lawson's letter was part of the Republican effort to discredit Callender after his publication of several scandalous stories about Jefferson, including Jefferson's relationship with Sally Hemings.

4. Ackerman, *Failure of the Founding Fathers*, 209–10; Ross E. Davies, "The Other Supreme Court," *Journal of Supreme Court History* 31, no. 3 (2006): 221–34, at 226; Keith Whittington, *Constitutional Construction*, 20–23, 43.

5. Chase to G. Morris, March 6, 1803, Samuel Chase Correspondence, Maryland Historical Society; quoted in Stephen Engel, "Before the Countermajoritarian Difficulty," 199 n. 84.

6. Ellis, *Jeffersonian Crisis*, 77–80; Wilentz, *Rise of American Democracy*, 126.

7. The summary fairly well reflects the description found in the proceedings of the US Senate, 8 *Annals of Congress* 2nd sess. (1834), 675–76.

8. *Founders Online*, National Archives, https://founders.archives.gov/documents/Jefferson/01-40-02-0278; original source: *Papers of Thomas Jefferson*, 40:371–73; quoted and discussed in Ellis, *Jeffersonian Crisis*, 80.

9. Ellis states, "[T]hroughout the spring and summer of 1803, the Republican press, led by the *National Intelligencer*, assailed Chase" (*Jeffersonian Crisis*, 81). However, the only mentions of Chase in the newspaper in 1803 were the four items discussed here.

10. Wilentz, *Rise of American Democracy*, 126; Ellis, *Jeffersonian Crisis*, 69–74.

11. Ellis notes that Elliot was part of the internal opposition among Republicans to John Randolph's management of the Chase impeachment proceedings (*Jeffersonian Crisis*, 86; see also 93).

12. Ellis, 82.

13. See chapter 2 for a fuller quotation of Chase's reasons.

14. Jane Shaffer Elsmere, "The Impeachment Trial of Justice Samuel Chase" (PhD diss., Indiana University, 1962), 73–74, revised, in book form, as *Justice Samuel Chase* (Muncie, IN: Janevar, 1980).

15. Malone (*Jefferson the President: First Term*, 470 n. 24) notes that Chase's memorial, dated March 24, 1804, and letter, dated March 29, 1804, were published that same day in the *New York Evening Post*. The *Washington Federalist* published the memo-

rial and cover letter on April 11, identifying it as a reprint from the *Baltimore Federal Gazette.*

16. Whittington, *Constitutional Construction.*

17. Malone, *Jefferson the President: First Term*, 470.

18. Ackerman, *Failure of the Founding Fathers*, 202–3. Like Ackerman, Elsmere ("Impeachment Trial," 83) notes but does not discuss the contents of Chase's public defense and fails to mention the *Intelligencer*'s critique of it at all. See also James Haw, Francis F. Beirne, Rosamond Beirne, and R. Samuel Jett, *Stormy Patriot: The Life of Samuel Chase* (Baltimore: Maryland Historical Society, 1980).

19. Ackerman, *Failure of the Founding Fathers*, 202–3. Elsmere adds that Chase's letter did "provide his friends with comfort and with ammunition to combat his enemies" ("Impeachment Trial," 83).

20. See, e.g., Robert McCloskey, *The American Supreme Court* (Chicago: University of Chicago Press, 1960).

21. In addition to its publication in these issues of the *Intelligencer*, Chase's answer can be found in the 1805 publication by Smith of *The Trial of Samuel Chase, . . . before the Senate of the United States, Taken in Shorthand by Samuel H. Smith and Thomas Lloyd, Entire Impeachment Trial Proceedings*, 2 vols. (Washington, DC, 1805). See also 8 *Annals of Congress* 2nd sess. (1834), 101–50. On the crucial role played by moderate Republican senators in Chase's acquittal, see Ellis, *Jeffersonian Crisis*, 80–81, 102–7.

22. See Peter Charles Hoffer and N. E. H. Hull, *Impeachment in America, 1635–1805* (New Haven: Yale University Press, 1984), 244.

23. Ackerman, *Failure of the Founding Fathers*, 214.

24. Laracey, *Presidents and the People*, 59.

25. In ads, the *Federalist* said it, too, was planning to publish a collection of the complete proceedings.

26. Raoul Berger, *Impeachment: The Constitutional Problems* (Cambridge, MA: Harvard University Press, 1973), 235–37.

27. Jeremy Bailey, "Constitutionalism, Conflict, and Consent: Jefferson on the Impeachment Power," *Review of Politics* 70, no. 4 (2008): 572–94, at 591–92.

28. Jeffrey K. Tulis, "Impeachment in the Constitutional Order," in *The Constitutional Presidency*, ed. Joseph M. Bessette and Jeffrey K. Tulis (Baltimore: Johns Hopkins University Press, 2009); Bailey, "Constitutionalism, Conflict, and Consent," 573–76. See Berger, *Impeachment*; Michael J. Gerhardt, *The Federal Impeachment Process: A Constitutional and Historical Analysis*, 2nd ed. (Chicago: University of Chicago Press, 2000).

29. Quoted in Bailey, "Constitutionalism, Conflict, and Consent," 577.

30. Engel, "Before the Countermajoritarian Difficulty," 198–202. See also Engel's fuller treatment in *American Politicians Confront the Court*. For earlier articulations of this idea, see Albert J. Beveridge, *The Life of John Marshall* (Boston: Houghton Mifflin, 1916–19), 3:159; Richard B. Lillich, "The Chase Impeachment," *American Journal of Legal History* 4, no. 1 (1960): 49–72, at 54–57. See also William Rehnquist, *Grand Inquests: The Historic Impeachments of Justice Samuel Chase and President Andrew Johnson* (New York: William McMorrow, 1992), 108–25; Whittington, *Constitutional Construction*, 57–65.

31. See, e.g., Ackerman, *Failure of the Founding Fathers*, 228; Whittington, *Constitutional Construction*, 24–25, 48–49, 66–67.

32. Dewey, *Marshall versus Jefferson*, 152–53; Ackerman, *Failure of the Founding Fathers*, 220.

33. Ellis, *Jeffersonian Crisis*, 99.

34. Ellis, 104. Ellis later elaborated on this opinion, asserting, "Actually, between Jefferson's letter to Nicholson in May 1803 and Chase's trial in March 1805 there is no evidence, aside from Federalist hyperbole, to indicate that the administration either was enthusiastic about, or even supported, the movement to impeach Chase." Ellis, "The Impeachment of Samuel Chase," in *American Political Trials*, ed. M. Belknap (Westport, CT: Greenwood Press, 1981), 57–78, at 65. See also McDonald, *Presidency of Thomas Jefferson*, 92–93.

35. McCloskey, *American Supreme Court*; see also Dean Alfange, "*Marbury v Madison* and Original Understanding of Judicial Review," *Supreme Court Review*, 1993, 329; Ackerman, *Failure of the Founding Fathers*, chap. 10.

36. See, e.g., Whittington, *Constitutional Construction*, 41; Ackerman, *Failure of the Founding Fathers*, 213; Engel, *Before the Countermajoritarian Difficulty*, 202.

37. Ellis, *Jeffersonian Crisis*, 86, 92–93; see also Ackerman, *Failure of the Founding Fathers*, 212–13.

Chapter 8

1. Malone, *Jefferson the President: First Term*, 260.

2. Malone, 266

3. Malone, 263–64.

4. Malone, 269.

5. Malone, 269.

6. Johnstone (*Jefferson and the Presidency*, 70) notes that Jefferson privately was contemplating using military force to seize New Orleans if negotiations failed.

7. Malone, *Jefferson the President: First Term*, 164.

8. McDonald, *Presidency of Thomas Jefferson*, 66.

9. On May 9, 1803, page 3 of the *Intelligencer* carried a report based on the "representation of Capt. Keilly," who had "arrived yesterday." While in port in Spain, he had witnessed the arrival of dispatches from the Spanish government with orders that they be put on board a ship immediately to sail "for any port in the United States." Within half an hour, he reported, a ship had sailed with the dispatches. The paper's note concluded with the observation that the ship had arrived in Baltimore "some time since," carrying the "*assurances* of a *continuation* of the right of deposit at New Orleans."

10. In the 1803 issues, see August 1 ("not one drop of blood lost"), August 26 ("Advantages of the Purchase of Louisiana"), August 29 ("The Price Contracted for Louisiana" was not "too dear"), August 31 ("Additional Arguments in Favor for Louisiana Purchase"); September 2 ("Further Evidence of the Federal Valuations of Louisiana"), September 28 ("Purchase of Louisiana"); October 3 ("Purchase of Louisiana"), October 5 ("Purchase of Louisiana"), October 19 ("Extract from a Pamphlet" suggesting that some of the Louisiana Territory could be traded for land held by "Indian nations" east of the Mississippi, as a place to resettle emancipated slaves, and as a "place of exile" for criminals), October 24 ("To the Senate of US"), October 28 ("Relating to Louisiana"); November 28 (under "Multiple News Items": the president received specimens of salt from Louisiana where there was reported to be large deposits).

11. See the issues of February 5 (celebratory resolution of citizens of Petersburg); March 2 (commentary on why the *Intelligencer* was carrying so many reports of celebrations), March 16 (reports of the "quiet" situation in Louisiana); April 18 (wildlife and

natural resources in the territory), April 27 (citizens' address to the governor of the territory and his reply); May 11 (circular from the governor to all military commanders in the territory), May 21 (celebrations and toasts), May 28 (poem by teenager); June 11 (oration by David Ramsay), June 13 (speeches and toasts), June 15 (ceremony with Governor Claiborne, toasts), June 20 (visit by the governor to a Catholic convent in New Orleans, address by the young ladies, assurances by the governor that the convent would "continue to prosper" under the new US government).

Chapter 9

1. See Onuf, *Mind of Thomas Jefferson*, 148–52.

2. Onuf, 152.

3. As promised, "Virginian" produced three more essays that were published first in the *Enquirer* and then in the *Intelligencer*, in that latter's issues of July 20, August 15, and September 10.

4. The *Intelligencer*'s commentary began by noting that the *Washington Federalist* was "edited by Elias B. Caldwell, *clerk of the supreme court of the United States.*"

5. See the discussion of the changing politics of the Fourth of July in Newman, *Parades and Politics of the Street*, chap. 3. In contrast, in the eight years of Jefferson's presidency, Christmas was mentioned just twice in the *Intelligencer*. Both times, on December 23, 1801, and January 22, 1808, the references were to "Christmas day" and nothing more. The first was in a note saying that the paper would not be published on that day; the second was a parenthetical reference to the day as a date signifier in a speech on the floor of Congress.

6. July 6 (Washington and Georgetown), July 9 (Baltimore), July 11 (New York, Alexandria, Petersburg, Philadelphia), July 13 (Boston), July 16 ("citizens of Powhatan county" and adjacent counties), July 20 (Orange Springs, Orange County); August 27 (New Orleans speech by Mr. Derbigby); October 19 (St. Genevieve, Louisiana).

7. Darshan Singh Maini, "Shakespeare's Leanings a Mystery," *The Tribune India*, February 1, 2004, https://tribuneindia.com/2004/20040201/spectrum/book7.htm; "Gaius Marcius Coriolanus," Wikepedia, https://en.wikipedia.org/wiki/Gaius_Marcius_Coriolanus

8. In a different twist, on February 27, 1804, the *Intelligencer* reprinted, from the *Washington Federalist*, a report of the toasts made at the celebration of Washington's birthday a few days earlier. To Republicans, probably the two most offensive toasts would have been the third one, directed to "The *Friends* of the People—not their *Flatterers* [Music, Yankey (*sic*) Doodle]," and the fifth one, directed to "The *Judiciary*—as free from *persecution* as from *patronage.*" The *Intelligencer*'s prefatory comment to the account complained, "It has been said that federalism has abated of its violence. Let the following toasts decide. . . . By this, it will be seen, that the memory of that great man [Washington] is attempted, impotently it is true, to be made as powerful an instrument of party malevolence, as his name, while living, was too successfully converted into a cover for many dangerous designs."

9. Later in 1804, the newspaper would devote quite a bit of attention to Alexander Hamilton's death in a duel with Burr. It printed an account on July 18 of the funeral ceremony for Hamilton and an account on July 20 of his death. On July 23, the paper published the extensive correspondence between the two that led up to the duel. Other issues that discussed the matter were published on July 25 and August 24.

10. Thus, they said, they had "thought it prudent to select a character on whom suspicion had not attached and whom we know above it: Morgan Lewis."

11. A few weeks earlier, on April 6, the *Intelligencer* had published a similar address to the "Republican Electors of Governor and Lieutenant Governor" in New York. On June 1 and 4, the paper carried similar addresses, as well as commentaries, to the voters in the District of Columbia, arguing why even the members of the district's city council should be aligned politically with the national government.

12. Cunningham, *Jeffersonian Republicans*, 256.

13. John Gerring, *Party Ideologies in America, 1828–1896* (Cambridge: Cambridge University Press, 1998), 292–93. In looking for "texts to represent the ideologies" of political parties in nineteenth-century America, Gerring consulted "all speeches, letters, and government documents authored" by the party's presidential candidates (293) but did not even consider the partisan, party-sponsored newspapers that, as Jeffrey Pasley showed (in *Tyranny of Printers*), were the backbone of party organization then.

14. Daniel Klinghard, *The Nationalization of American Political Parties, 1880–1896* (Cambridge: Cambridge University Press, 2010), vii–ix.

15. More recent studies of the history of partisan behavior in the early American republic tell a story of party-oriented behavior that seems almost indistinguishable from later periods up to the present. See, e.g., Wilentz, *Rise of American Democracy;* Jeffrey L. Pasley, *The First Presidential Contest: 1796 and the Founding of American Democracy* (Lawrence: University Press of Kansas, 2013).

16. Klinghard, *Nationalization of American Political Parties*, 8.

17. For example, response "No. I" in what the paper said was a "New Series Federal Misrepresentations" was published on April 11, and No. XV, the last in that numbered series, was published on July 23. The other dates were April 16, 18, and 25 and May 2 (No. VI; No. V not found); May 7, 11, and 30 and April 1 (No. X); April 4, 11, and 15 (No. XIII; No. XIV not found). The piece of April 16 defended the actions Jefferson was taking to free American sailors captured in the Mediterranean by pirates in Tripoli. Responding to Federalist criticism it reprinted from the *Charleston Courier*, the *Intelligencer* first attacked the patriotism of critics and then asserted that the likely ransom for the sailors would be far less than the "one or two millions" predicted by the *Courier*. For other examples, see No. IX (May 30, 1804), which assures its readers that claims about deficiencies in a new navy ship are "destitute of truth," and No. XIII (June 15), which simply denies the claim in a Federalist newspaper that the *Intelligencer* and the *Philadelphia Aurora* had "openly invited the murder of the First Consul Bonaparte."

18. The references to debt, seduction, and a Southern plantation owner sleeping with his slave are to the articles James Callender published in 1802 to embarrass Jefferson. Those to recompensing flattery or getting rid of an enemy could well have been to Callender's disclosures of Jefferson's past encouragement and financial support of his work as a rabidly Republican newspaper editor whose attacks had deeply offended prominent Federalists, including John and Abigail Adams. See Malone, *Jefferson the President: First Term*, 212, 423–24.

19. The *Intelligencer*'s vaguely worded response to Callender's charges echoes Smith's similar response in the issue of September 29, 1802, previously discussed in chapter 1. Although doing so might have seemed like an implicit acknowledgment that there was some truth to the innuendo, Smith could also have invoked his statement on December 9, 1801, in his "Address to Subscribers," that while his paper

"fears not to examine with intrepid calmness, the measures of public men, it will disdain to notice the foibles or the vices of private life."

20. Elsewhere in the commentary, the *Courier* argued that if a "chief magistrate . . . has been in the habit of not respecting himself, the law should compel him to respect his sacred office. If he is in habits of a low gross or vulgar kind, the law should compel him to relinquish them, or forfeit his office."

21. See Harvey C. Mansfield Jr., *Taming the Prince: The Ambivalence of Modern Executive Power* (Baltimore: Johns Hopkins University Press, 1989), 275–76.

22. As noted in chapter 3 of the present study, "Curtius" was the name of a young hero who gave his life to save the Roman Republic by leaping with his horse into a chasm in the center of the Forum that the priests had said would not close until the most precious thing in Rome had been cast into it. The essays are numbered I to XX; there was not a No. XIV published in the newspaper, but there was one in the compilation Smith published later in pamphlet form. In 1999, the Lawbook Exchange republished the 1804 Smith compilation of the essays.

23. Taylor's prominent Republican credentials and his well-known relationship with Jefferson have already been mentioned in chapter 6, in the discussion of his fourth "Curtius" essay, on the subject of judicial review.

24. The essays are probably beyond the interest of most readers. Some are discussed in this note to illustrate Taylor's approach, which was a mix of constitutional theory and partisan apologia. No. 4, published in the *National Intelligencer* on September 24, 1804, asserted that the president has only a "qualified agency" in the legislative function, the veto, which ought to be used sparingly in deference to the superior ability of Congress to reflect the will of the nation. The essay argued that for a president to "usurp" the legislative process in any other way, "by direct or indirect means," would be a grave, impeachable offense.

At the time, Taylor's reserved view of the legitimate role of presidents in the legislative process was shared by both Republicans and Federalists, at least officially. Hard political reality was different, however, as presidents, beginning with Washington, found it necessary to become involved with congressional affairs. See, e.g., Sidney M. Milkis and Michael Nelson, *The American Presidency: Origins and Development, 1776–2002*, 4th ed. (Washington, DC: CQ Press, 2003), chap. 4; Cunningham, *Process of Government under Jefferson*, chap. 9; Skowronek, *Politics Presidents Make*, 73–74.

Like his predecessors, Jefferson had been extensively but privately involved in the direction of Congress, by working with Republican allies there. Taylor's essay simply denied that involvement. His denials sometimes got a bit strained, as when Taylor claimed that even though Jefferson said, in his first Annual Message to Congress, that "of course" the question of the need for the additional judges would "present itself to the contemplation of Congress," that statement was not Jefferson's expression of the president's own opinion on the issue.

No. 18, entitled "Foreign Relations," is noteworthy because it provides a similarly reserved view of the president's war powers. Published on November 12, 1804, that essay praised Jefferson for keeping the nation out of war when American access to the port in New Orleans had been temporarily cut off. Taylor wrote, "Two alternatives were presented to us: war, or negotiation." Only Congress had the power to take the nation into war, Taylor argued, and until that decision, the President was obliged to keep the nation in a state of peace. A president who instead "carried the nation into a state of war," Taylor said, would commit a "shameful and criminal violation of this oath" that ought to result in impeachment.

Also of note is Taylor's praise in No. 19 for Jefferson's decision to involve the House of Representatives in legislation to carry out the terms of the Louisiana Purchase Treaty. As portrayed by Taylor, Jefferson's action was an act of deep political symbolism that affirmed both the populist roots of the American constitutional system and a limited, cautionary view of the powers of the national government. The treaty power was one of "vast importance," Taylor explained, that "from its very motive scarcely admits of constitutional restraint." Involving the House in the process of treaty implementation would be a check on the treaty power, he said.

25. On the modern-day phenomenon, see Kathleen Hall Jamieson and Joseph N. Cappella, *Rush Limbaugh and the Conservative Media Establishment* (Oxford: Oxford University Press, 2008).

26. Pasley, "1800 as a Revolution in American Culture," 135.

27. Kathleen Hall Jamieson and Joseph N. Cappella, *Echo Chamber* (New York: Oxford University Press, 2008), xiii.

28. Jamieson and Cappella, x.

Chapter 10

1. Johnstone, *Jefferson and the Presidency*, 250, 39.

2. Johnstone, 240, 39.

3. Skowronek, *Politics Presidents Make*, 69–70.

4. Skowronek, *Politics Presidents Make*, 71, 27.

5. Habermas, *Structural Transformation of the Public Sphere*. In chapter 2 of the present study, see the discussion of the 1803 *Intelligencer* essay regarding the key role newspapers play in a democracy.

6. Young, *Washington Community*, 33–37. For a critique of Young's assessment, see Johnstone, *Jefferson and the Presidency*, 125–27.

7. Of course, Federalists complained about newspaper bias. In its "Portencius" commentary on November 13, 1801 (previously discussed), the *Washington Federalist* said that "prejudice and party spirit" had deprived Americans of the "benefits of free discussion" in newspapers, because newspapers now only presented "one side or the other of every question." The commentary argued that since most people only read a newspaper that was aligned with their existing political outlook, they just became "more and more riveted in their own opinions, however erroneous the one and correct the other."

8. David Zarefsky, "Presidential Rhetoric and the Power of Definition," *Presidential Studies Quarterly* 34, no. 3 (2004): 607–19, at 611. As understood by rhetorical studies scholars, "rhetoric is not restricted to the spoken word" but includes "any means of symbolic inducement . . . if it is designed to influence or persuade an audience" (Medhurst, *Before the Rhetorical Presidency*, 2).

Index

Ackerman, Bruce, 11, 15, 29, 53–54, 63–64, 117, 124–26, 128, 199n42, 210n14, 228n18

Adams, Abigail, 226n39, 231n18

Adams, John, 48, 218n59, 223n44, 223n52
administration, 75, 92, 95, 102, 104,114, 116, 118, 121, 133, 159, 169, 175, 182, 188, 202n17
administration-sponsored newspaper, 31, 196n16, 202n16
annual message, 90–92, 95–98
appointments of attorneys and marshals, 100–104
Declaration of Independence draft, 24, 204nn46–47
Election of 1800, 41–54, 134, 211n28
Election of 1804 comparison, 183
midnight appointments, 99, 100, 118, 219n1, 220n15, 224nn8–9

Addresses
citizens, 80–84, 89
legislatures, 83–84

Alexandria Advertiser and Commercial Intelligencer, 197n19

Alien and Sedition Acts, 43, 75, 168, 209n91

Alvis, J. David, 104

American Philosophical Society, 20

America
democracy, 2, 93, 217n37
people, 7, 9, 65, 69, 73, 87, 103, 112, 116, 149–50, 168, 187, 189
political theory, 192
Republic, 3–4, 7, 9, 72–73, 163, 169, 172, 192, 231n15

American Revolution, 159, 171, 217n37

American Whig Party, 194n5

Ames, Fisher, 18

Ames, William, 21–22, 27, 201n6

Anderson, Benedict, 2

Anderson, Joseph, 157–58

Annual Messages
John Adams, 90–92, 95–98
Jefferson, 11, 15, 26, 76, 154, 156, 181–82, 187–88, 214n14, 217n50, 218n56, 232n24
Jefferson's delivery in writing, 90–98

anonymous, 3, 10, 13, 21–22, 24–25, 28, 107, 155, 187, 205n53, 206n71. *See also* pseudonym/pseudonymous

Anti-Democrat, 136, 204n49, 206n69

antidemocratic, 66, 68, 151

Appleby, Joyce, 18, 80–81, 194n5

Articles of Confederation, 54

Athens, 45, 53, 209n91